Volume 3
The Tennessee Series

GOVERNORS OF TENNESSEE, I
1790-1835

edited by
Charles W. Crawford

Memphis State University Press
Memphis, Tennessee

For Kermit Crawford, who would have been at home in this frontier land where men valued honor, pride, and loyalty.

Manufactured in the United States of America

ISBN 0-87870-075-7

TABLE OF CONTENTS

Introduction   vii
    by Charles W. Crawford

1. William Blount   1
    by Jill S. Broer

2. John Sevier   31
    by Lynette B. Wrenn

3. Archibald Roane   63
    by James Lee McDonough

4. Willie Blount   79
    by Mary B. Clark

5. Joseph McMinn   97
    by Nancy Boswell Kincaid

6. William Carroll   119
    by Harriet W. Stern

7. Sam Houston   149
    by James Alex Baggett

8. William Hall   179
    by Michael O. Sanders

CONTRIBUTORS

JAMES ALEX BAGGETT is Associate Professor of History and Political Science at Union University. He is the editor of the West Tennessee Historical Society *Papers* and served as a delegate to the 1976 Democratic National Convention. He is the author of numerous articles on Reconstruction.

JILL SCHAEFFER BROER is a Master of Arts candidate in history at Memphis State University. Her undergraduate education was in American Studies at Brown University.

MARY B. CLARK is a Master of Arts candidate in history and a graduate assistant at Memphis State University. She received her undergraduate education in history and sociology at the University of Central Arkansas.

NANCY BOSWELL KINCAID is a Master of Arts candidate at Memphis State University and a teacher at Central High School in Millington, Tennessee. She received her undergraduate education at Memphis State University.

JAMES LEE McDONOUGH is Justin Potter Distinguished Professor of History at David Lipscomb College. He is the author of two books and numerous articles on the Civil War.

MICHAEL O. SANDERS is a Master of Arts candidate in history at Memphis State University and a coach and history teacher at Elliston Baptist Academy. He received his undergraduate education at Memphis State University.

HARRIET W. STERN is a graduate student at Memphis State University and a teacher in the Memphis City School System. She has received degrees from Smith College and Memphis State University.

LYNETTE B. WRENN is a Doctor of Philosophy candidate in history and a teaching assistant at Memphis State University. After completing her undergraduate education in history at the University of North Carolina at Greensboro, she received a Master of Arts degree from Radcliffe College.

INTRODUCTION
by Charles W. Crawford

T ennesseans have traditionally maintained an interest in politics and a curiosity about the lives of their political leaders. While national and state issues, sectional interests, political ideology, and party loyalty have all been factors in the making of political fortunes, the dominant consideration of Tennessee voters often has been the personalities of the individuals seeking their support. This concern is never more pronounced than during an election for governor, for the governor is not only a symbol of the state, but a leader of the people.

Tennessee's governors have been pioneers, farmers, Indian fighters, soldiers, businessmen, editors, teachers, lawyers, and professional politicians. Collectively they have led their state through times of settlement, Indian fighting and removal, secession and defeat, and through eight wars. Their efforts, failures as well as triumphs, have directed the Volunteer State through almost two centuries of growth and development.

Each governor, on at least one election day, has been the most popular person in the state. Some of them have been heroic, others controversial. Some of them have left the capital more popular than when they were elected. Others have made the citizens of Tennessee most happy when they left office. They all have been interesting and colorful leaders. It is with this volume—the first in a set of five within the Tennessee Series—that their biographies begin.

Those interested in the history of Tennessee, whether scholars or general readers, have long recognized the inadequate historical consideration given to the state's governors. Although assorted biographies, monographs, and articles have been written about some of the state's chief executives, most readers seeking an inclusive approach to these holders of high office have relied on Robert H. White's *Messages of the Governors of Tennessee*, published by the Tennessee Historical Commission. This excellent series, however, is mainly documentary and currently ends with the administration of Governor John Isaac Cox. Therefore, in *Governors of Tennessee*, it is the editor's intention to provide a brief and accurate biography of each governor from 1790 to the present.

This volume, which spans the period from 1790 to 1835, begins when Tennessee was a cluster of fortified settlements dispersed along rivers, and it traces the development of the frontier region through territorial status and subsquent statehood. By 1835, after nearly four decades of statehood, Tennessee had become one of the most prominent members of the Union. Already economically prosperous, its citizens could look forward to the lucrative development of extensive natural resources, the expansion of agriculture, and the continued growth of a successfully established system of industry and commerce. Due to the successive efforts of its first governors, Tennessee also was on the threshold of a major undertaking to establish a statewide transportation network which would include railroads, turnpikes, and navigable river channels. During these decades, Tennessee also became recognized as one of the most politically influential states: Andrew Jackson occupied the White House; Hugh Lawson White prepared to run for the presidency in 1836; and two other residents of the state who would later become president, James K. Polk and Andrew Johnson, had begun their political careers.

Tennesseans, understandably, developed a remarkable devotion to politics, dating from their establishment of the Watauga Association, the first representative government west of the Appalachian Mountains. Their active involvement placed the state's citizens and their governors in the forefront of national leadership and brought excitement to state politics as well. In the following biographies of the governors of Tennessee, the colorful political history of the state emerges in lively detail.

1

WILLIAM BLOUNT
Governor of The Southwest Territory
(Tennessee), 1790-1796

by Jill S. Broer

On October 10, 1790, William Blount crossed the mountains to take up his post as first territorial governor of Tennessee. Accompanied only by one servant, Blount was armed with a copy of his commission from President Washington and a copy of the Northwest Ordinance of 1787 to guide him in his task of governing the territory. The new Constitution had been ratified the year before, and there were few, if any, guidelines for Blount to follow as he entered this frontier world.[1]

"The Territory of the United States South of the River Ohio," as Tennessee was officially called, theoretically covered a vast area. However, it consisted of only two pockets of settlement. A 150-mile strip called Washington District stretched from the Virginia border to the Little Tennessee River and was inhabited by 28,000 settlers. Hostile Indian territory separated it from Mero District, centered at Nashville along the Cumberland River with 7000 inhabitants. In 1791 Blount submitted to the United States government in Philadelphia the territorial census "as taken on the last Saturday of July, 1791, by the Captains of the Militia." This census recorded totals for Tennessee during Blount's first year as governor.

Free white males 21 and over	6,271
Free white males under 21	10,277
Free white females	15,365
All other free persons	361
Slaves	3,417
	35,691[2]

Although the territory claimed jurisdiction from the Appalachian Mountains to the Mississippi River, Spain actually controlled that river and its banks, and had various claims to other parts of the territory. The settled areas of Tennessee were thus mountain-bound in the east and blocked by the Spanish and the Indians to the west and south.[3]

Because of British restrictions on exploration west of the Appalachians, settlement had not begun in this area until the 1760s. At first only a few settlers moved into the area, and they did not encounter much hostility from the Indians. By 1782, however, settlers were pouring over the mountains. The Indians, fearing white encroachment, began to retaliate; the settlers built forts called "stations" where they huddled together for protection. Prior to 1795 one-third of those who settled on the frontier died violently and all "tilled fields with rifles beside them."[4]

In 1790 Blount had the responsibility of setting up a government, and the nearly impossible task of coexisting with the Indians. The man who faced these formidable obstacles was himself a product of the frontier, but in a different sense than were the buckskin-garbed Daniel Boone, Davy Crockett, or even the popular John Sevier. Blount has been described as an aristocrat, a cultured man. The Blount family of North Carolina were direct descendants of the English lesser nobility. Sir Walter Blount was a supporter of Charles I during the English Civil War. He had four sons, two of whom came to America in the late 17th century to make their fortunes. They came first to Virginia, then went on to the wilderness of North Carolina. Each generation of Blounts was successful in its own right, taking maximum advantage of the opportunities of the developing new world.[5]

William Blount was born on March 26, 1749, in Bertie County, North Carolina, the eldest son of Jacob and Barbara Gray Blount. In 1753, Jacob Blount took his young family to the developing region of Craven County, North Carolina. This area proved conducive to the ambitions of Jacob Blount; and his sons, as they grew older, took their places as community leaders and businessmen. William Blount and his brother, John Gray, were members of a powerful new class in late 18th-century America—successful businessmen who were also the social and political leaders. Blount was to become one of the most powerful of a group of land speculators who developed and governed what is now the state of Tennessee.[6]

Portrait of William Blount. *Photograph by George W. Hornal, courtesy Tennessee Department of Transportation.*

Blount was in his early twenties and just beginning in the family merchant business when North Carolina and the other colonies became embroiled in the revolution against England. Blount's world would never be the same. "It was this atmosphere of political and economic upheaval that set the mold of the mind and methods of William Blount . . . . In business and politics the times called for a leadership of expediency, gamble, and maneuver, and Blount's nature responded in a manner which became a lifelong pattern."[7]

Blount was appointed paymaster of the Third North Carolina Battalion, a position of great responsibility which brought him into contact not only with the soldiers, but also with central government officials in Philadelphia. During the unstable economic conditions of the war, the Blount brothers pursued lucrative careers as merchants in addition to fulfilling their military responsibilities. Inflation was rampant. Paper currencies issued by the various colonies fluctuated wildly in value. Dealing with the problems of trading and shipping under such circumstances appealed to Blount's gambling instincts and developed his business sense and the ability to manage people that would serve him well later in his career.[8]

In 1780, near the end of the war, the North Carolina legislature began to make preparations for the future. The problem of compensation for the soldiers was solved by setting up a reserve to pay them off in land rather than in cash. This reserve was to be in North Carolina's Tennessee lands. In 1781 Blount began his political career as a member of the North Carolina House of Commons. His first cause as a young legislator involved veterans. He secured a position on the soldiers' welfare committee, and thus had a hand in the disposal of their lands, often to his own advantage. The war finally over, Blount pursued ambitious plans for the future.[9]

During the war years Blount married Mary Grainger. They had one son, Cornelius. The family settled at their home, Piney Grove, not far from the other Blount brothers. But William Blount's ambitions kept him away from home much of the time. In 1782 he was elected by the legislature to serve as a member of the Continental Congress which served under the Articles of Confederation. Blount's future was to become more and more tied up with land—his own landholdings, the disposal of the western lands belonging to North Carolina, and the future of the Indian lands.[10]

The problem of what to do with lands belonging to the various states came up immediately at the Congress in Philadelphia. North Carolina owed $19 million in war debts to the central government. Other states which had paid their portions demanded that North Carolina's payment be made. Blount favored the suggestion that North Carolina give up its Tennessee land to pay this debt; as an aspiring speculator he knew that land values would rise, and as a North Carolinian he saw that giving up the land would relieve North Carolina of the burden of taxation necessary to protect Tennessee. However, most of Blount's fellow North Carolinians were opposed to the proposal, and it was dropped temporarily.[11]

In 1783 Blount was back in the North Carolina legislature. The prestige of attending the national government in Philadelphia had not diminished his economic and family interests in North Carolina, and state government was more influential at this time on the issues which directly affected Blount than was the weak confederation government. On his return to North Carolina, the aim of Blount's career was clear. His future was irrevocably tied up with land and politics. Although he and his brothers were involved in other business ventures, Blount dedicated more and more of his life to the amassing of land. It was this goal, for himself and for other speculators, that led his successful political career pursuits.[12]

The history of early Tennessee is the story of land speculators. They were the country's political and social leaders; they determined its future. As Blount, John Sevier, James Robertson, and later Andrew Jackson gained political control of Tennessee, they molded its policies toward one aim—the amassing of land from the Indians and for themselves. "The insatiable desire for territory by young and land-poor America cannot be fully comprehended unless it is understood that, in those days, the country was run largely by speculators in real estate."[13]

The end of the Revolution had brought a recession which had particularly affected North Carolina's predominantly rural population. Many families hoped to escape from poverty by crossing the Appalachians to the new lands. Speculators encouraged this settlement and strained their own credit resources to invest in the future of the Southwest, despite the fact that much of the land legally belonged to the Indians. From these complexities of economic problems, land grabs, and gambles, emerged the Franklin movement.[14]

The seed of the state of Franklin movement is said to have been planted by William Blount with the so-called "land grab" Act of 1783. This act, sponsored by Blount and his brother, opened for sale Tennessee lands from the mountains to the Mississippi River at the rate of ten pounds, or five dollars, per 100 acres. All lands were to be sold whether they were owned and inhabited by Indians or not. The only exceptions were a small Indian reservation and the reserve for military land grants in the Cumberland Valley. Even the military reserve was not completely safe from speculators because many soldiers could not afford to take up their claims and would sell their rights to large landowners. Thus North Carolinians took advantage of their state's territorial holdings. Nearly four million acres were entered in the land office as sold in only seven months. Through these purchases Blount was building up his empire. When North Carolina finally ceded Tennessee to Congress, the national government gained virtually nothing from the transfer. Almost all the land had already been taken.[15]

In 1784 Blount took the lead in pushing this cession act through the North Carolina legislature, although there was violent opposition from the Radical faction in the state. It was obvious that Blount's proposal primarily benefited the big land speculators who had invested in territorial land; however, because they were in power, the act was passed by the legislature.[16] Blount and his fellow speculators had been victorious. His land program had been a masterpiece of planning and politicking to achieve his goal. Nevertheless, he could not rest on these laurels, for at that moment an independence movement was rising in the territory that threatened all his well-laid plans. Neither Blount nor the North Carolina legislators realized how discontented the frontiersmen were with their treatment by the Easterners. They felt that North Carolina did not protect them properly, that their lands were being devoured by North Carolina speculators, and that they were mere pawns in the Easterners' game. In December of 1784, a convention met in Jonesborough in East Tennessee and declared the independent state of Franklin. They elected John Sevier governor and designated the state to include the three eastern counties of Washington, Sullivan, and Greene and to take in the Muscle Shoals area of the Tennessee River, a location which was claimed by Georgia and in which Blount and Sevier hoped to make fortunes. Davidson County in the Cumberland area did not participate in the Franklin movement, for its very existence was due to the military warrants issued by North Carolina. These settlers felt that leaving North Carolina might jeopardize their rights to this land.[17]

The Franklin movement threatened the security of Blount, Sevier, and other speculators' plans. Unlike Blount, Sevier lived among the frontiersmen and was popular in a way that Blount never was. Rather than lose this popularity, Sevier accepted his role as governor and took over the movement. To complicate matters further, Blount lost control of the North Carolina legislature, and in October of 1784 the Radical faction succeeded in repealing the cession act, again asserting ownership of Tennessee. Nevertheless, the state of Franklin, already launched on its course despite opposition from North Carolina, continued to pass its own legislation and make its own treaties with the Indians.[18]

Franklin's dream of being accepted into the United States grew dimmer as time passed. The Confederation Congress was divided on the issue, many members not wishing to offend North Carolina by supporting its recalcitrant possession. The necessary vote of two-thirds in Congress was impossible to achieve.[19] Franklin continued to exist outside of North Carolina and outside of the United States. Blount, who could do nothing but wait, pursued his political career, making plans for the future.

During this time relations between Indians and white men on the frontier were becoming more hostile. Immigrants were moving into the Southwest and pushing into territory belonging to the Indians. The state of Franklin became another invader, and the Indians felt that it had gone too far. Chief Alexander McGillivray of the Creeks proposed that the Indians protect themselves by forming an alliance with Spain against the United States. Congress decided it was time to act, and in 1785 sent a delegation to negotiate a treaty with the Southwest Indians.[20]

Governor Martin of North Carolina had planned to make a separate treaty with the Indians in an attempt to extract more land for his state's benefit. Fearful of the decisions that the United States commissioners might make, Martin gave Blount the title of North Carolina Indian Agent and sent him to interfere in the negotiations. Sensing trouble for his own financial interests, Blount was present in Hopewell, South Carolina, when the commission drew up the new treaty with the Indians. Blount took gifts worth 1000 pounds which were paid for by North Carolina to bribe the Indians to sell land to the state. However, the ploy was to no avail. The United States commissioners regarded the Indians as legal owners of the land and were prepared to deal fairly with them. Sensing this, the Indians rebuffed Blount's attempts at bribery. When the treaty was finished, virtually all of Tennessee was legally returned to the Indians. Blount had failed. Unless something could be done, all his investments were worthless. The commission, in its zeal to deal fairly with the Indians, had created many new problems and had solved none of the old ones. They had failed to deal with the problem of white settlers already living in the territory. Congress could not enforce the Hopewell treaty, which, though just, was impracticable and only worsened relations between the races in the Southwest. The Franklinites were furious because two-thirds of their state now legally belonged to the Indians.[21]

Blount's trip to Hopewell was his first experience with the frontier and the Indians. This treaty spelled doom to all his hopes and plans, but he and the other speculators counted on the weakness of Congress in enforcing such a treaty. Indeed, the wrath of the frontiersmen caused blatant disregard of the treaty of Hopewell. More settlers followed their fellow explorers into Indian country, the government powerless to stop them. The Indians continued to attack, accusing the United States of not living up to its part of the treaty.[22]

In North Carolina Blount was criticized for his inability to stop the disaster. It was rumored that he used the gifts intended for the Indians to purchase land for himself. A defensive Blount denied that he had used his position at Hopewell for personal gain. "I think it necessary to declare upon my word and honor that I have not purchased any land of any Indian . . . since June, 1785."[23] Despite criticism, Blount was appointed to represent North Carolina in Congress in New York. Following instructions from Governor Caswell, Blount tried to stop ratification of the Hopewell treaty by Congress on the grounds that North Carolina claims had been violated. But he was too late. The treaty had been recorded in the *Congressional Journal* and was therefore considered ratified.[24]

The legal return of Tennessee to the Indians had adversely affected land prices in the West, thus arousing the anger of every would-be landholder, not just the large speculators. At the same time, John Jay, who was negotiating a commercial treaty with Spain, urged Congress to give up American claims to free navigation of the Mississippi River for 25 or 30 years. The East supported Jay, but the West was appalled. The perennial problem of sectionalism was already developing. Congress backed down under the pressure, but the West was rapidly becoming alienated from the central government. Frontiersmen dreamed of ridding the West of the Spanish presence, but for the most part they produced only idle threats. Blount's own downfall would come of such a scheme, but the Westerners felt that it was their right to deal with these problems themselves; their own central government appeared to be their worst enemy.[25]

Things seemed even gloomier for Blount in North Carolina where a new Radical government had taken over the state and was conducting investigations into all hints of irregularity in land dealings, especially those regarding the military warrants. There were numerous indictments for fraud, including one involving Reading Blount, William's half brother. In these uncertain years Blount plunged deeper into land speculation in the Southwest. Historical investigations of Blount's career have shown that Blount and his firm did in fact cross the line from dubious dealings to outright fraud in obtaining Tennessee, as did many other speculators.[26] Blount often is called an early political boss because of his talent for manipulating people. Working through oral agreements, giving oral instructions, he rarely committed himself in writing. In every controversial situation, Blount himself seemed to fade into the background, but the outcome usually was managed by him behind the scenes.[27]

The year 1787 was one of disappointments for Blount. His opportunity for the office of President of the United States Congress was thwarted by the adverse publicity surrounding false land dealings. However, Blount enjoyed the prestige and the social life of Congress. While there he was appointed to represent North Carolina at the Philadelphia convention that was to draw up the new Constitution. Blount attended the convention, and although he did not distinguish himself there, he was won over to the Federalist cause. He saw the need for a strong central government. The convention finished its work and Blount was replaced in Congress so that he could return to North Carolina to lead the inevitable battle for ratification.[28]

In July of 1788 the state convention met and rejected the Constitution. Blount and many other old political masters had not been elected and therefore did not participate in this convention. Blount and the Federalists refused to accept defeat. Criticism was new and rankling to Blount; losing was worse. He continued to campaign for ratification. Finally elected to the state legislature again, he led the fight to call a new convention to reconsider the Constitution, and he continued to advocate cession of Tennessee to the federal government. When in 1789 Blount and the Federalists won their battle for a new state convention, Virginia and most other states had ratified the Constitution, and North Carolina had begun to lean in that direction. Through James Robertson's influence, Blount was elected to represent Tennessee County at the convention, despite the fact that Blount had never been to the territory. It was typical of Blount that he claimed traveling expenses as a delegate from the territory, although he had done no traveling. However, he was never reimbursed.[29]

Blount already had his eye on attaining one of the United States Senate seats from North Carolina, but he failed in this aim; Benjamin Hawkins was chosen instead. The Congressmen from North Carolina were John Ashe, John Steele, Hugh Williamson, and John Sevier. Blount did, however, use his influence to get his newest associate, Andrew Jackson, appointed attorney general of the Mero District. Not bemoaning his own loss for long, Blount sought the territorial governorship of Tennessee now that it was a federal territory. His friends in Congress urged President Washington to choose Blount over another candidate recommended by Patrick Henry of Virginia. Congressman Williamson wrote to Washington that Blount's landholdings in Tennessee were an asset to his candidacy because "he must be the more deeply interested in the Peace and Prosperity of the New Government."[30]

On June 8, 1790, President Washington issued Blount's commission for a three-year term as "Governor in and over the Territory of the United States South of the River Ohio."[31] Blount had achieved his goal. He was now governor with a formidable array of powers. He was also Superintendent of Indian Affairs, a vitally important position to the fledgling government of George Washington. The task of setting up a government in the territory was Blount's alone, with no representative assembly to limit his power. For William Blount the future was unlimited both in politics and in land development. He was now near the site of his land dealing; the field was open in the West; the future was rosy to those who had gambling instincts. Relations with the Indians, the Spanish, and even the British and French all affected the fate of the vast lands of the Southwest, and fortunes were made and lost with abandon.

On his way to his new post, Blount detoured to Mt. Vernon to visit briefly with President Washington. Because no capitol had been established in the territory, Blount settled temporarily at the home of William Cobb on the Watauga River. Thus the Cobb house served as the first capitol of Tennessee. Cobb was a wealthy farmer who maintained his comfortable life-style even in the Tennessee wilderness. President Washington appointed David Campbell and Joseph Anderson as judges in the territory. It was left to Blount to make all other governmental appointments, with the exception of the brigadier generals. However, Washington appointed Blount's recommendations, John Sevier for Washington District and James Robertson for Mero District.[32] Blount's two secretaries were Hugh Lawson White and half brother Willie Blount. His first order of business was to gain the support of the ex-leaders of Franklin who had hoped that Sevier might be made governor of the territory. Most of Blount's appointments, therefore, went to Sevier supporters. Blount and Sevier, both ambitious, nevertheless remained allies throughout Blount's administration.[33]

Blount visited each county in East Tennessee—Washington, Sullivan, Greene, and Hawkins. He reinstated the county governments under the jurisdiction of Tennessee, read formally the act of Congress accepting North Carolina's cession of Tennessee, and read his own commission as governor. Blount explained to the people that the territory would be governed "in a manner similar to that which they support northwest of the River Ohio."[34] One of the few differences was that slavery was allowed in Tennessee, one of the conditions of North Carolina's cession.[35]

In November, Blount led a party on the hazardous journey to Nashville to pay his official call there. Accompanying him were 25 riflemen, a group of Indians, and various other citizens. In Mero District, which included Davidson, Sumner, and Tennessee counties, Blount also made appointments. Nashville in 1790 was a primitive frontier, even in comparison with the eastern part of the territory. Residents stayed in forts for protection from hostile Indian attacks and lived primarily in log cabins.

J. G. M. Ramsey, early historian and Blount partisan, described

William Cobb's home, "Rocky Mount," served as the first capitol of the Southwest Territory. *Photograph courtesy the Rocky Mount Overmountain Museum.*

the new governor as having "courtly manners . . . a most commanding presence. His urbanity . . . his hospitality, unostentatiously, but yet elegantly and gracefully extended to all, won upon the affection and regard of the populace, and made him a universal favourite . . . . He was at once the social companion, the well-bred gentleman and capable officer."[36]

Blount brought to his new position a variety of experience in government and business in North Carolina. He desired the position of governor in order to be close to his own investments in land. It was more acceptable then for a governmental official to pursue his own interests, for the distinction "conflict of interest" was not clear-cut. Blount's letters to his brother are filled with ideas for money-making schemes, along with concern for governmental problems.[37]

The focus of his entire administration was Indian relations. Blount kept in contact with each tribe through interpreters and deputy residents from whom he received reports.[38] Treaties had been made and broken with the five tribes of the Southwest, and the Treaty of Hopewell was blatantly disregarded by the whites. As a federal appointee, Governor Blount was obliged to defend this treaty despite his personal opposition to it. The problem of white settlers inside Indian territory plagued the government. As settlers continued to pour into Indian territory, the tribes became increasingly resentful and retaliatory. It was obvious that the United States government could not stop the deluge of illegal settlers. The Cherokee had split over the issue of white encroachment, after which the five lower towns had seceded and, joined by other militant warriors, had formed the Chickamauga. Dedicated to retaliating against the whites, they became the most feared of the Southwest Indians.[39]

In 1790 the Treaty of New York was made with the Creeks, to be followed in 1791 by a treaty with the Cherokees. Newly-appointed Governor William Blount was designated to negotiate the pact. The stage was now set for the Treaty of the Holston, considered by Blount to be one of his major accomplishments as governor. President Washington was determined to handle the Indians with fairness and to solve the problems that plagued the Southwest.[40]

In the summer of 1791, after much persuasion on the part of Blount's agents, 1200 Cherokees arrived at the spot on the bank of the Holston River selected for treaty negotiations. Although there are no records of the proceedings, tradition says that Blount indulged his love of ritual as he sat in full military dress under the trees on the bank of the river. The chiefs were presented by an interpreter to James Armstrong who in turn introduced each chief by his Indian name to Governor Blount.[41] The haggling between Blount and the Indians went on for several days, but Blount was a tough bargainer and won most that he had hoped for from the Indians. The boundary was designated as a "line drawn straight from the point where the ridge between the Little and the Little Tennessee rivers struck the Holston eastward to the North Carolina line and westward to the mouth of the Clinch."[42] Blount also obtained unhampered use of the road between Washington District and Mero District, and of the Tennessee River. There was to be an exchange of prisoners; both sides promised to punish their own people who violated the agreement. For this the Indians were paid an annuity of $1000, which they considered unsatisfactory, but Blount promised an increase upon receipt of Congress' approval. The treaty was signed on July 2, 1791, by Governor Blount and 40 representatives of the Cherokees.[43]

Although no treaty ever solved the problem of Indian relations, the Treaty of Holston did clarify the boundaries and duties of each side. Enforcement of this treaty and of the one with the Creeks would mean that nearly all of Tennessee again would belong legally to the white settlers, with the exception of West Tennessee, still occupied by the Chickasaw, and of the Indian hunting grounds which separated East and Middle Tennessee.[44] Blount was proud of his accomplishment in dealing with the Cherokees. On July 8, 1791, he wrote, "The Chiefs left me well pleased and I have hopes that the Treaty will long be preserved on both sides inviolate."[45] Blount was optimistic about Indian-white relations, as were Secretary Knox and Washington. Blount felt his administration was off to a successful start.

It was just after the Holston treaty signing that Indian attacks began in the Nashville area. Many tribes did not approve of the Cherokees' concessions. Even the Indians who signed agreements often could not control their own men. This problem plagued Blount throughout his administration. He came to realize finally that conferences and treaties could not solve the impossible problem of the Indians and the white settlers. During his entire administration, Blount walked a tightrope between the settlers' desire for revenge and the Washington administration's insistence on peace. The story of Blount's governorship is told in the pages of letters to Secretary of War Knox; they explain the problems, outline plans, beg for permission to retaliate against Indian attacks by offensive action, and reflect plans for the inevitable Indian war. All these pleadings and tirades fell on deaf ears in Philadelphia. Knox was concerned with the Indian problem in the Northwest, not in the Southwest. He and Washington were determined that peace could be maintained in the Southwest, and they refused to listen to Blount's assertions to the contrary.[46]

Knox, representing President Washington, kept up a steady stream of letters to Blount, impressing upon him the government's interest in the Indians' welfare. "The Indians have constantly had their jealousies and hatred excited by attempts to obtain their lands—I hope in God that all such designs are suspended for a long period—We may therefore now speak to them with the confidence of men conscious of the fairest motives toward their happiness and interest in all respects. . . ." On this issue Washington and Knox were unyielding. They believed in treaty making and enforcing as the answer to the Indian-white conflict. As governor, Blount lived with the realities of the unpleasant situation. It took a maximum effort on his part, all of his well-known tact in dealing with men, and his famous ingenuity in dealing with governments, to keep both sides reasonably satisfied during his administration. In a letter dated January 31, 1792, Blount received another warning from Henry Knox on the use of force against the Indians. "The militia must not be called out excepting in cases of real danger. I am confident that this power will be used by you with a just regard to the interests of the United States . . . ."[47]

At the same time, in a letter dated February 1, 1792, the citizens of Tennessee County were petitioning General James Robertson.

> The Recent Murders & ravages Committed by Them [the Indians] on our Frontiers, too evidently proves their intentions on this quarter . . . . We are much afraid Sir that Government has not vested their Officers in this Country with Authority to Carry on Expedition against any Nation or village of Indians—yet we are Confident that something must be done with the Indians that does mischief on our Frontiers. . . . We are willing to pursue every Lawful Means to procure peace and Tranquility among us; . . . . We also think that a full representation of our greavences & Situation had better be immediately laid before Governor Blount.[48]

Many settlers always had misgivings about the motives of the federal government. They were suspicious of the government's defense of the Indians at their expenses and also of the government's anxiety to enjoy good relations with Spain, a power despised by the frontiersmen. Many settlers felt that they were being taxed to support a government which was betraying them to their two enemies. In August of 1792, Blount wrote to Secretary Knox expressing his concern over Spanish influence with the Choctaws.[49] The relations between the frontiersmen and the Spanish were perpetually uneasy and suspicious, the Indians often being caught in the middle. The settlers' almost frantic fear was that a strong power would completely cut off the Mississippi River and port of New Orleans, leaving American settlements stranded and mountain-bound.

These fears seem justified when in late 1791 Baron Hector Carondelet became Spanish governor of Louisiana with the avowed intent of using the Creek Indians against the United States. The federal government's major concerns at this time were the Indian problem in the Northwest and problems with Britain and Spain.

Federal officials, therefore, were never involved in nor fully informed about what was taking place in the Southwest Territory. Just as the United States government could not control the white settlers who went into the Indian territory, the Indian leaders could not control their warriors who conducted raids on white settlements.[50]

In 1792, early in his administration, Blount was still convinced that peace between settlers and Indians was possible, and he did his best to keep whites out of Indian Territory. On January 2nd of that year, Blount wrote James Robertson that the treaty should be "preserved inviolate and if this cannot be done I beg you to make examples of the first violators of it. It will be the Duty of the Attorney of the District Mr. [Andrew] Jackson to prosecute on Information in all such Cases and I have no doubt but that he will readily do it." Blount also praised Robertson for the "good treatment you gave the Creek chief."[51]

Also in 1792, building began on the capital which Blount named after his superior, Secretary Henry Knox. The area was owned by Colonel James White, who laid out the town into 64 lots according to Blount's instructions. In June, Knox County was formed from part of Hawkins County, and a jail and a courthouse were built at Knoxville, the new county seat. These buildings were constructed of logs in the fashion of a fort, with portholes to guard against Indian attacks. The first newspaper in Tennessee had already been established at Rogersville by George Roulstone in November of 1791. It was called the *Knoxville Gazette* in anticipation of the new capital to which its offices later moved. In 1793 the Blount family at last was able to build a house comparable to their home in North Carolina. They had been living in a log house on the Holston River since leaving William Cobb's home.[52]

In 1794 traveler Abishai Thomas wrote to John Gray Blount describing the territory and the town of Knoxville. "The Country is in a higher state of improvement than I counted on, and the Town has had a rapid growth, here are frame Houses & Brick Chimneys . . . there is in it ten stores & seven Taverns, besides tippling Houses, one Court House no prison which they boast of as not being an article of necessity. . . ."[53]

The Indian attacks continued, and Blount's popularity began to suffer. He arranged more conferences with the Indians. One such meeting in 1792 was at Coyatee and included Chief John Watts and

IE 43
BLOUNT MANSION

Built in 1792, this was one of the first
frame houses west of the Alleghenies. It
served as both the residence of William
Blount, Governor of the Territory South of the
River Ohio, and as capitol of that territory,
now the State of Tennessee. Born in North
Carolina, Blount was a delegate to the Constitutional Convention of 1787 and a signer
of the Constitution of the United States.

The William Blount Mansion, oldest frame house west of the Appalachians, was constructed in 1793. *Photograph courtesy the Governor
William Blount Association.*

the Chickamauga. Blount left this meeting assured that Watts would
be loyal to the United States; however, Watts also made secret
agreements with the Spanish. Later in the same year Blount attended an Indian conference, this time in Nashville with the Chickasaw and Choctaw for the sole purpose of distributing gifts to them.
Still there was no peace on the frontier.[54]

As the attacks continued, it became apparent to Blount that his
efforts were useless. He finally became convinced, as were most of
the frontiersmen all along, that a full-fledged war was the only answer to the conflict of interests between the settlers and the Indians.
He determined to protect the settlers until he could convince Knox
that an offensive war by the federal government was necessary.[55] But
Knox was adamant. Negotiations between the United States and
Spain over Florida and the Mississippi River were going on, and the
government wanted nothing to disrupt them. In September of 1792,
Blount learned that the Chickamauga and the Creek had declared
war on the settlers and were preparing to attack. Other chiefs sent
Blount a message that it was only a false alarm, and, believing them,
he ordered the militia disbanded. General Robertson, however, suspected a hoax and kept his men ready. The attack came on Septem-

ber 30th at Buchanan's Station south of Nashville. While the out-numbered settlers managed to fend off the Indians, who finally withdrew, the occurrence increased demand from the settlers for an Indian war.[56] Even then Knox would not agree to an offensive cam-paign. Congress was not in session at the time, and Knox insisted on postponing any move until Congress could consider it.[57]

Blount's position as a go-between made him increasingly unpop-ular, for all his attempts resulted in no promise of action from the federal government. The frontier population, especially around Nashville, was forced to live in crowded stations for protection. Whites began ambushing Indians, often attacking those friendly to the United States. In one incident whites attacked an Indian as he was leaving a visit with Blount. When a Chickasaw was murdered in Knoxville, Blount offered a reward for the capture of the killer; the governor himself attended the Indian's funeral.[58]

In addition to dealing with Indian problems, Blount was carry-ing on other business, both personal and official. He was involved even more heavily in land speculation. With his brother and other partners, he bought thousands of acres, using aliases and sometimes dubious means to obtain the land he wanted. Blount entered into an agreement with an acquaintance, Dr. Nicholas Romayne, to sell western lands to Englishmen.[59] Meanwhile, Blount conducted ter-ritorial business, making numerous appointments for positions in the new counties that were being set up in Tennessee.[60] He remained on good terms with the ever popular John Sevier and his followers. John Tipton, Sevier's enemy, was Blount's bitterest critic. Criticism increased as Indian attacks continued, and, in 1793, Blount decided to go to Philadelphia himself. He had not even gotten out of the territory when news came of an ambush by Captain John Beard and his party of the family of friendly Chief Hanging Maw. By the time Blount reached Philadelphia, Knox was in no mood to sympathize with the frontiersmen; instead he demanded an explanation for this attack. Blount's mission failed to move Secretary Knox even one step closer to war.[61]

Blount's understanding of both the Indians and the fron-tiersmen can be seen in a letter from him and Pickens to Knox re-garding the massacre by Beard. In what Blount called the Indian "Law of Blood for Blood," the guilty white men had to be punished, but it was obvious that a white jury would never convict them. Blount could offer Knox no solution to the predicament except a warning that, although gifts might satisfy the Indians temporarily, "families of the murdered or slain Indians will certainly at some time take Blood in satisfaction without regard to Age Sex or Innocence."[62]

Criticism of Blount had been building for various reasons, among them his not calling a territorial legislature even though it was believed that the territory had a large enough population to warrant one. For Blount, ruling unhindered had been the best way. Deciding the time was finally right, he called a meeting of the first Territorial Assembly on August 25, 1794. The upper house consisted of five councilors chosen by the president; members of the lower house were elected by the people of each county. Although life was much improved in the territory by 1794, only about 50 families lived in Knoxville. Occasionally the Assembly met in Carmichael's Tavern and the members boarded with various families and walked to meetings.[63] The most important debate was over taxation, the lower house insisting on higher land taxes in opposition to Blount and the upper house, which was guarding its personal financial interests. In this debate the lower house triumphed. The legislature also chartered two colleges—Greeneville in Greene County and Blount College in Knoxville—and they discussed the possibility of statehood. They also sent a "memorial" to Congress, requesting action regarding the Indian problem. The frontiersmen's view of the Indians was expressed in another letter to Congress several months later which deplored the policy of giving the Indians "large presents and annuities" because the Indians "considered it as an evidence of fear, or as a tribute paid to their superior prowess in war . . . . Fear, not love, is the only means by which Indians can be governed. . . ."[64]

After the legislature disbanded, Blount still faced the Indian problem. General James Robertson was planning to raid the Chickamauga, the Indians who most often attacked the settlements. Knox continued to refuse permission for offensive action, and Blount at last took things into his own hands. Blount secretly approved Robertson's expedition, but the plan was for Robertson to take full responsibility while Blount would officially disapprove. Robertson would then resign to appease government officials.[65] In August of 1794 Robertson and his troops destroyed the Chickamauga towns of Nickajack and Running Water in devastating, surprise attacks. The next month Blount wrote to Secretary Knox, "I assure you that if

General Robertson has given order for the destruction of these towns he is not warranted in so doing by any order from me."[66] It had taken Blount three years of disappointment since the Treaty of the Holston to resort to this deceptive method of dealing with the federal government.

The months after the Nickajack expedition were peaceful ones for the frontier. Blount, following Robertson's proposal, began to enlist friendly Chickasaw and Choctaw aid to protect the frontier from possible Creek attacks. The desired war would be fought against the Creeks, Blount hoped, with the other Indians on the American side.[67]

In 1795 Timothy Pickering replaced Henry Knox as Secretary of War. Pickering disliked Blount from the start and was convinced that Blount had contributed to the Indian problem in the Southwest. On March 23, 1795, Pickering wrote Blount, chastising him for virtually all of the problems with the Indians. Pickering refused to consider any offensive operations and refused to give the support of the United States to friendly Indians in their battles with the Creeks. "Upon the whole, Sir, I cannot refrain from saying that the complexion of some of the Transactions in the South western territory appears unfavorable to the public interests . . . . Congress alone are competant to decide upon an offensive war, and Congress have not thought fit to authorize it."[68] Pickering's actions further alienated Blount, who until then had been loyal to the Administration.

Support was growing for statehood for Tennessee. Blount had his eye on a seat in the United States Senate, for he realized that John Sevier would inevitably be elected governor of the new state because of his popularity with the people. Therefore, Blount called the territorial legislature into special session in June of 1795 to discuss the possibility of statehood. The legislature decided that a census should be taken as a first step toward obtaining statehood. The final count showed that the territory's population had more than doubled since the census of 1791.

Free white males 16 and over	16,179
Free white males under 16	19,944
Free white females	29,554
Other free persons	973
Slaves	10,613
	77,262[69]

The census showing more than enough residents to warrant statehood, the long awaited Constitutional Convention was held in Knoxville on January 11, 1796. Future leaders at the convention included Andrew Jackson, Joseph McMinn, Archibald Roane, and James Houston, father of Sam Houston. The Tennessee Constitution was more democratic than those of some other states in that the governor was to be popularly elected, representation in the legislature was apportioned by population, and the franchise was given to all freemen. On the conservative side, the Constitution set property qualifications for the offices of governor and legislator; it required all state officeholders "to believe in God and in future rewards and punishments"; and it placed restrictions on taxation. Blount was behind the taxation provision. The owner of large areas of choice lands, he supported low taxes and the taxing of all lands equally. This became part of the Constitution with the stipulation that town lots and slaves could be taxed at the equivalent of 200 acres.[70]

There were questions in some quarters about the short time in which the census had been taken and the Constitution written, but the people, led by Blount and Sevier, supported it. Sevier was elected governor. The first state legislature met on March 28, 1796, and elected Blount and William Cocke the first Senators from Tennessee. For Tennesseans at least, the territorial period had come to an end. There was still a battle to be fought in Congress, but for Tennessee, statehood had been accomplished. The new state was quite different from the place Blount had ridden into not quite six years before. The towns of Clarksville, Maryville, and Sevierville had been established, while the major towns of Nashville and Knoxville—the latter as state capital—had grown into places of civilization. When Blount came to the territory, Nashville had been a cluster of log cabins and Knoxville nonexistent.[71]

In the spring of 1796 Blount went to Philadelphia to use his influence in the fight for statehood. The year 1796 saw a crucial national election. Because Washington was retiring as president, the Federalist and anti-Federalist forces already were polarized. Sentiments in the West were notoriously anti-Federalist. The eastern-oriented John Adams party had no appeal for the frontiersmen. Tennessee's bid for statehood came at a sensitive moment in national politics and threatened to disrupt the balance between the factions in Congress. The Federalists who held a majority in the Senate were determined to delay Tennessee's application.[72]

Blount and Cocke arrived as Senators-elect from Tennessee, but their reception was not all that they had hoped for. In both houses of Congress Tennessee's application for statehood was referred to committee. When the debate came in the House, the Federalists attempted to postpone a decision by finding illegalities in the statehood-qualifying procedure used by Tennessee: they claimed that the census was illegal, that the territory should have been divided into several states, and that the territory should have waited for Congress to initiate statehood procedures. In effect, they charged that Tennessee should have waited for Congress to invite them to join the United States, instead of asking to enter.[73] There were some legitimate questions regarding the census which had reported 77,262 inhabitants of Tennessee. Because of its wording, *people* rather than *residents* could have included transients; the count happened to have been taken during a time of year when many people were traveling through the territory. In addition, sheriffs were paid a dollar for each group of 200 people counted and reported.[74] James Madison attempted to inject some common sense into the debate in the House of Representatives. He defended Tennessee's request as the right of its citizens, rebuking those who wanted to keep people out of the Union on unimportant legalistic interpretations. The final House vote was 43-30 in favor of Tennessee with opposition being almost entirely attributed to sectional and party reasons.[75]

The Federalist-controlled Senate postponed debate on the question for a month. On May 9, 1796, Blount and Cocke presented their credentials as Senators but were refused admission. On May 23rd the Senate voted by a small margin of 12-11 to give the two men chairs as spectators. The debate in the Senate was especially bitter, the Federalists grasping at every straw to keep Tennessee out. Blount's Tennessee enemies provided some of the ammunition; with him as spectator, the opponents of Tennessee statehood criticized Blount, his governing of the territory, and his general policies. The time for Senate adjournment was approaching with nothing settled when a key opponent, Senator King, resigned and Aaron Burr took his place on the committee. His sympathies were won over to the Westerners' cause, and the Senate approved Tennessee's application on May 31, 1796. In one final, insulting move, they denied by a vote of 11-10 to allow Blount and Cocke their seats in the Senate. The two would-be Senators were obliged to return to Tennessee and be reelected.[76]

The battle for statehood won, on June 1, 1796, the act admitting Tennessee into the Union was signed by the president.

> Be it enacted by the State and the House of Representatives . . . That the whole of the territory ceded to the United States by the State of North Carolina shall be one State, and the same is hereby declared to be one of the United States of America, on an equal footing with the original States, in all respects whatever, by the name and title of Tennessee . . . ."[77]

The victory came at great cost to Blount personally. He had been a staunch supporter of the Federalists since the 1789 battle for the Constitution. Whatever his personal faults, Blount had obeyed his superiors during his governorship, often at the expense of his own popularity at home, where the federal government—especially the Federalists—were violently unpopular. Blount felt that he had served well, but he received in return only criticism from Congress and snubs from the Federalists. Even Washington was now unfriendly to his former appointee. Blount was treated coolly by those in Federalist circles. The experience marked the end of Blount's loyalty to his old party and may have set the stage for the conspiracy against this government that brought Blount's political downfall.[78]

Blount was easily reelected to the Senate; at the same time, however, his personal fortunes were in trouble. Due to overspeculation, the entire land market suffered a collapse. Land prices dropped and cash became unavailable. War between Britain and Spain caused Americans to fear that Spain would give Louisiana to France for the price of France's support, causing land values in the West to plummet. Blount's associate, David Allison, was beginning to suffer financially, straining the resources of other speculators, including the Blount brothers and Andrew Jackson. As the economy worsened and Allison's collapse seemed inevitable, Blount became more desperate for a solution to his problems. The fear of a foreign power's denying free navigation of the Mississippi River had always haunted the frontier and now seemed perilously close to reality. This combination of circumstances made Blount open to suggestions that would relieve him of his difficulties.[79] One such plan involved John Chisholm, a Spanish-hating ex-soldier who had done other jobs for Blount. Chisholm later testified that he had originated a scheme

called crime was not considered as serious as it was in Philadelphia. When the Sergeant at Arms of the Senate arrived in Tennessee to escort Blount back to Philadelphia to face charges, Blount entertained him in style, but refused to go back with him. The Sergeant at Arms could get no assistance from Tennessee officials, for they were controlled by Sevier, Blount's old ally. The case was therefore heard without Blount.[89] Gradually Blount began to make a comeback in Tennessee. There was even a suggestion that he run for reelection to the Senate, but, despite the devotion of his followers, he had lost much of his great power. Nevertheless, Blount did plan to reenter politics. A rumor that Sevier might resign to take a federal appointment cast Blount's eye on the governorship. Although Sevier decided not to resign after all, Blount did win a seat in the legislature and became Speaker of the Senate. In the State Senate, Blount masterminded an attempt to impeach his enemy Judge Campbell, while ironically he himself was being impeached in the United States Senate. Blount's failure to remove Campbell meant the end of his great political influence in Tennessee.[90]

During March of 1800 several members of Blount's family contracted malaria. Blount himself caught a chill while staying up at night with his son Billy. He became seriously ill and died a few days later, leaving his wife with several small children. Despite his land investments, the family's financial situation was tangled and their holdings were virtually worthless. Blount's death occurred on March 21, 1800, just five days before his 51st birthday.[91]

Always an ambitious man, Blount continued buying land and making plans for expansion of his interests until the time of his death. He was ruthless in these endeavors, as were Jackson, Sevier, John Donelson, and the other big land speculators who settled the Southwest. Blount was never a man of the people, but people followed him. He was portrayed by early historians as a selfless servant of the people. He was not perfect, nor was he a villain. He was a businessman, a man of his times who took advantage of every opportunity that presented itself and dealt with every situation in a pragmatic way. He had no moral scruples about the plight of the Indians; he simply obtained their land whenever he could. He gambled on the fact that the white settlers would eventually take over all the land. Blount was a dedicated governor of Tennessee, taking his job seriously and obeying his superiors, even though he assiduously pursued his own interests on the side.

J. G. M. Ramsey in 1853 and Marcus Wright in 1884 extolled Blount's virtues, and in their histories of Tennessee claimed that Blount did nothing illegal in his conspiracy, only good for Tennessee. This one-sided view has been countered by opposition just as extreme. In 1930 Isabel Thompson condemned Blount for violating international law and villifying the American hero Washington.[92] It is true that Blount's letter to Carey was indiscreet, his plot illegal; but how far he had actually gone with it beyond the planning stages is not known. No army was raised; the plot was all talk when it was uncovered. The desire to eliminate the Spanish presence in the Southwest was a universal dream among the frontiersmen. Many schemes against the Spanish were dreamed of, even talked about, but Blount's was discovered. All of his investments depended on the removal of foreign powers from the area. He was therefore a desperate man and allowed himself to be carried away by this desperation.

Despite Blount's grandiose schemes, his investments were nearly worthless when he died. In addition, his great political power was gone. Andrew Jackson later took over what was left of the Blount political machine, and the struggle for power between him and Sevier erased much of the legacy of Blount from Tennessee politics. Blount has been nearly forgotten. He deserves better, for, despite his personal failings, he effectively represented government in a wilderness surrounded by hostile Indians and foreign power. Blount was "a tower of federal strength on the Spanish frontier."[93]

NOTES

1. William H. Masterson, *William Blount* (Baton Rouge: L.S.U. Press, 1954), p.180; Philip M. Hamer, ed., "Letters of Governor William Blount," *East Tennessee Historical Society Publications*, no. 4 (1932), p. 122.

2. Clarence E. Carter, ed., *Territorial Papers of the United States* (Washington: U.S. Goverment Printing Office, 1936), 4:81.

3. Masterson, pp. 185-186; J.G.M. Ramsey, *The Annals of Tennessee* (Kingsport: Kingsport Press, 1967), pp. 544-545.

4. Thomas P. Abernethy, *From Frontier to Plantation In Tennessee* (Chapel Hill: University of North Carolina Press, 1932), pp. 158-159; Randolph C. Downes, "Cherokee-American Relations in the Upper Tennessee Valley, 1776-1791," *East Tennessee Historical Society Publications*, no. 8, (1936), p. 41.

5. Masterson, pp. 2-3.

6. Ibid., pp. 4-7, Abernethy, p. 164.

7. Ibid., pp. 23-24, 29-30.

8. Ibid., pp. 32-35.

9. Ibid., p. 51.

10. Ibid., pp. 37, 56-57.
11. Ibid., pp. 57-60.
12. Ibid., p. 60.
13. Abernethy. p. 19.
14. Noel B. Gerson, *Franklin, America's "Lost State"* (New York: The Macmillan Company, 1968), pp. 1819.
15. Stanley J. Folmsbee, Robert E. Corlew, and Enoch L. Mitchell, *Tennessee: A Short History* (Knoxville: The University of Tennessee Press, 1969), pp. 79-80; Downes, p. 42.
16. Masterson, pp. 85-86.
17. Ibid., p. 92; Gerson, p. 30.
18. Abernethy, p. 89.
19. Folmsbee, Corlew, and Mitchell, pp. 83-84.
20. Masterson, pp. 100-101.
21. Ibid., pp. 106, 112.
22. Theodore Roosevelt, *The Winning of the West* (New York: G.P. Putnam's Sons, 1896), 4:154.
23. Walter Clark, ed., *The State Records of North Carolina* (Goldsboro, North Carolina: Nash Brothers, 1900), p. 767.
24. Ibid., p. 657.
25. Abernethy, p. 92; Arthur P. Whitaker, *The Spanish-American Frontier,* reprint 1927, (Lincoln: University of Nebraska Press, 1969), p. 9.
26. Masterson, pp. 118, 119; Roosevelt, p. 177.
27. Abernethy, p. 93.
28. Masterson, pp. 126-127.
29. Masterson, pp. 164-169.
30. Carter, pp. 19-20.
31. Ibid., p. 36.
32. Ramsey, pp. 542-544.
33. Masterson, p. 189.
34. "The Blount Journal" in Carter, *Territorial Papers,* pp. 429-477.
35. Roosevelt, pp. 133-134.
36. Ramsey, p. 542.
37. Alice Barnwell Keith, ed., "The John Gray Blount Papers" (Raleigh: North Carolina State Department, 1952).
38. Ramsey, p. 561.
39. Folmsbee, Corlew, and Mitchell, p. 101.
40. Roosevelt, p. 138.
41. Ramsey, p. 555.
42. Masterson, pp. 204-206; Ramsey, p. 556.
43. Carter, pp. 65-66.
44. Roosevelt, p. 138.
45. Keith, p. 170.
46. Carter, *Territorial Papers,* 5.
47. Ibid., p. 115.
48. Ibid., p. 117.
49. Ibid., pp. 171-172.
50. Masterson, pp. 215, 222.
51. Carter, p. 108.
52. Ramsey, p. 557.
53. Keith, pp. 447-448.
54. Masterson, p. 218; Ramsey, p. 562.
55. Masterson, p. 227.
56. Ramsey, pp. 562-564; Masterson, p. 229.
57. Carter, p. 195.
58. Masterson, p. 241.
59. Ibid., pp. 249-250.
60. "The Blount Journal" in Carter, *Territorial Papers,* pp. 429-477.

61. Masterson, pp. 241-248, 252-253.
62. Carter, p. 296.
63. Ramsey, pp. 623-624.
64. Carter, p. 355.
65. Masterson, p. 268.
66. Carter, p. 356.
67. Masterson, p 270.
68. Carter, p. 389.
69. Ramsey, p. 648; Charlotte Williams, "Congressional Action on the Admission of Tennessee to the Union," reprinted in *Tennessee Old and New* (Kingsport: Kingsport Press, 1946), p. 31. [ed. note: total correct; enumeration reflects error in source]
70. John D. Barnhart, *Valley of Democracy* (Bloomington: Indiana University Press, 1953), pp. 106-120.
71. Masterson, p. 286.
72. Williams, p. 32.
73. Ibid., pp. 40-41.
74. Ibid., p. 35.
75. Ibid., p. 42.
76. Ibid., pp. 44-50.
77. Carter, pp. 424-425.
78. Masterson, p. 297.
79. Ibid., pp. 299-301.
80. Ibid., pp. 303-305; Arthur P. Whitaker, *The Mississippi Question, 1795-1803* (Gloucester, Mass.: Peter Smith, 1962), p. 108.
81. Keith, p. 535.
82. Masterson, p. 307.
83. Isabel Thompson, "The Blount Conspiracy," *East Tennessee Historical Society Publications,* no. 2 (1930), pp. 7-10.
84. Masterson, pp. 313-320.
85. Ibid., pp. 322-323.
86. U.S. Congress, "Proceedings in the Impeachment of William Blount," Philadelphia, 1799, p. 11.
87. James L. Highsaw, comp., "Papers of Willie Blount" from the Draper Collection.
88. U.S. Congress, p. 102.
89. Masterson, p. 334.
90. Ibid., pp. 332-333.
91. Ibid., pp. 340-342.
92. Marcus Wright, *Some Account of the Life and Services of William Blount* (Washington: E. J. Gray, 1884); Thompson, p. 10.
93. Arthur P. Whitaker, *The Spanish-American Frontier,* p. 20.

BIBLIOGRAPHY

BOOKS
Abernethy, Thomas Perkins. *From Frontier to Plantation in Tennessee.* Chapel Hill: The University of North Carolina Press, 1932.
Barnhart, John D. *Valley of Democracy.* Bloomington: Indiana University Press, 1953.
Caldwell, Mary French. *Tennessee: The Dangerous Example.* Nashville, Tennessee: Aurora Publishing Company, 1974.
Carter, Clarence Edwin, ed. *Territorial Papers of the United States: The Southwest Territory.* Vol. 4. Washington: U.S. Goverment Printing Office, 1936.
Clark, Walter, ed. *The State Records of North Carolina.* Goldsboro, North Carolina: Nash Brothers, 1900.
Folmsbee, Stanely J; Corlew, Robert E.; and Mitchell, Enoch L. *Tennessee: A Short History.* Knoxville: The University of Tennessee Press, 1969.

Gerson, Noel B. *Franklin: America's "Lost State."* New York: The Macmillan Company, 1968.
Masterson, William H. *William Blount.* Baton Rouge: Louisiana State University Press, 1954.
Ramsey, J. G. M. *The Annals of Tennessee,* 1853; reprint ed., Kingsport, Tennessee: Kingsport Press, 1967.
Roosevelt, Theodore. *The Winning of the West,* Vol. 4. New York and London: G. P. Putnam's Sons, 1896.
Whitaker, Arthur P. *The Mississippi Question, 1795-1803,* 1934; reprint ed., Gloucester, Massachusetts: Peter Smith, 1962.
_____. *The Spanish-American Frontier, 1783-1795,* 1927; reprint ed., Lincoln: University of Nebraska Press, 1969.
Wright, Marcus J. *Some Account of the Life and Services of William Blount.* Washington, D.C. E. J. Gray Publishers, 1884.

MANUSCRIPTS
Highsaw, James Leonard, comp. "Transcripts from the Lyman C. Draper Manuscripts Relating to the History of Tennessee from 1769 to 1850." Compiled for the D. A. R. and the Cossitt Library from papers in the Wisconsin State Historical Society, Madison, Wisconsin, June-September, 1914.
Keith, Alice Barnwell, ed. "The John Gray Blount Papers." Raleigh: North Carolina Department of Archives and History, 1952.
United States Congress. "Proceedings in the Impeachment of William Blount." Philadelphia, 1799.

ARTICLES
Downes, Randolph C. "Cherokee-American Relations in the Upper Tennessee Valley, 1776-1791." *East Tennessee Historical Society Publications* no. 8, 1936.
Hamer, Philip M., ed. "Letters of Governor William Blount." *East Tennessee Historical Society Publications* no. 4, 1932.
Thompson, Isabel. "The Blount Conspiracy." *East Tennessee Historical Society Publications* no. 2, 1930.
William Blount Mansion Association. "The Blount Mansion." Knoxville, Tennessee: Knoxville Lithographic Company, n. d.
Williams, Charlotte. "Congressional Action on the Admission of Tennessee into the Union." In *Tennessee Old and New: Sesquicentennial Edition, 1796-1946,* sponsored by The Tennessee Historical Commission and The Historical Society, Vol 1. Kingsport, Tennessee: Kingsport Press, 1946.

2

JOHN SEVIER
Governor of Tennessee,
1796-1801 and 1803-1809

by Lynette B. Wrenn

This testimonial from the Tennessee General Assembly in 1809 marked the conclusion of John Sevier's sixth term as governor of Tennessee:

> The long and uninterrupted continuance of that confidence and undiminished affection of a grateful people, are proofs of your merit to which we are sensible our testimony can add but little weight. In whatever situation you may be placed hereafter, doubt not that you will continue still to merit the esteem and affection of the freemen of Tennessee Accept, Sir, our warmest wishes for your future welfare and happiness.[1]

While Sevier had enemies, no Tennessean during his lifetime surpassed him in popularity. Born a British subject on the American frontier, he fought for independence from a country that sought to dam the tide of westward movement and became a powerful member of the political and military hierarchy of the old Southwest during the pioneering days when Indians claimed most of the Tennessee country. By the time of his death in 1815, white settlers had spread from the Appalachian Mountains to the Mississippi River.

Land and the expectation of rapidly appreciating land values were the primary motivations that lured men down the valleys of Virginia and over the mountains from North Carolina to Tennessee. Land ownership conferred status and political privileges as well as material rewards. Only the desire for land can explain the determination of settlers who daily faced the loss of life and property and fought tenaciously to hold and extend their possessions at the expense of the Indians. The man who could lead his neighbors in successful military forays against the natives and who shared the conviction that the soil should belong to white men would win the loyalty of these people. Such a man was John Sevier who, through his military prowess and gift for making loyal friends, became governor of the state of Franklin, first governor of Tennessee, and United States Representative from East Tennessee.

The best evidence suggests that the future governor of Tennessee was born on September 23, 1745, in the Shenandoah Valley of Virginia, to Valentine Sevier, a recent immigrant of French and English parentage. John's grandfather is believed to have been a Huguenot who fled from France and religious persecution to England, where he married an English woman and changed his name from Xavier to Sevier. Valentine, one of his two sons, who had come to Baltimore around 1740, then made his way to western Virginia where he pursued those traditional modes of getting ahead on the frontier—farming, trading, tavern keeping, and land speculating.

After a brief formal education, Valentine's first-born child, John, followed the same pattern with even greater success. The uncertainty of life on the frontier brought an early maturity; at 16 John Sevier married Sarah Hawkins, who, before her death, bore him ten children. In addition to farming, Sevier helped his father run a store, and, at the age of 19, on land purchased near his birthplace, laid out the town of New Market, sold lots, and built a tavern. John Sevier had learned early that the real rewards were to be reaped in the buying and selling of land.[2]

Attracted by hunters' tales of abundant game and rich lands, colonial settlers prepared to move westward following the defeat of France in 1763, but a British proclamation of that year forbade settlement beyond the crest of the Appalachians. In 1768 the treaties of Fort Stanwix with the Iroquois and Hard Labor with the Cherokee Indians appeared to open additional areas to white settlement. The first settlers arrived in present-day Tennessee at this time and began to farm in the Holston Valley.[3] During this time the entire Sevier clan, including the parents, located north of the south fork of the Holston River, which in the 1770s was considered a part of Virginia and was governed by that state.[4]

Meanwhile, the Watauga squatters under James Robertson's leadership formed the Watauga Association in 1772 for purposes of self government, land distribution, and defense, and they leased their lands for ten years from some of the older Cherokee chiefs for

Portrait of John Sevier. *Photograph by George W. Hornal, courtesy Tennessee Department of Transportation.*

about $6000 in goods. The Proclamation of 1763 forbade the purchase of lands from the Indians but was silent on the subject of leasing from them. The first two years of the Watauga Association were a time of peace with the Indians that brought in hundreds of new settlers.

In 1775 Judge Richard Henderson of North Carolina met a delegation of Cherokees at Sycamore Shoals, near the Watauga Community, and, in defiance of the King's proclamation, purchased thousands of acres in Kentucky and the Cumberland Valley. Following his example, the Wataugans bought 2000 square miles of land from the Indians. John Sevier was one of seven white men and four Cherokee chiefs who signed the deed of purchase on March 19, 1775.[5] He acquired a patent for some of this land and moved his wife and children to Watauga in 1775. Sevier enjoyed a position of prominence immediately, being made clerk of the Watauga Association and a member of the five-man governing court the year he arrived. After the outbreak of the American Revolution, pioneers along the Watauga and Nolichucky rivers, doubtless hoping to legalize land purchases the Crown considered illegal, cast their lot with the patriots. The Watauga settlers constituted themselves the Washington District and named a 13-member committee of safety on which John Sevier served.[6]

In the ensuing struggle, Cherokee loyalty went to the British, who hoped to use the Indians to immobilize the people on the frontier. Many Cherokees viewed the struggle among white men as an opportune moment for regaining their former lands. British Indian agents urged families living along the Watauga and Nolichucky rivers to withdraw lest the innocent suffer. Instead the settlers stalled for time while they quickly strengthened old and built new fortifications and stationed a militia company between themselves and the Cherokees. Hostilities soon began when, on July 21, 1776, a small force under the command of Captain James Robertson and Lieutenant John Sevier successfully withstood a siege by several hundred Indians at the Watauga fort near Sycamore Shoals.[7]

To keep their back country enemy quiet during the struggle for independence, militia units of Virginia, Georgia, and the two Carolinas campaigned aggressively against the Indians in four separate engagements, known during the remainder of 1776 as the Cherokee War. The virtually horseless and poorly-armed Cherokees were no match for their mounted foes. Near starvation forced many of them to agree to the Treaty of Long Island in July of 1777; it granted to North Carolina the lands purchased by the men of the Watauga and Nolichucky settlements in 1775 in return for a promise that the line would "remain through all generations."[8] Dissident Cherokees under Chief Dragging Canoe relocated on Chickamauga Creek, and, together with the Upper Creeks and other dissatisfied Indians, continued their struggle against white intruders.

The isolated Wataugans petitioned Virginia in the summer of 1776 to take them under her jurisdiction; Virginia declined. The settlers then looked to North Carolina and were instructed to send delegates to the state Constitutional Convention in November. One of the five chosen was John Sevier. He attended the convention at Halifax, North Carolina, and signed the Constitution. Sevier represented the District of Washington in the lower house of the first North Carolina General Assembly and was among 21 justices of the peace named for the district. In 1778 North Carolina renamed the District of Washington "Washington County" and appointed John Sevier clerk of the county court. When Sullivan County was carved out of Washington County in 1779, Evan Shelby was made colonel of its militia, and Sevier became colonel of the Washington County militia.

For 20 years John Sevier led his people in a perpetual round of Indian wars. During most of these years he lived at Plum Grove on the Nolichucky River and was referred to as "Nolichucky Jack," or just "Chucky Jack." Settlers were flowing westward in a steady stream; eventually they settled within "one day's walk" of the closest Cherokee villages.[9] Horse stealing, robbery, and murder by Indians and encroachment and broken treaties by whites kept the frontier in turmoil. Sevier adopted an aggressive method of frontier warfare and was so successful with it that he is said to have fought 35 battles and never lost one.

With several hundred mounted men and experienced scouts ranging ahead, Sevier and his force frequently took the Indians by surprise. They fought on foot, firing from behind trees, and usually deployed in the Indian half-moon formation. A few scouts would attempt to decoy the Indians through the open space, and Sevier then would close the gap behind them. After killing or dispersing the natives, Sevier and his men burned their villages and destroyed or carried off their stores of corn and livestock. Sometimes just the rumor that Sevier was near caused the Indians to flee in panic. With this scorched earth policy the destitute natives were pushed back inexorably and forced to agree to new treaties that legitimized the gains of their adversaries.[10]

The Revolutionary War Battle of King's Mountain further enhanced Sevier's military reputation. A few months after the British launched their Southern campaign with the capture of Charleston, Major Patrick Ferguson, commander of a troop of Southern loyalists and British regulars, threatened to come over the mountains in 1780 and "lay their country waste with fire and sword."[11] When this message reached Isaac Shelby, the colonel rode to the Nolichucky where John Sevier was celebrating his marriage to Catherine Sherrill with a barbecue and horse race for his neighbors. The two colonels decided to intercept Ferguson before he could cross the mountains. Men of Washington and Sullivan counties, refugees from east of the mountains, and a large party of Virginians traveled over the mountains into the Carolina country where they were joined by other patriots. British and American forces met at King's Mountain, South Carolina, on October 7, 1780, and the over-mountain men won a decisive victory. This victory heartened patriots throughout the Carolinas and had a correspondingly dispiriting effect on the Tories. The defeat of the British at King's Mountain began the series of military reverses that led to Yorktown. The grateful state of North Carolina voted to present a sword and pistols to both Sevier and Shelby but delayed the presentation until 1813 when the United States again was fighting Great Britain. Being known as one of the heroes of King's Mountain added to Sevier's popularity and renown.[12]

On the trip home from King's Mountain, the frontiersmen, accompanied by a large body of prisoners, halted long enough to try some of the Tories for murder, theft, and other offenses. Thirty-two were condemned to die, and before Sevier and Shelby could stop the proceedings, the sentence for nine had already been carried out by hanging.[13]

A year after King's Mountain, Colonels Sevier and Shelby, along with a sizable force of Westerners, helped General Francis Marion clear South Carolina of the British and the Tories. Rumors that the Indians planned to attack the settlements in their absence caused

Sevier to lead an expedition against them immediately upon his return. At Boyd's Creek on the French Broad River, in territory that
later became Sevier County, Sevier and his men destroyed all but two
of the area villages and are said to have burned 1000 huts and seized
50,000 bushels of corn. In the next two years Sevier led additional
campaigns against the Indians that brought a plaintive cry from one
of their chiefs: "We are the first people who ever lived on this land; it
is ours, and why will our elder brother take it from us?"[14]

In the final years of the War for Independence, the land situation
in Western North Carolina became chaotic. When, in 1777, the state
opened land offices in each county, speculators picked up more than
a million acres of land in Washington County, largely in areas
claimed by the Indians. Loyalist lands were put up for auction in
1779 and men, especially those in influential posts such as John
Sevier, used depreciating state and continental bills to enlarge their
landholdings. Rampant speculation, accompanied by numerous
charges of illegal procedure, prompted North Carolina in 1781 to
close county land offices in the West. During the following year the
legislature created a new land office in Nashville to handle Cumberland Valley lands set aside for compensation to North Carolina
soldiers. Speculators profited from this arrangement, buying the
claims of veterans who could not go to Nashville to file, or who did
not have the resources to homestead. With complete disregard for
Indian holdings, all other unsettled lands in the western section of
the state were opened to entry in 1783. North Carolina's attitude was
that Indian loyalty to the British nullified their claims to all except
the small area south of the Holston, French Broad, and Big Pigeon
rivers where the Cherokees lived. During the seven months that this
land office in Hillsboro, North Carolina, remained open, entries
were recorded for approximately four million acres of land in
present-day Tennessee. Most of the land went to large-scale
speculators like William Blount who alone had the credit, political
contacts, and inside information necessary to put together large
holdings. Many opportunities for fraud existed and were
exploited.[15]

While the full extent of John Sevier's land ownership has not
been determined—he was not in the same class as William Blount—it
is known that between 1786 and 1795 he acquired title to more than
70,000 acres in his own name, much of it in the Cumberland Valley.

He and his partners owned other large properties. Lands along the Holston, Watauga, and Nolichucky rivers came into Sevier's possession prior to 1777; as one of three Commissioners of Confiscated Estates in 1778, he increased his estate by purchases of confiscated property.[16]

Eastern speculators who expected to profit without sharing the dangers of frontier life incurred the odium of the West. Sevier's speculative activities, however, did nothing to diminish his popularity, for all pioneers in a sense were speculating in land. Important military and political positions gave him a far greater chance for aggrandizement than the ordinary pioneer, but Sevier lived in their midst, led them successfully against the Indians, and labored to build up the West country. He helped finance militia operations, opened his corn cribs to hungry families, and sold land to newcomers on moderate terms.

Sevier's dream of acquiring a large estate in the Muscle Shoals area of the Tennessee River, his greatest speculative project, ended in failure. When a 1783 survey revealed that land in the "Great Bend" of the river lay south of the North Carolina boundary, prominent North Carolinians, William Blount and Richard Caswell, formed a company to buy the territory from the Indians and to establish a colony there. They brought Western leaders such as John Sevier into the company, for the usual mode of operation in land deals was for Easterners to supply most of the capital while Western leaders located suitable land and made local arrangements. William Blount persuaded Georgia to establish Houston County in the "Great Bend." Georgia then made Sevier a member of the seven-man commission responsible for examining the land and appointed him colonel of the Houston County militia. The chimera of a colony at Muscle Shoals became an obsession with Sevier. It carried him through the dark days of Franklin and he never gave up his interest in the "Bend" area, as letters throughout his governorship testify.[17]

Only after most of the Tennessee country was in private hands, with the balance in the North Carolina treasury swelled by land payments, did the North Carolina legislature heed the pleas of Congress that she cede her western lands to the nation. Residents of Eastern North Carolina, in particular, were then ready to let Congress assume the burdensome costs of Indian defense west of the mountains. By a narrow margin, North Carolina assembly delegates voted in 1784 to transfer their western lands to the public domain. The state gave Congress one year to act on the cession and attached two conditions: that slavery could not be abolished without local consent and that all land entries under North Carolina law had to be honored. In a subsequent act North Carolina retained jurisdiction over her western lands for five more years.

The act of cession ignited a separatist movement in the transmontane region. It was fueled by multiple resentments, as well as by clear-sighted realism. When North Carolina in 1776 defined her boundaries, one clause stipulated that "it shall not be construed so as to prevent the establishment of one or more governments westward of this State, by consent of the Legislature."[18] The men on the frontier knew that Congress would establish procedures for the admission of new states, and also were well aware of efforts in southwestern Virginia to create a separate state. While Congress deliberated and North Carolina relinquished responsibility, the people beyond the mountains, without even a separate militia or superior court, knew that they stood alone against the Indians, hundreds of miles from the state capital. They were conscious, too, that the Indians were unusually restive because promised treaty goods had not been delivered by North Carolina. The Westerners had been referred to in the East as the "offscourings of the earth," and many south of the French Broad River stood to lose their land if the union with North Carolina persisted. Emboldened by the successful Watauga experiment in self-government and embittered by North Carolina taxing policies that seemed to favor the eastern part of the state, these pioneers determined to act.[19]

Delegates from the three western counties of Washington, Sullivan, and Greene met in Jonesborough during the late summer of 1784, elected John Sevier president, and discussed the formation of an independent state. Separated from these counties by a forest wilderness of about 150 miles and feeling a closer identity with Kentucky settlements to the north, the Cumberland region did not participate in the state-making experiment. Before the new state could be organized on a permanent basis, however, North Carolina repealed her act of cession. News of this action did not travel across the mountains, however, until after delegates to a convention in December declared their independence and adopted a new Constitution.

John Sevier did not support the separatist movement initially, although he had corresponded in 1782 with Arthur Campbell, the Virginia leader who desired to create a western state. Among other things, Sevier feared that independence would end his partnership in the Muscle Shoals venture. With word of North Carolina's repeal came news of concessions for the West; Sevier communicated these developments with the expectation and hope that they would "satisfy the people with the old state."[20] The North Carolina legislature appointed Sevier brigadier general of a newly created western military district and established a superior court across the mountains as well. When it became evident to him that the movement could not be stopped, Sevier accepted the position of leadership that his countrymen accorded him rather than lose his popularity with them. In time Sevier realized that the possibility existed for the Muscle Shoals region to be included within the boundaries of the new state. When petitioned to recognize the new state, Congress was asked to include the "Big Bend," as well as parts of Virginia and Kentucky, in the state of Franklin. This project was no secret, for one resident wrote in December of 1784 that the new state was controlled by "a few crafty landjobbers, whom you know, are aiming at purchasing the great bent of Tenasee from the Indians and if not successful that way, to . . . drive the natives (Cortez-like) out by force."[21] Once he had made the commitment to Franklin, Sevier, for whatever reason—pride or profit—remained loyal to the state after many of its most ardent early supporters abandoned the cause.

In March of 1785, the first General Assembly of Franklin elected Sevier governor for a three-year term. At the same time the assembly sent William Cocke to Congress to plead their cause. As a conciliatory gesture toward the mother state, the Franklin assembly voted in August to honor North Carolina land claims and to return all money collected by former North Carolina officials. They then sent a representative to North Carolina to state their case for independence. North Carolina alternately threatened and conciliated but would not agree to a separation. Without North Carolina's assent, Congress declined to grant statehood, and this refusal destroyed the unity of Franklin. The rift between those for and against the new state widened when Governor Sevier convinced the assembly to retain the provisional Constitution rather than accept a more democratic instrument of government proposed by one group of delegates.

After North Carolina withdrew her cession offer, many Westerners refused to run the risk of being declared rebels. An offer of pardon from the "Old North State" caused them to return to her allegiance. A faction favoring North Carolina coalesced around John Tipton, a Washington County leader who had originally helped to form the government of Franklin. An ugly feud which erupted between Tipton and Sevier and their followers came close to civil war in 1788. North Carolina had strengthened the Tipton group in 1786 and 1787 by offering to forgive taxes due the state since 1784 and by appointing some of the group to represent North Carolina as judges and sheriffs within Franklin. Tiptonites stood for election to the North Carolina assembly in 1786 and won several seats in the legislature, where they made it impossible for Franklin to present a united front for independence.

The interrelated problems of territorial expansion and Indian relations also occupied Sevier's attention during his term as governor of Franklin. One of his first official acts was to force some of the Cherokee chiefs in June of 1785 to relinquish their claims to territory that lay inside the "Cherokee Reservation" acknowledged by North Carolina in 1783. Congress undercut Sevier's gains from this Treaty of Dumplin Creek and infuriated citizens of Franklin by negotiating two treaties at Hopewell, South Carolina—the first with the Cherokees in November of 1785, and the second with the Chickasaws in January of 1786. In return for surrendering their claim to the Cumberland and Holston territories, Congress confirmed in these treaties the right of the Indians to all other lands in present-day Tennessee and gave the Indians authority to punish and remove trespassers. This meant that many people who had obtained land in accordance with North Carolina laws of 1783 now found themselves living inside Indian territory, for Hopewell restored Indian rights to the soil that North Carolina had voided after the Revolutionary War. Hopewell left even Greeneville, capital of the new state, in Indian country. When the Cherokees went to war to remove white trespassers, as the Treaty of Hopewell authorized, Governor Sevier led an expedition against their towns. A second invasion brought capitulation in August of 1786, and the Cherokees were forced to accept the terms imposed at Dumplin Creek.

The remaining years of the "lost state of Franklin" were bloody ones. Congress had unleashed the Indians but lacked the power to enforce the Treaty of Hopewell. North Carolina ordered white squatters to move out of Indian country and then encouraged them to remain. White expansion continued with the sanction of the Franklin government, the Indians fought back, and both sides exacted vengeance in barbaric ways. Aggression bred aggression. Judge David Campbell spoke for the people of Franklin when he exclaimed, "Have not all Americans extended their back settlements in opposition to laws and proclamations?"[22] The attitude of the Cherokees was expressed by a chieftain who said:

> We well remember, whenever we are invited into a treaty, . . . and bounds are fixed, that the white people settle much faster on our lands than they did before. It must certainly be the case, they think we will not break the peace directly, and they will strengthen themselves and keep the lands. . . . You told us at the treaty, if any white people settled on our lands we might do as we pleased with them.[23]

Against this backdrop of violence, the state of Franklin disintegrated. An attempt by Sevier and Evan Shelby early in 1787 to work out a compromise between the new state and the old failed. When Sevier's term as governor came to an end on March 1, 1788, he was not reelected. Evan Shelby refused to accept the governorship, and no further offer was made. Finally the legislature stopped meeting. Sevier retreated southward to live among his loyal supporters in Greene County where land titles had been negotiated by the governor of Franklin. There remained to him one hope that Franklin might survive—the offer in April of 1786 from Georgia of lands at Muscle Shoals in return for military aid against the Creek Indians. It had taken Sevier only one week to recruit 1500 militiamen, lured by the promise of land, for service in Georgia. Had the scheme materialized it might have unified and revitalized the state; its collapse, however, hastened the end. After nearly two years of waiting for marching orders, Georgia ratified the federal Constitution in February of 1788; Congress then took over the task of pacifying the Creeks, and the men of Franklin were not needed.

As the state of Franklin expired, a strange interlude occurred that is known to history as the "Spanish Conspiracy." Discouraged by the failure of Congress to secure free navigation of the Mississippi River after its closure by Spain in 1784 and by a Congressional Indian policy that protected Indians and left thousands of white settlers on Indian lands without legal title, Sevier, a private citizen once again, began correspondence with Don Diego de Gardoqui, Spanish chargé d'affaires at New York. James Robertson of the beleaguered Cumberland settlements and James Wilkinson in Kentucky were also writing to Spanish officials. Sevier's objectives are not known with certainty, but it is probable the he hoped either to persuade Spain to open the Mississippi to navigation and pacify the Indians in the Muscle Shoals area or to use the threat of a Spanish alliance to win concessions from the government in Washington. Navigation of the Mississippi, peace with the Indians, and a colony in the bend of the Tennessee were the goals which Sevier hoped to achieve by one method or another. He held out the possibility of an alliance between Franklin and Spain, but Spain called his bluff by inviting the frontiersmen to move to Spanish colonies. Requirements for Spanish citizenship and conditions of life in her colonies were too alien to the self-governing protestants of the old Southwest, and when North Carolina made a second offer of her western lands in 1789 and the prospect of statehood seemed sure, the "Spanish Intrigue" came to an end.[24]

The beginning of 1788 found John Sevier in the South making plans for a war against the Indians. During his absence from home, John Tipton ordered the seizure of several of Sevier's slaves in payment for delinquent North Carolina taxes. With a band of about 50 men, Sevier went to Tipton's house in Washington County and placed it under siege. Other men came to the aid of Tipton and, in an ensuing skirmish, several lives were lost. The Tiptonites captured two of Sevier's sons and Tipton threatened to hang them. Moderation prevailed among Tipton's followers, however, and Sevier evidently had little desire to plunge the country into civil war.[25]

Sevier's career reached its nadir in the weeks following his encounter with Tipton. North Carolina officials suspected him of deliberately inciting white settlers south of the French Broad River to launch an Indian war in order to revive his waning popularity. Some historians concur in this judgment, although the encroaching settlers had suffered so many Indian attacks that they needed little urging. During the campaign an unusually barbarous act occurred. Under a flag of truce, Sevier invited several Cherokee chiefs to confer with him. After putting a guard around their tent, he left the camp. One of the men with Sevier was John Kirk, the only survivor of a recent Indian massacre which had left 11 members of his family dead. In Sevier's absence Kirk entered the tent and tomahawked the chiefs one by one. The Indians, accepting their fate with dignity, sat and waited for the blows to fall. Young Kirk had the support and sympathy of the other men. Possibly not even Sevier could have prevented the act of vengeance. It is probable that he left rather than accept responsibility for what was going to happen.

When North Carolina Governor Johnston sent an order for Sevier's arrest on charges of treasonably raising troops to subvert the laws of North Carolina, John Tipton carried out the order personally when other officials declined to act. Tipton arrested Sevier in October of 1788, and sent him over the mountains to Morganton, North Carolina. There he was permitted to remain 'with friends while awaiting trial. North Carolina authorities wisely looked the other way when relatives and friends effected Sevier's escape. The North Carolina legislature cleared Sevier on charges of treason, but debarred him from office. However, after he swore allegiance to North Carolina in February and was elected by Greene County to the State Senate in August of 1789, the assembly seated him and restored his commission as brigadier general. Elevation of the popular Sevier to a place of honor seemed to many state leaders the surest method of quickly pacifying the West. Then, too, Sevier had powerful friends in William Blount, Richard Caswell, and their associates. He voted with the majority of the legislature when North Carolina agreed at last to cede her western lands to Congress.

Sevier became the first representative to Congress from the Washington and Mero districts, and consequently, the first representative from the Mississippi Valley. He proceeded to New York, and on June 16, 1790, took his seat in the Second Congress. Because of the delay in ratifying the Constitution, no representatives from North Carolina sat in the First Congress under the new federal Constitution. With the exception of his vote in favor of a national bank, John Sevier consistently supported Jeffersonian measures. He voted against an excise tax and national assumption of state debts, and he supported a permanent capital on the Potomac.

Congress accepted North Carolina's western lands in 1790 with conditions attached that slavery not be abolished and that North Carolina land claims be honored. Congress then organized Tennessee as the "Territory of the United States South of the River Ohio" and governed the territory under the provisions of the Northwest

Ordinance. There was keen competition for the top territorial positions, for they carried with them vast opportunities for political and economic advancement, as well as honor and status. People of the territory organized a campaign to promote John Sevier's candidacy for governor,[26] but his association with the Franklin adventure and his aggressiveness toward the Indians cost valuable support. President Washington later said of Sevier that he "never was celebrated for anything (that ever came to my knowledge) except the murder of Indians. . . ."[27] William Blount, a Federalist whom Washington knew personally, desired the post to protect the vast Blount possessions in the territory, and he secured the appointment as territorial governor and Indian agent.

Sevier served the territory as brigadier general of Washington District, and, after 1795, served as a member of the five-man Legislative Council—the upper house of the territorial legislature. Blount and Sevier worked together harmoniously, although it must have been difficult at times for the most popular man in the territory to subordinate himself to a newcomer. Blount appointed many Sevierites to territorial office, however, and from the former business associates evolved a cooperative political relationship.

As they had earlier, Indian relations constituted the major preoccupation of the territorial period. Failure of the United States to enforce the Treaty of Hopewell angered the Cherokees. The territorial gains achieved by Governor Blount south of the French Broad River in the Treaty of Holston, July 2, 1791, further increased Indian resentment. Moreover, incessant horse stealing and Indian raids left the whites frustrated and hostile. Neither chiefs nor territorial leaders had much control over the actions of their people. Blount was caught between the popular clamor for preventive war and the administration's insistence on defensive measures alone. Working with Blount, John Sevier and James Robertson counseled for patience, while the governor tried to convince the Washington administration to adopt a more aggressive policy. After a gruesome massacre at Cavet's Station near Knoxville, the territorial secretary, in Governor Blount's absence, authorized Sevier to conduct an offensive campaign. At the battle of Etowah—the site today of Rome, Georgia—Sevier in 1793 punished the Cherokees and Creeks severely. This was his final Indian campaign. The successful Nickajack expedition mounted by the Cumberland settlers against the Creeks and Mad Anthony Wayne's victory over the Northern Indians further pacified the frontier. Spain, now courting the United States, agreed in Pinckney's Treaty to open the Mississippi to navigation.

Improved Indian relations and transportation to market made the Southwest a magnet for new settlers, thereby raising the prospect of statehood. Blount and Sevier both began to plan for this eventuality—Sevier because he knew that no one could deny him the governorship in a state election and Blount because he believed that the settlers could suppress the Indians more decisively than Congress had done. Blount realized, too, that the popular Sevier could not be forever denied the top political post. The territorial assembly carried out a census that showed the territory to have a free population of 66,649, more than enough people to qualify for statehood. An election on the question of whether to seek admission to the union brought overwhelming support, although Davidson and Tennessee counties in the Mero District voted four to one against, probably because the eastern counties would dominate the new state. Governor Blount called for the election of delegates to a Constitutional Convention which met in January of 1796.

For the most part, Blount and his adherents got the kind of Constitution they wanted, including the stipulation that all land except city lots be taxed alike. They created a government in which the legislative body had the greatest amount of power. Most state and county officials were to be elected by the legislature. The governor had no veto and only limited appointive powers. The governor's salary was set at no more than $750 a year. In March, Tennesseans chose members of the state legislature and elected John Sevier their first governor. The legislature, meeting at the end of the month, selected William Blount and William Cocke as the state's two senators, chose four presidential electors, and prepared for the election of two representatives.

The Federalists in Congress, reluctant to strengthen Thomas Jefferson's support in an election year, tried to delay the admission of Tennessee. A compromise reducing the number of representatives from two to one and her electors, consequently, from four to three, enabled the measure to pass. Tennessee became the 16th state to enter the Union.

When John Sevier was inaugurated on March 30, 1796, he became governor of a state in which three-fourths of the soil was still claimed by Indians. The traditional frontier problems of land titles and Indian relations thus continued to be the most urgent concerns. The boundary line agreed upon in the 1791 Treaty of Holston had not yet been surveyed when Sevier took office. He followed William Blount's policy of delaying the survey in order to give settlers beyond the line as strong a claim as possible. Nevertheless, the survey began in 1797 even though General James Winchester, Tennessee's representative on the three-man commission, did not appear. The completed line left several hundred families inside Indian country, and the Adams administration sent troops to supervise their withdrawal. An Englishman traveling from New Orleans to the east coast visited an "encampment" of evicted families on the Clinch River and reported that

> The inhabitants firmly opposed being removed from their settlements, . . . as they all hate the Indians, and think a little deviation from justice is a thing to be overlooked where their two interests clash with each other.[28]

Sevier labored to prevent the settlers from forcibly resisting removal while he assured them of his continuing concern for their welfare. Simultaneously, the governor undertook to convince the federal government to acquire additional lands by treaty. "The lands they inhabit is of little or no use to the natives," Sevier wrote to Secretary of War McHenry, and "I am confident their claim could be extinguished on very easy terms. . . ."[29] Sevier bypassed protesting United States officers and freely issued passes to the dispossessed settlers so that they could return to their claims at intervals.

Sevier sent Colonel James Ore as his unofficial emissary to the Cherokees and instructed him to say to the Indians that they could get more goods from an increased annuity than by hunting and thus take better care of their elderly and helpless. Ore was to urge the Cherokees to abandon hunting and take up farming if they wished to become rich like the white men who had prospered and multiplied much more than the Indians. "By the law of Nations," Sevier added, "it is agreed that no people shall be entitled to more land than they can cultivate."[30]

A first attempt to negotiate with the Cherokees in the autumn of 1798 failed. Sevier blamed this on the commissioners' ignorance of the Indians and not on their lack of good will and determination. The governor spent much time writing to the commissioners and seeking their understanding of Tennessee's point of view. He attended the second conference; largely due to his presence, the Cherokees agreed to the first Treaty of Tellico on October 2, 1798. Tennesseans were not satisfied, but the treaty did make it possible for most of the evicted settlers to return to their homes. Land as far south as the Little Tennessee River and between the Clinch River and the Cumberland Plateau was ceded.

By the time Sevier became governor in 1796, 20 years of punitive expeditions had left the Indians too poor and weak to fight back in an organized way, but individual acts of robbery and murder by both whites and Indians menaced Sevier's goal of preserving peace as an encouragement to large-scale immigration. "There has never been a time when war could have been more ruinous to this Country," Sevier wrote to a man on the border after some Indian guns had been stolen, "and should the report of war get circulated abroad, all this promising prospect of population immediately ceases."[31] A rapidly growing population would both insure rising land values, Governor Sevier believed, and exert pressure against the natives that would eventually drive them out of the state completely.

In accordance with his determination to pursue a policy of peace, Sevier, shortly after his inauguration, wrote to Cherokee chiefs and warriors that he would keep the peace and "if ever war is again known in your land it will not be our fault."[32] At the same time he told the Tennessee legislature that

> The present appearances of Indian affairs has a pacific colour, and should proper methods be adopted by your legislative aid and interposition so as to prevent violations and encroachments, I have no doubt but peace and tranquility will abound, throughout the government.[33]

A steady stream of letters flowed from Sevier's hand throughout his governorship urging peace, promising justice, expressing sympathy, counseling patience, and begging restitution of Indian guns or white horses and slaves. "Let not a few foolish and bad people, on either side," he wrote the Cherokees, "cause you to let go the white chain of peace that keeps our nations bound up, and united so firmly to each other."[34]

During Sevier's second term as governor, relations between France and the United States deteriorated. President Adams planned, as part of a military preparedness program, to make Sevier a brigadier general and commander of southern forces. Because Sevier intended to accept the commission and step down from the governorship, the threat of war engaged his attention for months. He recommended that the administration use American regular troops rather than the militia to fight the war. The Cherokees were warned not to aid the French, and the legislature was advised to rewrite the militia law. The governor offered Tennessee iron to President Adams, as well as several companies of cavalry and mounted troops. Sevier did not miss the opportunity of urging the administration to delay removing squatters, for the country needed to be unified at a time of national danger. The threat of war passed, however, and Sevier continued as chief executive.

When John Sevier's third term as governor ended in 1801, he was not eligible for reelection. During the administration of his successor, Governor Archibald Roane, opposition to Sevier that had been building for some time became quite open and bitter. Andrew Jackson emerged as Sevier's most outspoken critic. During the territorial period, William Blount had drawn into his orbit a number of men who now challenged the leadership of Sevier. Besides Jackson and Roane, other important members of the Blount group were Willie Blount, William's half brother and a future governor, John and Thomas Overton, James Winchester, and Daniel Smith, who had been territorial secretary. As long as William Blount lived he was able to work with both Sevier and Jackson and to keep their clashing personalities somewhat in check, but death two years after his impeachment by the United States Senate removed Blount's restraining hand in 1800.

Ambitious for advancement, Jackson sought military office as the surest road to power in frontier Tennessee. Sevier and Jackson, both understanding the critical importance of military office and paying close attention to key militia elections, began to find themselves on opposite sides in several key contests. The clash between the popular, older Sevier and the rising young challenger spawned the famous Jackson-Sevier feud.

According to state law, each militia company elected its own field officers, a colonel and two majors. Field officers in each of the three military districts—Washington, Hamilton, and Mero—chose their district's brigadier general. In turn all of the field officers together elected a major general as the state's commanding officer. Each district had a cavalry division which held elections at different times. All officers received their commissions from the governor.

During the 1796 Mero District militia elections, Governor Sevier tried to secure the election of a Colonel Ford. Middle Tennesseans who had opposed Sevier in the gubernatorial contest earlier that year, and a number of the old cavalry officers, rallied behind James Winchester. In a move to qualify cavalry officers elected the same day to participate in the election for brigadier general, Governor Sevier sent signed blank commissions for James Robertson to complete. When some question as to the constitutionality of this procedure arose, Joel Lewis, a Sevier partisan in Mero, produced a letter from Sevier defending the practice. Andrew Jackson branded the procedure a "dangerous precedent" and, according to his account, replied that he was sorry to be compelled "to expose the Ignorace of the governor in his attempting to negociate his Constitutional duties" to others.[35] Robertson then refused to complete the commissions, and Winchester won the election as brigadier general of Mero District. The furious Sevier, in a letter to Lewis that the latter made public, referred to Jackson as "a poor pitifull petty fogging Lawyer."[36] A month later, when Jackson ran for the top position of major general of the Tennessee militia, Sevier backed Conway, the winner.

When Jackson heard of the insulting remarks that had been made about him and demanded an explanation, Sevier, regretting what he had written in haste, tried to heal the breach. He admitted to Jackson that his utterance was "the language of a man who thought himself highly injured" and added revealingly that "like yourself when passion agitates my Breast, I can not view things in the calm light of mild philosophy."[37] After an exchange of conciliatory letters between the two men, the controversy appeared to die down, and Governor Sevier, on the recommendation of the Blounts, appointed Jackson to fill a vacancy on the Tennessee Supreme Court.

On his way to Philadelphia in the fall of 1797, Jackson heard some information about fraudulent land practices in the old Nashville land office. He passed this word along to a North Carolina senator who in turn communicated the story to the governor of his state. As a result, Governor Ashe requested the state legislature to investigate the Nashville land office opened by North Carolina in 1783 to grant land to revolutionary soldiers or their assignees. At the same time, Ashe asked Governor Sevier to send papers from the Martin Armstrong office in Nashville to North Carolina. Sevier informed Ashe that only copies should be taken, not the original documents. Sevier's refusal to turn over the papers to North Carolina may have been a dodge to protect himself from charges of fraud, but he also acted on legal advice that Tennessee land records had to remain in the state where they would be readily available as evidence in land cases.

There is evidence that Blount, Sevier, Stockley Donelson, and other Tennesseans involved in large-scale land deals arranged an abortive attempt to steal incriminating papers stored in the North Carolina comptroller's office. Desperate to halt the trial in 1800 of North Carolina Secretary of State James Glasgow, which might bring their own involvement in the land office to public attention, the speculators allegedly sent William Tyrell, one of their accomplices, to North Carolina to destroy evidence. This effort to obstruct justice also failed. James Glasgow lost his office and was fined heavily, and Blount, Sevier, Donelson, and Tyrell were implicated. Through the efforts of Blount and Sevier the report of the North Carolina legislature on the operations of the Nashville land office was suppressed in Tennessee, but copies of several letters from Sevier to Glasgow came into Jackson's hands and were used against Sevier in the gubernatorial campaign of 1803.[38]

With the death of Major General Conway in 1801, Sevier aspired to command the Tennessee militia, but the famous Indian fighter found himself challenged by the militarily inexperienced Jackson. Governor Roane broke a tie vote in the latter's favor, and Jackson became the new major general. An infuriated Sevier determined to recapture the governorship. Using Jackson's letters, Roane charged in one of the bitterest gubernatorial elections in Tennessee history that Sevier had stolen thousands of acres of land. While still governor, Roane called on the legislature to investigate his evidence. His intention probably was to gather evidence for a criminal indictment or impeachment. Sevier supporters were able to eliminate charges of fraud against him and to keep the report from being printed in the *Senate Journal*, but the final report contained evidence that pointed toward him. Sevier also was able to keep the report quiet, and he took his revenge out on Jackson. By an act of the legislature, Tennessee was divided into two military districts, each with its own major general. Jackson's authority had been cut in half.

Jackson's charges were that Sevier had used his official positions to commit acts of bribery, destruction of official records, and forgery of new records in order to secure valuable lands near the Obed River in Middle Tennessee. Whether Sevier was guilty of Jackson's charges—and historians disagree on this point—the affair must be understood primarily as a political struggle between the two men in which Jackson used the charge of fraud to discredit his political opponent. Carl Driver, Sevier's most recent biographer, examined all the evidence carefully and concluded that while the "innocence or guilt of Sevier is not possible of determination . . . he took advantage of the technicalities of the laws to acquire these two large tracts of lands."[39] The remark of a Jackson partisan during the gubernatorial election campaign that "if the records are true, our late Chief Magistrate gave himself great latitude" is probably a fair assessment of Sevier's conduct.[40]

The climax of the Jackson-Sevier feud came in October of 1803 at the height of the legislative investigation. During a confrontation on the streets of Knoxville, Sevier made an insulting reference to the circumstances of Jackson's marriage that brought a challenge from the younger man. Sevier apparently preferred to avoid a duel, and it may be that Jackson soon realized that Sevier's death would destroy him politically in Tennessee. At first the governor did agree to meet Jackson—but outside of Tennessee, for dueling had been made illegal in the state during the Roane administration. Jackson demanded satisfaction in Knoxville where the insult occurred, and when Sevier would not accept this demand, Jackson published Sevier as "a base coward and poltroon" in the *Knoxville Gazette*.[41] A final encounter at Southwest Point near Kingston, where the two men brandished pistols and shouted insults at each other, brought the tragicomic episode to an end. Jackson at this time was 36 and Sevier 58. For a moment, Sevier had frustrated Jackson's ambitions and had survived a serious attack on his own reputation.

Further evidence of this feud appeared in the summer of 1803. Upon orders from Secretary of War Dearborn, Governor Sevier began to mobilize a troop of Tennessee militia for service in New Orleans in the event that Spanish officials refused to transfer Louisiana to the United States. Because the troops were to go first to Natchez, Sevier recruited primarily in the Mero District, but selected an East Tennessean to command them. This action brought charges of favoritism against Sevier from Middle Tennessee and almost halted recruiting. Jackson protested to Dearborn that the militia units had the right to choose their own officers and that the governor had usurped this prerogative. He suggested that Congress pass a law confirming local militia regulations. Sevier, on the other hand, fulminated in letters to the Secretary of War and to Tennessee Congressmen that "every obstacle" had been thrown in his way.[42] The militiamen eventually reached Natchez, and, as no need arose for their services, returned home; but the episode drove the two men further apart.

On one level the Jackson-Sevier feud was a consequence of the personal rivalry between two proud, ambitious and impetuous men. In another respect, however, their rivalry reflected the sectional feeling that has always been characteristic of the state. Physical separation of East and Middle Tennessee by the Cumberland Mountains and miles of Indian-infested wilderness gave the two sections a consciousness of separate identities. This awareness was aggravated by their different histories during the Franklin period and by East Tennessee's political domination of the less populated Cumberland area. Boom years and a rapidly growing population in Middle Tennessee followed the opening of the Mississippi River in 1795. Contemporaries were well aware of the growing importance of this section of the state and of the impending reversal of roles.[43] Jackson's attempt to displace Sevier as political leader of Tennessee is symbolic of the rivalry between the two major divisions of the state at that time.

During Sevier's fourth term as governor, following his defeat of Roane in 1803, the complicated problem of jurisdiction over the public lands of Tennessee was largely resolved. Prior to the creation of the Southwest Territory, North Carolina issued warrants for millions of acres of Tennessee land on the grounds that the Indians lost their land rights when they allied with the British. North Carolina continued to make land grants based on these warrants. Following the final North Carolina cession of her western lands in 1789, however, Congress claimed the right to dispose of the vacant lands of the territory, as she did those of the Northwest Territory; and Congress took the position that the Indians possessed all the land except the areas they had given up by treaty. From his first year as governor, Sevier claimed for Tennessee the right to dispose of her own unappropriated lands without further interference from Congress or North Carolina. In 1803 the Tennessee General Assembly sent John Overton to North Carolina where he worked out a compromise, recommended by Governor Sevier and adopted by the Tennessee legislature. Congress agreed to a settlement that gave Tennessee the right to dispose of lands west of the Tennessee River and south of the Duck and Tennessee rivers, an area that constituted the Chickasaw hunting grounds. Most land east and north of this line was turned over to Tennessee on the conditions that the state satisfy all of North Carolina's Revolutionary War claims and that 200,000 acres of land be set aside for the support of two colleges and for an academy in each county. The Tennessee legislature hastily agreed to these terms without realizing just how many North Carolina grants still existed.

Throughout his governorship John Sevier demonstrated a consistent interest in building roads and improving river navigation. As Indian problems receded into the background during his last three terms, his interest in promoting internal improvements could be given fuller expression. East Tennesseans, relying heavily upon their numerous rivers for trade and transportation, requested year after year that these rivers be cleared of the debris that hampered boat and barge traffic. In his fourth inaugural message, Sevier recommended the clearing of rivers and building of roads, but his powers were limited constitutionally and no legislative action followed. Governor Sevier also called for federal aid for navigation, and when he became a United States Representative he continued to be sensitive to these needs. He wrote in 1814 that once the war was over he was certain the national government would help East Tennessee build roads and clear their rivers.

During the remainder of his time as governor, Sevier persisted in his endeavors to clear Tennessee soil of Indian title as rapidly as possible. With white squatters and holders of warrants for land in Indian territory exerting continuing pressure, Congress speeded up its efforts to acquire land through negotiation. The wilderness area between East and Middle Tennessee was acquired in 1805 as a result of the second Treaty of Tellico, and in the following year the Cherokees were forced to cede a large area in southern Tennessee. By the time Sevier went out of office in 1809, the Cherokees had been stripped of most of their land in the state.

After a term in the State Senate following his mandatory retirement as governor in 1809, Sevier was elected to Congress as a representative from East Tennessee. There was talk in Greene County of another campaign for governor, but Sevier realized that, with the growing population of Middle Tennessee, his chances would be slim. In the ten years after the census of 1800 the population of Middle Tennessee grew to nearly 160,000, an increase of almost 500 percent, while that of the eastern section grew by only about 32 percent. Sevier represented East Tennessee in the Congress from 1811 until his death in 1815. As a Westerner and a War Hawk, he supported the War of 1812 and expansion into "the Canadys" and the Floridas. When he called for the extermination of the Creeks, his old enemy Jackson responded. After the war was over Sevier wrote to his constituents that the United States had "had to declare war or submit"; and, with the pride that so many Americans felt at the conclusion of the conflict, he added, "We have proved to the world that we are capable of self government, and have, indeed, astonished all Europe at our feats, both on land and sea."[44]

While in Washington Sevier amused himself by gambling at whist, visiting in Georgetown, and attending performances at the theater and circus. He even reported seeing a rope dancer. He went to balls and parties in the capitol and attended President Madison's levees. The French minister was a frequent companion of the representative from Tennessee, which may help to account for his attendance at Catholic services that so disturbed later historians. His Washington years were plagued with ill health. He complained of rheumatism or arthritis, and his journal is filled with fascinating home remedies for "ague, rheumatism, tape worms, dropsy, pluricy, fluenzy and appoplexy."

President Madison appointed Sevier as one of three commissioners charged with surveying the boundary between the United States and the Creek Nation. Sevier spent the summer in the field and died of fever on September 24, 1815, at the age of 70. He was buried on the bank of the Tallapoosa River in Alabama country. In 1887, following a campaign to honor the hero who had been overshadowed by the reputation of Andrew Jackson, the remains of John Sevier were returned to Knoxville and the state of Tennessee erected a monument in his honor.

After Sevier's death his personal attributes and legendary exploits were kept alive and magnified by word of mouth and by sympathetic annalists who eulogized their subject and glossed over his less heroic qualities. It is not easy to remove the layers of myth and uncover the real man. That the five-foot, nine-inch Sevier was handsome is evident from his portraits. George Washington Sevier described his father as fair skinned and fair haired, blue eyed, of slender build, and weighing about 190 pounds in his prime. He never joined a church but attended meetings of a variety of denominations. He also was unquestionably ambitious, hot-tempered, and a gifted natural leader not always overly scrupulous in the methods he used. Endowed with the ability to mingle freely and on equal terms with the rough pioneers of East Tennessee, he also was able to move with dignity in the social and political circles of Knoxville and the national capital. One contemporary said of Sevier that "he knew how to get along with the people better than any man I ever knew."[45] While he had implacable enemies, such as Andrew Jackson and John Tipton, his popularity was phenomenal. The sketchy "journal" that Sevier kept sporadically from 1790 until his death in 1815 reveals a man in motion. He traveled about continually visiting family, friends, business and political associates, and attending various county and superior courts, military musters, and the General Assembly in Knoxville. In addition, there were details of farm life to attend to. From an early date Sevier owned slaves; there is no evidence that he ever questioned the institution.

Sevier's attitude toward Indians is a matter of record and is typical of American frontier opinion. On occasion he referred to the natives as "this banditti" and as a "degenerated set of savage murderers and assassins of American Liberty." He also described them as "vagrant, lawless, debauched and immoral" and sincerely believed that "nothing but a sufficient conviction of being chastised will ever deter those itinerant nations from their common desperate and rapacious practices."[46] He treated individual Indians, especially women and children, with consideration, but for Indians en masse he felt contempt.

Few details of John Sevier's personal life have survived. When Sarah Hawkins, his first wife, died, Sevier married Catherine Sherrill, better known as "Bonnie Kate." Part of the Sevier mythology is the often-told story that romance blossomed after John Sevier helped Kate over the walls of the fort at Watauga when Indians caught her outside milking a cow. Eight more children were born to

Sevier by this union. It appears to have been a close-knit family. One son died at the hands of the Indians and three others gave lengthy interviews to Dr. Lyman Draper in 1844 which, with their letters to Dr. Draper, form the basis for much that is known about their father's personal life.

John Sevier spent his entire adult life in public service; while his motives were not unmixed, he was universally known for his openhanded liberality. Anecdotes of his generosity abound which, even discounting for exaggeration, are impressive. He is said to have used his own livestock and provisions lavishly in helping to equip the militia for service against the Indians and in the Revolutionary War. In the case of the Battle of King's Mountain, however, it is known that Sevier persuaded the entry taker to surrender the public funds that he had on hand. A. W. Putnam, the historian of Middle Tennessee who married one of Sevier's granddaughters, repeated the traditional belief that "He supplied arms, ammunition, and provisions for many of his expeditions from his own resources."[47] The only payment Sevier received for military service was for the Etowah Campaign of 1793, when he held a United States commission. Even then it took years of pressure before the federal government reimbursed Sevier and his men. George Washington Sevier said that his father lost heavily by standing bond for friends and that he could never resist helping those down on their luck, including a family with 24 near-naked boys whom Sevier helped to clothe. "His house, his camp, his provisions, horses, [and] means were open to all his friends," a Knoxville acquaintance testified, and J. G. M. Ramsey, whose father was secretary of Franklin and a close friend and neighbor, recorded that Sevier's "house was always open and not unfrequently crowded with his old soldiers and comrades in arms...."[48]

Sevier, for all his vast acres, apparently was not a wealthy man. As governor he did not have the means to live in Knoxville on the lavish scale that William Blount had enjoyed. An attempt to build a brick dwelling in Knoxville had to be abandoned for lack of funds, and Sevier and his family lived in rented quarters. His last residence, located on a farm near the frontier south of Knoxville, was a modest log dwelling surrounded by various out-buildings and known as Marble Springs. It stands today as a memorial to Tennessee's first governor and as a reminder of the rigors of frontier living.

Marble Springs, his farm located south of Knoxville, served as the last residence of John Sevier. *Photograph courtesy the Tennessee Historical Commission.*

John Sevier has been called the most popular man in Tennessee, not excepting Andrew Jackson. This was unquestionably true for the eastern counties of the state, the region that dominated Tennessee until about 1810. For the people of the eastern mountains, Sevier was a hero and remained so after his death. He was their generous neighbor, their protector against the Indians and the British, and he was their friend. For as long as the eastern communities dominated political life, Sevier was the leader of the state; however, after a perilous beginning, the Cumberland settlements grew in importance and eventually overshadowed the older region to the east. With the growing importance of Middle Tennessee came the challenge to Sevier's leadership symbolized by the rise of Andrew Jackson. No one recognized this political reality more clearly than Sevier himself.

The life of John Sevier is more than the story of an individual; it is the history of early Tennessee. Sevier moved to the Holston River just three or four years after the first permanent settlers, and he participated in every phase of the pioneer period from the Watauga Association through statehood. He was the state's first hero, as well as its first governor. Though no ordinary man, Sevier personified the pioneer jack-of-all-trades who was in turn farmer, surveyor, land speculator, Indian fighter, trader, and political leader. He had flourished with the frontier, which by the time of his death was rapidly vanishing in Tennessee.

NOTES

1. Carl S. Driver, *John Sevier, Pioneer of the Old Southwest* (Chapel Hill: University of North Carolina Press, 1932), p. 201.
2. Ibid., pp. 1-15.
3. Stanley J. Folmsbee, Robert E. Corlew, and Enoch Mitchell, *Tennessee, A Short History* (Knoxville: University of Tennessee Press, 1969), pp. 49, 53-54; John Anthony Caruso, *The Appalachian Frontier, America's First Surge Westward* (Indianapolis: The Bobbs-Merrill Co., 1959), p. 108.
4. John D. Barnhart, *Valley of Democracy, The Frontier Versus the Plantation in the Ohio Valley, 1775-1818* (Bloomington: Indiana University Press, 1953), p. 7.
5. Ben Allen and Dennis T. Lawson, "The Wataugans and the 'Dangerous Example' ", *Tennessee Historical Quarterly*, no. 26 (1967), p. 142.
6. Ibid., p. 143.
7. The fort is variously referred to as Fort Watauga, Fort Caswell, and Fort Lee.
8. Folmsbee, p. 69.
9. Francis M. Turner, *Life of General John Sevier* (New York: The Neale Publishing Company, 1910), p. 149.
10. For details of Indian campaigns and fighting techniques see J. G. M. Ramsey, *The Annals of Tennessee to the End of the Eighteenth Century* (Kingsport, Tennessee: Kingsport Press, 1926) originally published, 1853.
11. Folmsbee, p. 71.
12. Ramsey, p. 246.
13. Driver, p. 57
14. Ramsey, p. 271.
15. For information on land speculation in Tennessee, see Thomas P. Abernethy, *From Frontier to Plantation in Tennessee, A Study in Frontier Democracy* (Chapel Hill: University of North Carolina Press, 1932). It is helpful to understand the process of land acquisition. A rough survey had to be made and the survey or "entry" recorded with an entry-taker. The claimant would be given a warrant for an official survey. The surveyor's plat would be sent to the Secretary of State and a land grant issued. Finally, the grant had to be recorded in the registrar's office of the county where the land was located; Abernethy, pp. 50-51.
16. Driver, pp. 67-70.
17. For an account of the Muscle Shoals venture see Abernethy, *From Frontier to Plantation* and Arthur Preston Whitaker, *The Spanish-American Frontier: 1783-1795* (Gloucester, Mass.: Peter Smith, 1962), originally published, 1927.
18. Turner, p. 61.
19. Ramsey, p. 270.
20. Folmsbee, p. 81.
21. James W. Hagy and Stanley J. Folmsbee, "Arthur Campbell and the Separate State Movements in Virginia and North Carolina," *East Tennessee Historical Society Publications* no. 42 (1970), p. 31.
22. Randolph C. Downes, "Cherokee-American Relations in the Upper Tennessee Valley, 1776-1791," *East Tennessee Historical Society Publications* no. 8 (1936): 43.
23. Ibid., p. 47.
24. Whitaker, pp. 90-113.
25. James R. Gilmore, *John Sevier As A Commonwealth-Builder* (New York: D. Appleton & Co., 1887), p. 156.
26. William H. Masterson, *William Blount* (Baton Rouge: Louisiana State University Press, 1954), p. 176.

27. Driver, p. 132.
28. Francis Baily, *Journal of a Tour in Unsettled Parts of North America in 1796 and 1797* (Carbondale: Southern Illinois University, 1969), originally published London, 1851, pp. 262-263.
29. Sevier to Dearborn, August 22, 1797, in Samuel C. Williams, ed., "Executive Journal of Governor John Sevier," *East Tennessee Historical Society Publications,* no. 2 (1930): 145.
30. Sevier to Orr, May 12, 1798, "Executive Journal," (1932), 4: 151-152.
31. Sevier to Col. Samuel Weir [Wear], May 5, 1796, in "Executive Journal," (1929), 1:108.
32. Sevier to Cherokee chiefs and warriors, April 2, 1796, in Ibid, pp. 101-102.
33. Sevier to General Assembly, April 11, 1796, in Ibid., p. 103.
34. Sevier to Cherokee Nation, May 4, 1796, in Ibid., p. 107.
35. Jackson to Sevier, May 8, 1797, in John Spencer Bassett, ed., *Correspondence of Andrew Jackson,* (Washington: The Carnegie Institute, 1926), 1:32.
36. Ibid.
37. Sevier to Jackson, May 8, 1797, in Ibid., p. 31.
38. Masterson, pp. 332-333.
39. Driver, pp. 165-166.
40. S. Williams to Jackson, July 20, 1803, in Basset, *Correspondence of Jackson,* 1:66.
41. Jackson to Sevier, October 9, 1803, in Ibid., pp. 73-75.
42. Jackson to Dearborn, November 12, 1803, in Bassett, *Correspondence of Jackson,* 4:77; Sevier to Congressmen Cocke, Anderson, Rhea & Campbell, February 1, 1804, in "Executive Journal," (1935), 7:137; Sevier to Dearborn, February 8, 1804, in Ibid., p. 138.
43. Gilbert Imlay, "A short description of the state of Tenasee, lately called the territory of the United States south of the river Ohio," in *Tennessee Old & New, Sesquicentennial Edition, 1796-1946* (Kingsport, Tenn.: Kingsport Press, Inc., 1946), p. 2.
44. "Transcriptions from the Lyman C. Draper Manuscripts Relating to the History of Tennessee From 1769-1850," made by James Leonard Highsaw for the Daughters of the American Revolution, 1914, Memphis Public Library, pp. 75-76.
45. Cora Bales Sevier and Nancy S. Madden, *Sevier Family History with the Collected Letters of General John Sevier, First Governor of Tennessee and 28 Collateral Family Lineages* (Washington, D. C., 1961), p. 17.
46. Sevier to Tenn. Senate and House, December 3, 1798, in "Executive Journal," (1933), 5:171; Sevier to Daniel Smith, June 2, 1800, in Ibid., (1934), 6:114; Sevier to Secretary of War, July 20, 1796, in Ibid., (1929) 1:113.
47. A. W. Putnam, *History of Middle Tennessee or Life and Times of General James Robertson* (Nashville: Southern Methodist Publishing House, 1859), p. 287.
48. Sevier, p. 18; Ramsey, p. 710.

BIBLIOGRAPHY

BOOKS

Abernethy, Thomas P. *From Frontier to Plantation in Tennessee, A Study in Frontier Democracy.* Chapel Hill: University of North Carolina Press, 1932.

Bailey, Francis. *Journal of a Tour in Unsettled Parts of North America in 1796 and 1797.* London, 1851; reprint ed., Carbondale: Southern Illinois University, 1969.

Barnhart, John D. *Valley of Democracy, The Frontier Versus the Plantation in the Ohio Valley, 1775-1818.* Bloomington: Indiana University Press, 1953.

Bassett, John Spencer, ed. *Correspondence of Andrew Jackson,* 6 vols. Washington: The Carnegie Institute, 1926.
_____. *The Life of Andrew Jackson.* Archon Books, 1967. (Originally published, 1911).

Caruso, John Anthony. *The Appalachian Frontier, America's First Surge Westward.* Indianapolis: The Bobbs-Merrill Co., 1959.

Dixon, Max. *The Wataugans, Tennessee in the Eighteenth Century.* Tennessee American Revolution Bicentennial Commission, 1976.

Driver, Carl. *John Sevier, Pioneer of the Old Southwest.* Chapel Hill: The University of North Carolina Press, 1932.

Folmsbee, Stanley J.; Corlew, Robert E.; and Mitchell, Enoch. *Tennessee, A Short History,* Knoxville: University of Tennessee Press, 1969.

Gilmore, James R. *John Sevier As A Commonwealth-Builder.* New York: D. Appleton & Co., 1887.

Hamer, Philip M., ed. *Tennessee, A History, 1673-1932.* New York: The American Historical Society, 1933.

Haywood, John. *The Civil and Political History of the State of Tennessee From Its Earliest Settlement Up to the Year 1796, Including the Boundaries of the State.* Nashville: Publishing House of the Methodist Episcopal Church, South, 1891.

Heiskell, S. G. *Andrew Jackson and Early Tennessee History,* 3 vols. Nashville: Ambrose Printing Company, 1920-21. (Originally published, 1918-20.)

James, Marquis. *Andrew Jackson, The Border Captain.* New York: Grossett & Dunlap, 1933.

Lacy, Eric Russell. *Vanquished Volunteers: East Tennessee Sectionalism From Statehood to Secession.* Johnson City: East Tennessee State University Press, 1965.

Masterson, William H. *William Blount.* Baton Rouge: Louisiana State University Press, 1954.

Putnam, A. W. *History of Middle Tennessee or Life and Times of General James Robertson.* Nashville: Southern Methodist Publishing House, 1859.

Ramsey, J. G. M. *The Annals of Tennessee to the End of the Eighteenth Century.* Kingsport, Tenn.: Kingsport Press, 1926. (Originally published, 1853.)

Sevier, Cora Bales and Madden, Nancy S. *Sevier Family History With the Collected Letters of General John Sevier, First Governor of Tennessee and 28 Collateral Family Lineages.* Washington, D. C., 1961.

Turner, Francis M. *Life of General John Sevier.* New York: The Neale Publishing Company, 1910.

Whitaker, Arthur Preston. *The Spanish-American Frontier: 1783-1795.* Gloucester, Mass.: Peter Smith, 1962. (Originally published, 1927.)

Williams, Samuel Cole. *History of the Lost State of Franklin.* Johnson City: The Watauga Press, 1924.

MANUSCRIPTS

Highsaw, James Leonard, comp. "Transcripts from the Lyman C. Draper Manuscripts Relating to the History of Tennessee from 1769 to 1850." Compiled for the D. A. R. and the Cossitt Library from papers in the Wisconsin State Historical Society, Madison, Wisconsin, June-September, 1914. Memphis Public Library.

ARTICLES

Allen, Ben and Lawson, Dennis T. "The Wataugans and the 'Dangerous Example.' " *Tennessee Historical Quarterly* no. 26, 1967.

Cannon, Walter Faw. "Four Interpretations of the History of the State of Franklin." East Tennessee Historical Society *Publication* no. 22, 1950.

DeWitt, John H., ed. "Journal of John Sevier." *Tennessee Historical Magazine* no. 5, 1919; no 6, 1920.

Downes, Randolph C. "Cherokee-American Relations in the Upper Tennessee Valley, 1776-1791." *East Tennessee Historical Society Publications* no. 8, 1936.

Fink, Paul M. "Some Phases of the History of the State of Franklin." *Tennessee Historical Quarterly* no. 16, 1957.

Goodpaster, A. V. "Dr. James White." *Tennessee: Old and New,* Vol. 1. Nashville, 1946.

————. "Genesis of the Jackson-Sevier Feud." *Tennessee: Old and New,* Vol. 1. Nashville, 1946.

Hagy, James W. and Folmsbee, Stanley J. "Arthur Campbell and the Separate State Movements in Virginia and North Carolina." *East Tennessee Historical Society Publications* no. 42, 1970.

Imlay, Gilbert. "A short description of the state of Tenasee, lately called the territory of the United States south of the river Ohio." *Tennessee: Old and New,* Vol. 1. Nashville, 1946.

Jones, Thomas B. "The Public Lands of Tennessee." *Tennessee Historical Quarterly* no. 27, 1968.

Nelson, Selden. "The Tipton Family of Tennessee." *East Tennessee Historical Society Publications* no. 1, 1929.

Temple, Oliver Perry. "John Sevier." *Tennessee: Old and New,* Vol 1. Nashville, 1946.

Williams Samuel C. "The First Territorial Division Named for Washington." *Tennessee: Old and New,* Vol. 1. Nashville, 1946.

3
ARCHIBALD ROANE
Governor of Tennessee, 1801-1803

by James Lee McDonough

*T*he coming of the 19th century was a time of political change and contrast in America, or so it must have seemed when judging from appearances. In the so-called "Revolution of 1800," the philosopher-Democrat Thomas Jefferson, a tall and agrarian liberal, had defeated the conservative and rotund John Adams for the presidency of the United States. The inauguration of Tennessee's second governor in 1801 was almost like a microcosm of the national scene with its marked contrast between the new and the old.

Of no more than average height, "plain in his dress," and, according to a contemporary observer, with "the simplicity of a child in his manners," 41-year-old Archibald Roane was a cultivated, scholarly individual.[1] Fond of literature and well-versed in the classics, Tennessee's new governor was perhaps the best-educated man in the state. Certainly he was quite different from his predecessor, the tall, aggressive and charismatic John Sevier, Revolutionary War hero and longtime Indian fighter. In accordance with Tennessee's Constitution, Sevier had had to retire from the governor's chair after three successive terms in office, thus giving Roane the opportunity to succeed him.

Born about 1760 in what is now Dauphin County, Pennsylvania, Archibald Roane was the oldest child of Andrew and Margaret Roane, who emigrated from Ireland in 1739.[2] His father, who made a living as a weaver, died at an early age, leaving four children to the care of a brother, John Roane, who was a Presbyterian minister. Archibald proved to be a good student and received a legacy from his uncle of 20 pounds that was to be applied toward a college education. After studying for a while at Dickinson College near Carlisle,

Pennsylvania, he left school and joined the Continental Army where he served until the end of the Revolutionary War. Archibald claimed the distinction of being with George Washington on the night of December 25, 1776, when the ragged American army crossed the Delaware River in high, freezing winds, marched nine miles to Trenton, New Jersey, and caught the British asleep and befuddled in one of the great victories of the war. Roane also was on hand in 1781 when 7000 British troops marched out of Yorktown and stacked their arms in surrender while the bands played "The World Turned Upside Down."[3]

When the war was over Roane moved to Rockbridge County, Virginia, and taught for a year at Liberty Hall Academy. Then he went to Greene County and opened a grammar school. He also studied law and began to practice the legal profession while continuing to operate the grammar school. In 1788 he married Ann Campbell, the daughter of David and Mary Hamilton Campbell of Abingdon, Virginia. One of her brothers, also named David, later became the governor of Virginia.[4]

Soon after his marriage Roane moved to what is now part of East Tennessee, then a North Carolina frontier region where lawyers were in demand. He was one of five young men, in a group that included Andrew Jackson, who stood in a rustic log courthouse in Jonesboro and were admitted to the bar of Washington County, North Carolina, in May of 1788. When Tennessee became a territory of the United States two years later, Roane was the first attorney general of the Hamilton District, and when Tennessee was admitted into the Union in 1796, Roane was a member of the convention which framed the Constitution for the new state. For the next several years he served as a judge in Tennessee's Superior Court of Errors and Appeals.[5]

At the turn of the century Roane was certainly setting an example of the life he heartily recommended to his younger brother-in-law. "Your determination still to persevere in the acquisition of useful knowledge is truly laudable," he wrote, "but when you have made the acquisition remember that it is not for yourself alone. That society of which you are a member has a claim, and requires you to use it for the promotion of its interests." On another occasion, while endorsing the study of law, not merely to acquire knowledge but to engage in the profession with "vigour and perseverence," Roane affirmed

Portrait of Archibald Roane. *Photograph by George W. Hornal, courtesy Tennessee Department of Transportation.*

his belief in "a duty to yourself, to your connections, and to your country, not to bury your talents in the earth, but to look forward to the time when you may be called by your fellow citizens to assist in moving the wheels of government."[6]

Probably Roane himself was already hearing the "call" from his fellow Tennesseans as the time approached to select a new governor. Roane had obviously rendered significant public service over the preceding decade. No one available for the position was as well-educated as he, and, while not outstanding as a public speaker at the bar, he had acquired an enviable reputation as a good lawyer and an able judge. His marked strength was a mind that quickly identified the important and strong points of a case, with a facility to organize and present them in a brief and lucid manner.[7] In 1801 Roane was elected governor of Tennessee.

The state grew and prospered under his direction, and was divided into three Congressional Districts: Washington, Hamilton and Mero. Several new counties were created: Anderson County, named for Senator Joseph Anderson; Roane County, named for the new governor; Claiborne County, named for W. C. C. Claiborne; and Jackson County, named for Andrew Jackson. The state seal was also designed. Produced by William and Matthew Atkinson of Knoxville, who were paid $100 for manufacturing both the seal and the press to use it, Governor Roane first applied it on April 24, 1802. Some of the most important laws passed during his administration were acts to prevent frauds and perjuries, to permit county courts to set slaves free, to appoint one attorney general for the state, to prevent dueling, and to prohibit the disturbance of public worship.[8]

The times were violent and uncertain, as the governor's correspondence clearly reveals. Stabbings, shootings, and robberies were common occurrences. One of the worst perpetrators of such depredations appears to have been a man, "well mounted and armed with pistols," called "Trainum"; in tandem with a companion lacking an ear (that extremity presumably lost in some despicable scrape), he was the object of much anxiety and several of Roane's letters. The "infamous Mason," as Roane referred to another villain, was likewise a source of many problems. When informed that Mason had been killed, Roane wanted confirmation, and he asked "by whom was so good an act done?"[9] Presumably, the governor must have thought some type of commendation was in order.

There are also continual references to Indian problems in the Roane papers. For a while apprehension was widespread that an Indian war might erupt in the new Jackson County. In Anderson County many of the settlers were dissatisfied with the federal government's role in dealing with Indian difficulties. They thought that the government seemed to favor the Indians. In a letter dated April 13, 1803, Governor Roane repeated his earlier advice to Anderson County citizens to move from the lands secured to the Indians by treaty. He cautioned the residents that they were subject either to prosecution in federal courts or removal by federal troops if they continued to occupy land recognized by the United States as the legal property of the Indians. Apparently the governor attempted to pursue a just and unbiased policy in dealing with the Red Man. Upon learning that a Creek Indian had been killed in Jackson County, allegedly by two men named Richmond and Irwin, Roane wrote to Colonel R. J. Meigs, agent for the War Department: "My present impressions are that it was an unwarrantable Act, perhaps such a one for which the offenders ought to atone with their lives."[10]

One of the chief concerns of Roane's administration was the construction of the proposed Natchez Road, an endeavor involving problems not only with villains ("gangs of banditti" according to the governor) and Indians, but also with the good citizens of Williamson County. Three years before Roane became governor, Spain had surrendered all claim to lands north of the 31st parallel. The United States in the same year created Mississippi Territory with Natchez as its capital. Significant in military and diplomatic affairs because of its strategic location, and possessing vast commercial and economic potential in its plantations, the Natchez region required better communication with the East and the nation's capital. In 1801 President Jefferson ordered the army to clear out a road between Nashville and Natchez. The task was accomplished under the general direction of General James Wilkinson, commander of the American army in the West. He conducted a survey and secured permission from the Choctaw and Chickasaw Indians to open up the road, although work was begun before consent was obtained.[11]

The road was to be cut from Nashville in a southwestern direction by the shortest feasible route to the Indian boundary line. Thus the road would pass west of Franklin, chief site of settlement in Williamson County. The Williamson County Court strongly objected to being bypassed; in a letter dated June 18, 1802, Governor Roane pleaded the county's case before Secretary of War Henry Dearborn. The road through Franklin, he said, would be only about three or four miles longer than a direct route from Nashville to the Indian boundary line. Because "the general approbation of the citizens most immediately concerned" would be gained by building along the lengthier route, the governor diplomatically expressed his hope that their request might be granted.[12] Roane's plea was to no avail. On July 9, 1802, the Secretary of War replied: "We ought by all means in our power to guard against any unnecessary extension of the distance. It ought not to be expected that a great public road made for the purpose of connecting two distant countries, and national purposes, should be diverted from the shortest and best route to accommodate the inhabitants of a single county."[13]

Nevertheless, the citizens of Williamson County had partial satisfaction. Beginning in 1802, the postal service riders, making one trip a month each way between Nashville and Natchez, began going directly south to Franklin and from there in a southwesterly direction climbing to the crest of Duck River Ridge.[14] Also, Governor Roane's suggestions to the War Department for coping with the brigands who infested the Natchez Road (the term *Natchez Trace* was not used until the 1820s[15]) were appreciated and put into effect.

The governor advocated that some "houses of entertainment" (inns) and a few military posts be established along the road. He also suggested that a reward be offered for information leading to the apprehension of the ruffians who robbed and murdered travelers. A note of urgency characterized Roane's letter to the Secretary of War, written June 9, 1803. Referring to recent killing and terrorization on the road, whether at the hands of white men, Indians, or both (as some alleged), he warned that if similar cases occurred and it appeared that the offenders belonged to "any tribe of Indians I doubt that the frontier citizens would wait for the orders of Government . . . ." After this clear implication, the governor closed with a statement vowing to do all in his power "to preserve that peace with the Indians which is so necessary to our prosperity."[16] In a letter dated July 18, 1803, Secretary Dearborn began by assuring Governor Roane that "The President of the United States is desirous of affording every aid in his power for rendering the intercourse between Tennessee and Natchez as safe and convenient as circumstances will permit." To this end the president was authorizing the establishment of several houses of entertainment at different parts of the road, a detachment of troops on the Tennessee River, together with a small detachment at the Duck River to help protect travelers, and he was offering a $400 reward "to any citizen or Indian who shall apprehend one or more of the banditti who have been guilty of attacking, robbing and murdering persons on the road . . . between Nashville and Natchez . . . ."[17] The reward also would be paid for intelligence leading to the detection and apprehension of the criminals.

The first house of entertainment was built in 1804, by which time there were perhaps 3000 or 4000 people traveling the road annually. By 1820 more than 20 were in operation, usually managed by half-breed Indians or white men with Indian wives. Although rather crude affairs, they facilitated travel and eased somewhat the discomforts of a long passage through the wilderness.[18]

While the work on the Trace progressed, the State of Tennessee was opening a road from Nashville to Southwest Point (now Kingston). The objections and haggling of the Cherokee Indians, which had continued for a decade, were, in the governor's words, "a serious inconvenience to this State."[19] Roane, in spite of his education and his attempts to be fair, shared the common bias of the day against the Indian, stating that "it is a well known fact and shamefully obvious that all the . . . tribes are accustomed and habituated to licentiousness, and educated to a vagrant, lawless, debauched and immoral life, and nothing but a sufficient conviction of being chastised will ever deter these itinerant nations from their common desperate and rapacious practices."[20]

Several letters in the governor's papers deal with the construction of this Cumberland Turnpike, as it was known, and the Indian problems. The Cherokees finally consented to the opening of the road which, together with the Walton Road that was soon constructed, greatly facilitated travel between Knoxville and Nashville.[21]

In those early days of Tennessee's history, not all of the state's boundary lines were firmly established. The long-running dispute over the line separating Tennessee from Virginia was finally settled during Roane's administration. On the authority of the legislature in 1802, the governor appointed John Sevier, Moses Fisk, and George

Rutledge as commissioners for Tennessee. Creed Taylor, General Joseph Martin, and Peter Johnson were appointed by Virginia. The two commissions fixed a compromise line midway between the older surveys, known as "Walker's line" and "Henderson's line." This compromise was ratified by both states and, while at least two attempts were later made to change it, the line set in Roane's administration has survived to the present.[22]

Tennessee's controversy with Kentucky over the boundary line proved more annoying and long lasting than that with Virginia. In fact, it was not settled until many years after Roane was dead. A point of interest in Roane's administration was the desire of at least some Kentuckians, living south of Green River, to become a part of Tennessee. To that end a Memorial and Resolution of the Tennessee legislature was passed and John Overton was appointed by Governor Roane as a commissioner to the State of Kentucky with full power and authority to conclude such a transaction. Roane also addressed a letter to James Garrard, Governor of Kentucky, attempting to pave the way for the region south of Green River to be annexed to Tennessee. Nothing ever developed from this effort, with the exception of bad feelings toward Tennessee on the part of some Kentuckians who thought their southern neighbor was becoming greedy for additional land.[23]

The Tennessee-North Carolina boundary was also a source of longtime dispute. Soon after Tennessee was admitted to the Union in 1796, North Carolina appointed a commission to permanently establish the boundary line in conjunction with a commission from Tennessee. When Tennessee's legislature took no action, North Carolina proceeded alone to locate the line. In 1802 Governor Roane requested North Carolina's governor, James Turner, to send a certified copy of the North Carolina commission's report. This was done under date of July 10, 1803.[24] No further action was taken until 1805 when the Tennessee legislature passed an act stating that the line established by North Carolina was incorrect. The boundary remained a point of controversy, off and on, until the early 20th century.[25]

Much more dramatic—and of far greater import—was the situation in Louisiana. In the secret Treaty of San Ildefonso (1800), Napoleon Bonaparte had negotiated the transfer of Louisiana from Spain to France, although formal possession by France was long delayed.

Then came news, like the proverbial bombshell bursting upon the old Southwest, that the Spanish Intendant at New Orleans had on October 16, 1802, proclaimed that the right of deposit at that great mart of ocean commerce was suspended. Governor Roane's reaction was typical of that of many Westerners. Reflecting upon the results of the French Revolution, he wrote to David Campbell: "Has [the Revolution] not been injurious to the cause of liberty? To what ultimate object does the aspiring genius of Bonaparte tend? Must we consider the obstructions to the Mississippi trade as a measure of his system or merely dictated by a whimsical, capricious Intendant who is too obstinate to correct his own errors? It will require more than a disavowal of the measures of the Intendant to induce me to believe that he acted only from himself, or was more than an agent in the whole business."[26]

Alarmed by the actions of the Intendant, President Jefferson feared for a time that Napoleon might force a reconsideration of his basically peaceful foreign policy, perhaps even requiring him to use force in support of the indignant Westerners. Roane received a letter from the president with respect to the militia of Tennessee; it instructed that special attention be given to prepare the men for action if necessary. On April 7, 1803, Governor Roane sent letters to Brigadier Generals James White, George Rutledge, and James Winchester, informing them of the president's wishes and stating: "It will be necessary and proper that vigorous exertions be used on your part to carry into effect the Militia system in conformity with the existing laws, and that you endeavor to have your brigade instructed in military discipline and a knowledge of tactics . . . . The citizens of Tennessee will always be willing to aid in rectifying any wrongs done to their country and have full confidence that the constituted authorities will call for and direct that National force as soon as it becomes necessary."

Fearing that some Tennesseans might not be inclined to wait but might take hostile actions at once, the governor warned: "If any unauthorized attempt should be made within the bounds of your brigade to proceed . . . against the Province of Louisiana you will take the most prompt and effectual measures to restrain such attempt."[27] The Tennesseans were willing to wait, believing that if negotiations failed, then an expedition against Louisiana would be authorized by the federal government. That would be soon enough to take by force what, in their opinion, they had been deprived of unjustly.[28]

Fortunately, the timely purchase of the entire Louisiana territory ended the possibility of an armed intervention, and Roane, like nearly all Southerners and Westerners, rejoiced in the great acquisition. "I can not but partake in the general satisfaction which pervades the breast of every true American in contemplating the prosperous situation of the United States," he wrote to David Campbell. "The Government administered with prudence and firmness, the finances increasing, and a new world added to her jurisdiction" were the basic reasons for his satisfaction. "A number of people have already gone to Louisiana," he said, "and crowds will flock there as soon as proper regulations shall be made to enable them to procure lands."[29]

Although the Tennessee militia was not used against Louisiana, it was that institution which involved the governor in the most controversial act of his administration—and one of the most important events in the rise of Andrew Jackson. On February 5, 1802, the brigadier generals and field officers of the Tennessee militia met for the purpose of electing a new major general to command them. When the votes were counted, there was a tie between John Sevier and Andrew Jackson. Governor Roane broke the tie, casting the deciding vote in favor of Andrew Jackson. The vote·was one of the most critical events in Jackson's military career and probably cost Roane the victory in his bid for reelection as governor in 1803.

To fully understand what occurred it is necessary to go back as early as 1796 when elections for officers of the state militia were held. At that time, in the election for major general, Andrew Jackson and George Conway of Greene County were the candidates. John Sevier was governor and used his influence against Jackson, saying that he never had and never would vote to select any inexperienced person—Jackson had never held military office except that of judge advocate of the Davidson County regiment—to the command of the state militia. Conway was elected and Jackson was angry, making some derogatory remark about Sevier, who then responded in like manner.

"The scurrilous expressions of a poor, pitiful, pettyfogging lawyer" was reportedly the phrase that Sevier employed to describe Jackson. His Scotch-Irish blood rapidly overheating, Jackson demanded redress for what he called "the injury done his private character and feelings." Sevier decided not to press the matter, writing Jackson a moderating explanation, and a shaky peace was established between the two men.[30]

The reconciliation between Jackson and Sevier, such as it was, did not last long. Major General Conway died in 1801 and Sevier, out of the job of governor, decided to take over the militia once again. He was surprised to learn that Andrew Jackson was challenging him for the post. For several years Jackson had been working hard to cultivate the militia and arrange his election. The result was 17 votes for Sevier and 17 votes for Jackson. Then Jackson, according to several accounts, played his trump card and won the backing of Governor Roane.

More than four years earlier, Jackson, serving out a partial term as United States Senator, secured information of wholesale land frauds perpetrated through the land office in Nashville. An investigation was conducted, fraudulent transactions on a large scale were uncovered, North Carolina's Secretary of State was forced to resign from office, and a number of Tennesseans were implicated, among them Jackson's brother-in-law, Stockley Donelson. But most significant for Jackson's purposes was the evidence he secured that seemed to implicate Sevier in extensive land frauds involving forgery and bribery. "When you set a bear trap," Jackson was reported to say, "you never can tell what particular bear is going to blunder into it." However, Jackson bided his time, not making immediate use of his information. Then, in 1802, with the 17-17 tie vote for election of the new major general, Jackson unveiled his "bear."[31]

He presented the evidence implicating Sevier to Governor Roane, and Roane cast the deciding vote for Jackson as major general—both took place on the same day, according to some Tennessee historians. Insufficient evidence precludes certainty as to which came first, but Roane possessed the papers implicating Sevier soon after, if not before, he broke the tie vote for major general in Jackson's favor. Sevier, 20 years Jackson's senior, 30 years a soldier and a Revolutionary War hero, as well as an Indian fighter, had been defeated by a 35-year-old lawyer with no known military experience. Sevier was enraged.[32]

Denied the military post he had cherished, Sevier determined to regain the governor's chair from Roane. When he announced his candidacy in 1803, however, Roane released the information, courtesy of Jackson, charging that Sevier had forged 165 warrants for 640 acres each and had bribed North Carolina's Secretary of State, James Glasgow. The political explosion that followed culminated in one of the bitterest campaigns for governor that Tennessee has ever known. Jackson took it upon himself to champion the cause of Roane, and thereby his own cause as well—that of becoming the most powerful leader in Tennessee.[33]

The *Knoxville Gazette* of July 27, 1803, carried a celebrated article, contributed by Jackson, containing the specifics of the accusations against Sevier. Then Sevier, "evading, denying, confusing," as historian Marquis James described Sevier's campaign, "stormed the settlements as the persecuted friend of the poor."[34] It worked! Maybe the majority were not convinced of Sevier's guilt; perhaps they did not care if he was guilty. "Nolichucky Jack," as the popular leader was fondly called, was elected governor once more, by a vote of 6780 to 4923 for Roane.[35] It would be his fourth term.

A few hours before he retired from office, Roane transmitted to the legislature the documents upon which the charges of forgery and bribery against Sevier were based, and a joint committee began an investigation. Jackson and Sevier continued to growl and snarl at one another, the former referring to the latter as, among other things, "a base coward and poltroon," while Sevier, who once said that Jackson was "the most abandoned rascal in principle my eyes ever beheld," picked up on a Jackson reference to his "public services" and remarked that the only "service" he knew anything about was Jackson's "taking a trip to Natchez with another man's wife." Jackson was fighting mad and for a while it seemed likely that the two antagonists would fight a duel, despite the fact that the legislature in 1801 had passed an act to outlaw the practice.[36]

The ironic fact of the entire situation is that if Sevier had been elected major general of the militia in 1802, he probably would not have made the bid for governor in 1803. Roane would then have won reelection, probably without significant opposition. Furthermore, the rise of Jackson's military career would have been seriously delayed, if not halted.

The legislature's investigation of Sevier was unsatisfactory, obviously hampered by the bias of both pro-Sevier and anti-Sevier members. The joint committee concluded that he was guilty, but the

Senate rejected the committee's findings. The House accepted the committee's statement of facts, which contained an implication of Sevier's guilt, but refused to approve the committee's statement of guilt.[37]

What is the truth of the matter? Carl S. Driver, biographer of Sevier, concludes a lengthy analysis of the evidence by writing that "the innocence or guilt of Sevier is not possible of determination."[38] Marquis James, in his biography of Jackson, concluded that "Jackson had made Sevier's guilt plain to any thinking person, overlooking only the fact that in the glamorous presence of Nolichucky Jack people did not think."[39] Jackson had many faults, not the least of which was continually carrying a chip on his shoulder, and, undoubtedly, he wanted to wrest power in Tennessee from the grasp of the popular Sevier. Nevertheless, Jackson was probably right in his charges against the man. Sevier's efforts to explain away the damning evidence seem contrived. Certainly Roane believed that Nolichucky Jack was guilty.

Regardless of whether Sevier was guilty or innocent, Roane was no longer governor of Tennessee. His intellectual qualifications earned him respect from some people, but they were not an essential ingredient for a leader of that early period in the state's history. The settlers wanted men of action, men who revealed a fighting prowess, not scholarly thinkers. Partly for this reason, Roane lost his second bid for the governorship to the people's hero, John Sevier, who remained in office until 1809. Roane had a high sense of justice and integrity and could be attractive in conversation with a friend; but, a rather taciturn man generally, most people probably never saw him as he really was.[40]

Although well-educated for his day, Roane wrote relatively few papers. By far the most revealing of his extant correspondence was that with the Campbell family. He seems Jeffersonian and physiocratic in his belief that "every man in the western country," regardless of what other occupation or profession he may pursue, "ought to have a farm and have it well managed." Roane was convinced that a man's marriage contributed to better citizenship. "I suppose the reason," he philosophized, "is because he feels himself of more importance in [civil society] and holds his rights and privileges in higher estimation." In regard to financial retrenchment, he commented that "economy in the expenditure of public money is certainly an amiable trait in Republican Government, but like many other virtues, may be carried to a blameable excess . . . ." On happiness Roane wrote that the emotion is largely dependent on one's own mind: "If we are disposed to be content, we will very probably be so."[41]

Perhaps the major interest in Roane's life was teaching and to that profession he returned for a while after he left the governor's chair. At one time he was the instructor of Hugh L. White, who became a candidate for president of the United States in 1836. Roane also served as trustee of Greeneville College, Blount College (now the University of Tennessee), and of Washington College in Washington County, the first three incorporated colleges in the state.[42]

He was appointed circuit court judge in 1811 and held that office until 1815 when he was again appointed a judge of the Tennessee Supreme Court. Roane died on January 18, 1819, preceding his widow by 12 years. He was an Episcopalian. His grave in Pleasant Forest Cemetery near Campbell's Station was unmarked for almost a hundred years until the state erected a monument in his memory in June of 1918.[43]

NOTES

1. "Biographical Sketch," in the David Campbell Papers, original in the Duke University Library, Durham, North Carolina. Microfilm copy in the Tennessee State Library and Archives, Nashville. Hereafter cited as TSLA.
2. Allen Johnson, ed., *Dictionary of American Biography* (New York, 1929), 15:640-641.
3. "Biographical Sketch," Campbell Papers, TSLA; Margaret I. Phillips, *The Governors of Tennessee* (Gretna, Louisiana, 1978), pp. 16, 18; John M. Blum and others, *The National Experience: A History of the United States* (New York, 1963), p. 114; Inscription on Tombstone, from an article in the *Knoxville Journal and Tribune*, June 27, 1918.
4. "Biographical Sketch," Campbell Papers, TSLA.
5. Hazel Lander, article on Archibald Roane, in the Archibald Roane Papers, TSLA; Robert H. White, *Tennessee: Its Growth and Progress* (Nashville, 1944), p. 527.
6. Roane to David Campbell, June 7, 1800 and October 11, 1800, Campbell Papers, TSLA.
7. "Biographical Sketch," Campbell Papers, TSLA.
8. John Trotwood Moore and Austin P. Foster, eds., *Tennessee, The Volunteer State, 1769-1923* (Nashville, 1923), I: 296-301.
9. Roane to Moses Fisk, November 28, 1801, Moses Fisk Papers, TSLA; William H. Harrison to Roane, August 18, 1803, and James Garrard to Roane, June 27, 1803, Roane Papers, TSLA; Roane to John Campbell, June 7, 1800, Roane to David Campbell, October 11, 1800, and Roane to Maria Campbell, December 27, 1800, Campbell Papers, TSLA; Roane to Henry Brazeale, August 22, 1803 and Roane to Colonel R. J. Meigs, August 21, 1803, Roane Papers, TSLA; Roane to James Winchester, August 26, 1803, James Winchester Papers, TSLA.
10. Roane to Henry McKinny, April 28, 1802, Cherokee Collection, TSLA; Roane to Citizens of Anderson County, April 13, 1803, Roane Papers, TSLA; Roane to R. J. Meigs, April 30, 1802, Cherokee Collection, TSLA.

11. Dawson A. Phelps, "The Natchez Trace: Indian Trail to Parkway," *Tennessee Historical Quarterly* (September, 1962), pp. 205-206.
12. Roane to Henry Dearborn, June 18, 1802, Roane Papers, TSLA.
13. Dearborn to Roane, July 9, 1802, Roane Papers, TSLA.
14. Phelps, p. 215.
15. Ibid., pp. 216-217.
16. Roane to Dearborn, June 9, 1803, Roane Papers, TSLA.
17. Dearborn to Roane, July 18, 1803, Roane Papers, TSLA.
18. Phelps, pp. 204-205, 208.
19. Roane to Joseph Anderson (U.S. Senator from Tennessee), February 19, 1802, Roane Papers, TSLA.
20. Address to the House of Representatives, 1801, Roane Papers, TSLA.
21. Roane to Thomas N. Clark, September 6, 1802, William Walton, William Hale and Thomas Clark to Roane, August 24, 1802, and T. A. Smith to Roane, August 3, 1802, Roane Papers, TSLA. Phelps, 206.
22. Moore, *Tennessee*, I, 296, 379, 380.
23. Roane to Overton, November 8, 1801, November 14, 1801, Roane Papers, TSLA. Roane to Garrard, November 4, 1801, Murdock Collection, TSLA.
24. Moore, p. 384.
25. Ibid., pp. 384-385.
26. Roane to David Campbell, April 20, 1803, Campbell Papers, TSLA; Blum, p. 166.
27. Roane to White, Rutledge and Winchester, April 7, 1803, Roane Papers, TSLA.
28. Winchester to Roane, April 15, 1803, Roane Papers, TSLA.
29. Roane to Campbell, February 25, 1804, Campbell Papers, TSLA.
30. Philip M. Hamer, ed., *Tennessee–A History, 1673-1932* (New York, 1933), 1:202-03; Will T. Hale and Dixon L. Merritt, *A History of Tennessee and Tennesseans* (Chicago and New York, 1913), 1:233-34; John S. Bassett, *The Life of Andrew Jackson* (New York, 1931), pp. 57-58.
31. Hamer, p. 204; Hale and Merritt, p. 234.
32. Robert Remini, *Andrew Jackson and the Course of American Empire, 1767-1821* (New York, 1977), p. 119; Moore, p. 303; John Carter's affidavit respecting the papers of the Entry Office of Washington County, sworn and subscribed, February 10, 1802, Roane Papers, TSLA.
33. Hamer, p. 205.
34. Marquis, James, *Andrew Jackson: the Border Captain* (Indianapolis, 1933), p. 99.
35. Hamer, p. 205.
36. Moore, pp. 305-306; Hamer, p. 205; James Parton, *Life of Andrew Jackson* (Boston, 1866), 1:233.
37. Hamer, pp. 209-210.
38. Carl S. Driver, *John Sevier: Pioneer of the Old Southwest* (Chapel Hill, 1932), p. 165.
39. James, p. 99
40. "Biographical Sketch," Campbell Papers, TSLA.
41. Roane to David Campbell, October 11, 1800, Roane to John Campbell, June 7, 1800, and Roane to Maria Campbell, December 27, 1800, Campbell Papers, TSLA.
42. Phillips, p. 19.
43. *Dictionary of American Biography*, p. 641; Phillips. p. 19.

BIBLIOGRAPHY

BOOKS
Bassett, John S. *The Life of Andrew Jackson.* New York, 1931.
Blum, John M. and others. *The National Experience: A History of the United States.* New York, 1963.
Driver, Carl S. *John Sevier: Pioneer of the Old Southwest.* Chapel Hill. 1932.
Hale, Will T. and Dixon L. Merritt. *A History of Tennessee and Tennesseans.* Chicago and New York, 1913.
Hamer, Philip M., ed. *Tennessee–A History, 1673-1932.* New York, 1933.
James, Marquis. *Andrew Jackson: The Border Captain.* Indianapolis, 1933.

Johnson, Allen, ed. *Dictionary of American Biography.* New York, 1929.
Moore, John Trotwood and Austin P. Foster, eds. *Tennessee, the Volunteer State.* Chicago, 1923.
Parton, James, *Life of Andrew Jackson.* Boston, 1866.
Phillips, Margaret I. *The Governors of Tennessee.* Gretna, Louisiana, 1978.
Remini, Robert V. *Andrew Jackson and the Course of American Empire, 1767-1821.* New York, 1977.
White, Robert H. *Tennessee: Its Growth and Progress.* Nashville, 1944.

MANUSCRIPTS
Murdock Collection. TSLA.
Nashville, Tennessee. Tennessee State Library and Archives. David Campbell papers.
Nashville, Tennessee. TSLA, Cherokee Collection.
Nashville, Tennessee, TSLA, Moses Fisk Papers.
Nashville, Tennessee. TSLA. Archibald Roane Papers.
Nashville, Tennessee. TSLA. Jas. Winchester Papers.

NEWSPAPERS
Knoxville *Gazette,* July 27, 1803.
Knoxville *Journal and Tribune,* June 27, 1918.

ARTICLES
Phelps, Dawson A. "The Natchez Trace: Indian Trail to Parkway," *Tennessee Historical Quarterly.* September, 1962.

4

WILLIE BLOUNT
Governor of Tennessee, 1809-1815

by Mary B. Clark

Willie Blount, the third governor of Tennessee and half brother of the only governor of the Southwest Territory, contributed almost 50 years of public service to his adopted state. Governor for three consecutive terms and the first chief executive to lead Tennessee through a war, he shared a close association during his periods of greatest service with two other men, Andrew Jackson and William Blount, whose contemporary and historical reputations overshadowed his own. Consequently his own achievements, although substantial, have received comparatively little attention. Two of his three terms of office were occupied almost entirely with problems of the War of 1812. It was during this time that the nickname "The Volunteer State" was first given to Tennessee, partly as a result of Blount's competence at wartime administration. Although the general belief for many years was that the title was adopted during the Mexican War, it is now accepted that the appellation came into being during the governorship of Willie Blount.[1]

The Blount family was prominent in the early history of the nation as well as of Tennessee. As early as the American Revolution the Blounts were highly situated in North Carolina political circles. Willie's father, Jacob, and his older half brother, William, had fought with Governor William Tyron to suppress the rebellion of the Regulators in 1771. After service in the American Revolution, William, the more ambitious brother, was selected in 1782 as a delegate to the Continental Congress, and he became an extensive land speculator in the area which was to become the Southwest Territory.[2] It was this interest in land and politics that was to bring both brothers to the Tennessee country.

The movement of this distinguished family from the Tidewater section of North Carolina to the wilderness west of the Appalachian Mountains was a continuation of their tradition. Reportedly of direct Cavalier descent, their ancestry is traced in the *Goodspeed* history of 1887 to the invasion of England in 1066 by William the Conqueror. Although this historical account may be subject to some error, the details cited are certainly voluminous. The name originally was Le Blount. As a result of the successful Norman invasion the two Le Blounts accompanying William became owners of large estates. The family later migrated westward across the Atlantic to Virginia and then on to North Carolina.[3] A recent biographer recounts that Jacob Blount of Blount Hall in Craven, County, North Carolina, married Hannah Baker, widow of William Baker of South Quay, Virginia, on November 26, 1765. She was the daughter of Colonel Edward Slatter, an influential settler. Jacob's first wife had died leaving him with eight children.[4]

Willie (pronounced Wylie) was one of five children born to Jacob and Hannah. He was born on April 18, 1768, at Blount Hall. Because his father was a man of considerable wealth, Willie and the rest of the children were brought up in a manner corresponding to their father's status.[5] The elder, William, was determined that Willie should study law. Jacob, who wished to have his younger son remain at home, objected to this study.[6] William's influence seems to have been dominant, for Willie did study at the College of New Jersey and King's College, now known as Princeton and Columbia universities. He then returned to North Carolina where he read law with Judge John Sitgraves at New Bern.[7]

The relationship of the two brothers remained close. In 1790, when William managed to secure appointment by President George Washington as governor of the newly created Southwest Territory, Willie also moved to the Tennessee country as his brother's private secretary. Because the wilderness territory had no capitol and no cities, Governor Blount established his headquarters in the William Cobb house at Rocky Mount. Willie shared these accommodations with his brother, his brother's wife, and their two children. Located on the Watauga River near present-day Johnson City, the William Cobb home is now maintained as a historical museum. When the capital was fixed at the newly-created settlement of Knoxville two years later, the entire Blount family moved there. At Knoxville

Portrait of Willie Blount. *Photograph by George W. Hornal, courtesy Tennessee Department of Transportation.*

William built his home, the Blount Mansion, reportedly the first frame house west of the mountains.[8] Today it is a historical memorial and a tourist attraction.

In 1794, while still serving as his brother's private secretary, Willie secured a license to practice law, and in 1796, when William guided the Southwest Territory into statehood, the first legislature of the State of Tennessee elected Willie one of the three judges of the Superior Court of Law and Equity—a position which, at the age of 28, he declined.[9] In spite of his young age, however, Willie Blount was at the time one of the best-educated and most politically knowledgeable men in the state. As private secretary to the territorial governor, he enjoyed close associations with the most powerful and influential men of this growing frontier. Among them were Andrew Jackson, John Sevier, James White, Samuel Doak, Archibald Roane, William Hall, and Joseph McMinn.[10] Much of the political leadership during Tennessee's first half century of statehood was exercised by these men, as well as by others in the circle of the Blount family's influence. Probably the most critical problem Tennessee faced during the territorial period was that of Indian relations, and, because the territorial governor was also Superintendent of Indian Affairs, Willie Blount was well-informed on this subject. Many of the Indian problems during the younger Blount's gubernatorial administrations were similar to ones he had experienced as private secretary to William Blount from 1790 to 1797.[11]

Although the Blount family's political power declined during the first four years of statehood, Willie remained steadfastly loyal to his older brother, William. In the territorial period William Blount had exercised almost absolute political power and had built a political organization of remarkable effectiveness, but his efforts had not made him popular with the people of the area. Realizing that he could not defeat the frontier hero, John Sevier, in an election, William Blount arranged to be selected by the legislature as one of Tennessee's United States Senators. Even this office was unsuccessful for him. In 1797 he was expelled from the Senate for his leadership in a conspiracy to give aid to England in a seizure of Louisiana and the Floridas from Spain. Returning to Tennessee he used the power of his political organization to win election to the State Senate and to be selected as its speaker, the second highest political office in the state. Had his untimely death not occurred in 1800, he might well have become governor after Sevier left office.

Still devoted to his brother, Willie became the guardian of William's children and assumed responsibility for his estate. He found his brother's financial affairs in serious disarray. Although still a large landowner at the time of his death, William had met severe financial reverses. Together with many other prominent Tennesseans, he had become involved in extensive speculations managed by a persuasive business promoter, David Allison. When the Allison business empire collapsed, William was left with settlement obligations amounting to several hundred thousand dollars. Willie attempted to restore financial order, to satisfy creditors, and to get the scattered family holdings on a paying basis. In order to pursue these efforts, he found it necessary in 1802 to move to Montgomery County where he established a large and successful plantation on land owned by the family.[12]

Meanwhile, he had married Lucinda Baker, daughter of Major John Baker and his wife, Ann, of Bertie County, North Carolina. Willie and Lucinda later had two daughters, Eliza Ann and Lucinda. Records from North Carolina list Lucinda Baker's year of birth as 1750, which would have made her 18 years older than Willie—a situation which even then was somewhat unusual.[13] Lucinda's maturity and effective management of the household probably contributed greatly to the success of her young husband as he struggled to become a wealthy planter and salvage his family's bankrupt estate.

Willie Blount's efforts, which were quite likely aided by prominent friends, were successful. His plantation prospered and the value of his landholdings increased in proportion to the rapidly growing population of the Cumberland Valley during the first decade of the century. He continued to maintain the friendships formed during the years he had served his brother. During this time the initial political division of the state between supporters of William Blount and John Sevier continued, although no single leader emerged to succeed the older Blount brother. Archibald Roane achieved only a limited success and Willie, although he carried the family name and a detailed knowledge of the political organization, was handicapped by his youth and financial problems. Andrew Jackson, a favored lieutenant in the organization, had also suffered political losses after the death of William Blount; however, he was driven by a relentless will and ambition that would later carry him to greater success than any of his associates, but his later rise to prominence would not begin until Willie Blount had won the governor's office. During these years of domination of state politics by John Sevier, Willie Blount maintained his statewide network of friendships, served as a charter trustee of Blount College—later to become the University of Tennessee—and became a trustee of Cumberland College. By 1807 his financial affairs were sufficiently recovered that he accepted an opportunity to return to public life as a member of the General Assembly from Montgomery County.[14] There he soon won acceptance as a leader among the remaining members of the Blount political faction.

Although his enemies had never been able to defeat Sevier in an election, they found themselves in a favorable situation in 1809. Sevier was unable to run again for the governor's office, for he had just completed a series of three consecutive terms—the maximum allowed by the Constitution of 1796. Encouraged by this opportunity, Willie's friends united in his support. Their efforts were successful. He was elected governor by a 3000 vote majority over his elderly opponent, William Cocke, a former United States Senator and hero of the Cherokee war fought during the American Revolution. Since there were few issues of consequence in this race, Blount evidently won because of his personal popularity, although it must be assumed he had learned something from his successful brother's passion for meticulous political organization. Willie Blount demonstrated his ability again by winning subsequent elections in 1811 and 1813.[15]

During this period of his return to state politics, Willie Blount apparently won something that had always eluded his brilliant and aristocratic older brother—genuine popularity with the people. James G. M. Ramsey, in his *Annals of Tennessee,* claims that "Willie's popularity with the masses has rarely been equalled."[16] But he also benefited from sectionalism in the rapidly growing state. By 1809 Tennessee had changed considerably from the time, almost two decades before, when the Blounts had first arrived. The population had increased by almost 800 percent, most of this growth being in Middle Tennessee. This was the area represented by Blount, while Sevier's greatest support had been from East Tennessee. The census of 1810 revealed a population of 261,727, the Nashville Bank had been chartered, churches were becoming numerous, and private schools were being organized. The days were thus passing when an East

Tennessee frontiersman and Indian fighter such as John Sevier could dominate the politics of the state.[17]

Despite the changes that had taken place in his state when he was inaugurated in 1809, Governor Willie Blount felt a sense of timelessness governing problems which confronted his office. The perennial Indian problem was still foremost on the governor's agenda. Increases in the white population of the state had not solved the problem which had actually become worse as greater numbers of settlers demanded, and sought to take, lands belonging to the Indians. When they resisted this seizure of their lands, the whites became even more aggressive. There were armed attacks and counterattacks by both sides, with the whites often accusing the British of inciting the Indians to violence. Blount's Indian policy was consistent through all of his years in office. He invariably took the side of his voting constituents against the Indians' claims to their lands. His two objectives were to secure the relinquishment of territory held in Tennessee by the Chickasaws and Cherokees and to suppress and control the two tribes, Choctaws and Creeks, who owned the land through which the trade route between Tennessee and the Gulf Coast passed.[18] Because the state could not take direct action against the federally recognized Indian holdings, Blount wrote to James Robertson, then serving as a commissioner to the Cherokees, arguing in favor of Tennessee's claims to land they held.[19] Blount recommended giving the land west of the Mississippi, and thus outside of Tennessee, to the Cherokees and Chickasaws. He offered the dubious argument that, because any foreign power at war would surely plan to take the western area, friendly Indians there would be of great value to national defense. He advised Secretary of War William Eustis that "In my judgement, it would be as easy to tame a flock of black birds whilst permitted to fly at large, as to reclaim those Indians as tribes at any reasonable expense whilst settled where they are in the present dispersed manner of their settlement."[20]

While in office, Governor Blount also wrote repeatedly to the War Department about hostile actions by the southern tribes, the Creeks and Choctaws, against Tennessee settlers and travelers.[21] Feeling that these tribes were incited by more aggressive northern Indians, he asked that rangers and regular troops be sent into the area between the Tennessee and Arkansas rivers to cut communication between the northern and southern Indians.[22] The Secretary of War refused those requests, but Blount continued to send complaints about alleged offenses by the Creeks.[23] Despite Governor Blount's persistent attention to these problems, his efforts did not produce success during his tenure in office. The federal government, concerned less about the demands of land-seeking Tennessee voters than about its treaty promises, was slow to implement the policy of removal—the final solution to the Indian problem. It was only after Blount had left office that the southeastern Indians were deprived of their ancestral lands and removed across the Mississippi. It is reasonable to assume, however, that Blount's continued advocacy of this policy helped to bring it about. He therefore deserves a share of the credit, or the blame, for this action.

Another perplexing problem remaining from the territorial days when Blount assumed office in 1809 was that of land claims. The chaotic and overlapping land policies of North Carolina, the federal government, and Tennessee had produced uncertainty about many of the landholdings in the state. This problem was further complicated by the actions of squatters who had simply moved onto land they desired and developed it as their own. Because they were numerous and had the right to vote, they were never without spokesmen in state government.

Governor Blount took several specific actions to aid in settling questionable matters concerning land titles. He turned to the legislature for direction in handling a problem inherited from the Sevier administration: registrars in both areas of the state—not including the Chickasaw lands of West Tennessee—had issued various land grants in the name of Governor John Sevier, but these documents had not received his signature before he left office. Blount sought and received regulations from the General Assembly to protect landowners from legal questions about inconsistency between the wording of their papers and the signature of the governor.[24] He was concerned also about the uncertainty of land titles in the area of the Tennessee-Kentucky boundary, which had not been drawn when he took office. In 1809 he secured authorization from the legislature to purchase a set of surveying instruments for the state and to employ a mathematician to decide the exact line of latitude between the two states. This dispute, however, was not settled until after he had left office.[25]

Other domestic issues also received attention from Governor Blount before he became enmeshed in the requirements of wartime administration. One of his enduring contributions was in the area of governmental reorganization. Especially concerned about reform of the judicial system, he won support from the Seventh General Assembly of Tennessee in dividing the state into five judicial districts, abolishing the Superior Court of Law and Equity, and establishing the Supreme Court of Errors and Appeals.[26] He instituted a policy of requiring that reports of county taxes be published and instituted a movement for reform in the law governing punishment of writers of counterfeit bank notes—an important matter in a state with an infant banking system. His interest in business development led him to support the establishment of the first state bank in 1811. It was during his administration also that provision was made for a state residence for the governor.[27]

Blount's vision of commercial development motivated him to become an early advocate of the building of roads to connect Tennessee with surrounding areas. He devoted special interest to a road between Tennessee and Georgia. Most of these ideas were not to be implemented until after he left the governor's office, but it was during his administration that the "turnpike road" was built from Nashville to Knoxville.[28] In 1811, in order to turn the attention of Tennessee to the problem of internal navigation, he laid before the General Assembly an act passed by New York which dealt with that question. During the same year he secured directions for the Tennessee delegation in Congress to work for the passage of bills calling for the establishment of free navigation of the "boatable" waters between Tennessee and Mobile and the construction of a road from Tennessee to that city. In 1813 he corresponded with the governor of Alabama about these proposed improvements.[29] Throughout his terms as governor, Blount sought support for his conviction that improved communication and transportation facilities were necessary for the development of the economy of Tennessee. He reported to the legislature in 1811 that "Attention in us in these things is more important in the future growth of our infant state, than time devoted to the idle whimsies of foreign relations. . . ."[30]

Despite these forcefully expressed sentiments in favor of internal improvements, most of Governor Willie Blount's time in office was claimed by the requirements of foreign relations, namely the War of

1812; the last two of his three terms of office occurred during this effort—which he fully supported. Aware from his frontier days of the uses of military force, he supported the message sent in 1811 by the General Assembly to the president pledging Tennessee's willingness to support him in the event of war. Upon learning of the declaration of war, Blount wrote to Felix Grundy, acting Secretary of War, assuring him that "My feelings as an American citizen are more to my mind since the receipt of your last informing that Congress had done their duty in declaring war than they have been since before the first violation of our rights. . . ."[31]

From the day he had become governor Blount had known that he could count on loyal support in the command of the state militia. His long-standing friendship with Andrew Jackson was continued as they corresponded frequently about the training of troops and the preparation for war. As early as 1810 Jackson had written the governor proposing that, in the interest of the discipline of the troops, the militia officers should be appointed rather than elected and that the men should be divided into two classes, 18 to 28 years of age and 29 to 40 years of age. He further suggested that the two groups should each have two months of training. No official action came from these proposals; however, Jackson unofficially put this plan into practice thereby insuring the readiness of Tennessee troops.[32]

As has already been noted, Tennesseans were highly sensitive to the Indian problem. Many of the people believed that England—either directly or through her ally, Spain—was responsible for the restiveness among both northern and southern tribes. Therefore, they felt that a war against England could be an essential part of securing the borders against the Indians. A successful war could also result in large additions of territory to gratify the settlers' desire for land. Blount wrote Jackson, "I hope you will purge the camps of the Indians of every Englishman to be found there."[33]

In 1812, with the Creeks in the Alabama area threatening trouble, Congress finally authorized the organization of companies of rangers for the frontiers. When Governor Blount asked that Tennessee be allowed such a company, the request was granted by the Secretary of War. The governor accepted the services of Captain David Mason and his company and directed them to range north of the Creek lands "so as to cut off or check the too frequent intercourse between the Creeks and the northern Indians."[34]

Neither Blount nor Jackson felt that enough was being done in Washington to meet the Indian threat. This feeling seemed justified when a party of Creeks killed seven persons and captured several others in a surprise attack on a settlement near the mouth of the Duck River. Expressing the indignation felt by his constituents, Blount demanded of Benjamin Hawkins, Federal Agent to the Creeks, and of Secretary of War Eustis the return of the prisoners and the surrender of the Indians. Because no action was taken by Washington, Blount sent out a company of rangers. He warned, "The Executive will feel himself bound on all proper occasions to exercise his authority, but more especially will it be exercised when the object is to afford protection against Indian depredations to the inhabitants of the State."[35]

Jackson reported to Blount that he could move 2500 volunteers in three days against the Creeks if the president would only give the governor power to authorize this action. However, while they were waiting for an answer from Washington, the welcome news that the United States had declared war against England reached Tennessee. Jackson became impatient with Blount's lack of authority to order an immediate campaign against the Creeks. It seemed to him that the United States government was so absorbed in foreign affairs that the Indian problem in the South was being ignored. He repeatedly urged Blount to make another request.[36] Accordingly, the governor again wrote the Secretary of War on June 25, 1812, telling of Jackson's offer of 2500 trained men for instantaneous service and informing him of the general's offer to have the Tennessee militia in Quebec within 90 days.[37] Blount also sent a personal pledge of Tennessee's enthusiasm for supporting the war.[38]

Morale was high throughout the state. The governor shared his feeling about the conflict with the legislature and the people in a war message in which he declared that "our cause is a good one . . . the crisis demands our aid to preserve, maintain and hand them [American liberty and independence] to posterity by the force of arms." He also requested that volunteers over the age of 45 be provided with compensation.[39] Tennesseans apparently were virtually unanimous in their support of the war effort. The editor of *Niles Register* praised the Tennessee militia as "ready to go anywhere to avenge the injured republic and meet and punish the barbaric foe. . . . The East may be a place of wisdom, but patriotic strength is in the West."[40]

Governor Blount devoted personal attention to the conduct of the war, giving directions freely to officers commanding Tennessee troops. He urged General James Winchester to greater efforts to ensure that his militia would be among the first ready and equipped for fighting. In writing to General George W. Campbell, he promised that Tennesseans were ready to "use their purses for wadding and run their silver into bullets. . . ."[41]

On November 11, 1812, Blount notified General Andrew Jackson that the War Department had asked for 1500 men from the state and asked him to recruit them from his militia. Jackson, beginning the tradition of the volunteer state, quickly organized a force of more than 2000. The Secretary of War authorized Blount to draw on the War Department for $10,000 to pay the expenses of the men until they joined General James Wilkinson in New Orleans. Although the militia went no further than Natchez before being ordered to return, the governor had drawn on the War Department for more than $35,000 before the troops were mustered out of service at Nashville.[42]

This first year of the war was disappointing to the militant Tennesseans who had found no opportunity to fight the enemy. In 1813, however, their prospects improved as the war expanded to include hostilities with the Creek Indians, a tribe long considered by the Tennessee settlers to be their enemies. This part of the war began violently on August 30, 1813, when a Creek army captured Fort Mims on the lower Alabama River in the southern part of the Alabama country and massacred the several hundred settlers and friendly Indians there.[43] The outrage felt by Tennessee citizens was shared by their governor who proceeded, apparently before he received proper authorization from Washington, to call for the mobilization of 3500 men. The response to Blount's order was so enthusiastic that two armies were raised, one commanded by General Andrew Jackson of Middle Tennessee and the other by General John Cocke of East Tennessee.

It was Andrew Jackson's army that was successful in locating and destroying the enemy. After establishing a supply base on the Tennessee River in northern Alabama, he cut a road through the forests into Creek territory. There he built Fort Strother and from that sanctuary launched attacks which in the fall of 1813 and the spring of 1814 reduced the fighting strength of the Indians.[44] His decisive victory came on March 27, 1814, when his army assaulted the major Creek center of resistance at Horseshoe Bend on the Tallapoosa River, near the present city of Montgomery, killing all but about 50 of an estimated 800 warriors and making prisoners of the 500 women and children.[45] In the summer following this battle Jackson gathered the surviving leaders of the Creek nation and forced the signing of a treaty which deprived them of their lands and opened the way for their removal to the West.[46]

Governor Blount had raised the Tennessee volunteers with the understanding that he would borrow $300,000 on the credit of the state to pay their expenses. When he received official authorization for raising the militia from Washington, he assumed that the United States government would relieve Tennessee of all financial obligations for the war expenses. When he was unable to get further assurances regarding finances, he refused to delay the mobilization but raised the money himself by securing endorsements from his friends for the requisitions. In many cases this was the only way he could persuade the banks to honor them. Any risks he may have taken were justified by the outcome, for the national government did eventually meet all of the state's financial obligations for the war. Also, Blount's original authorization of $10,000, which had been stretched to more than $35,000, was paid in full. Blount has received considerable praise for his unusual initiative in raising in excess of $300,000 on his own authority to enable Tennessee to move rapidly into the war. He received thanks from many citizens, as well as from the president, three secretaries of war, General Andrew Jackson, and the General Assembly of Tennessee. Such major financial support would have been a noteworthy contribution from any state governor.[47] It is interesting to note, however, that after the war was over, Blount asked the United States government to pay him a commission on the money he had raised. It was not until years later—on April 14, 1830, when Blount's friend, Andrew Jackson, was president—that Congress was willing to pay this claim. Blount was paid one-half of one percent for handling, endorsing and depositing the $250,000 in Treasury notes sent him November 4, 1814, and June 30, 1815. He was paid two and one-half percent for drawing the remainder on his own responsibility and for assuming personal financial risk.[48]

The Creek war had been conducted almost entirely by Tennes-

9. Elizabeth H. Peeler, "The Policies of Willie Blount as Governor of Tennessee, 1809-1815" (Thesis: Vanderbilt, 1936), p. 5.
10. Walker, p. 48.
11. Noel B. Gerson, *Franklin: America's "Lost State"* (New York, 1968), p. 150.
12. Masterson, p. 346.
13. Walker, p. 130.
14. John Dobson, ed., *Tennessee Beginnings* (reprint: Spartanburg, South Carolina, 1974), pp. xiv-xvii.
15. Peeler, p. 6.
16. James G. M. Ramsey, *Annals of Tennessee to the End of the 18th Century* (reprint edition: New York, 1971), p. 136.
17. Stanley J. Folmsbee, Robert E. Corlew, Enoch L. Mitchell, *Tennessee: A Short History* (University of Tennessee Press: Knoxville, 1969), pp. 116, 140.
18. Elizabeth H. Peeler, "Policies of Willie Blount as Governor of Tennessee, 1809-1815," *Tennessee Historical Quarterly* no. 1 (1942), pp. 309-327.
19. A. W. Putnam, *History of Middle Tennessee or Life and Times of General James Robertson* (University of Tennessee Press: Knoxville, 1971), p. 594.
20. Peeler, Thesis, pp. 12-14.
21. Ibid., pp. 20-24.
22. Putnam, p. 597.
23. Peeler, Thesis, pp. 26-27.
24. Ibid., p. 8.
25. Ibid., pp. 10-12.
26. Ibid., p. 44.
27. Ibid., pp. 36-38.
28. Ibid., pp. 51-56.
29. James Phelan, *History of Tennessee* (Boston and New York, 1888), p. 276.
30. Allen Johnson, ed., *Dictionary of American Biographies* (New York, 1929), 2:391.
31. Peeler, Thesis, pp. 58-59.
32. Abernethy, p. 222.
33. W. A. Walker, Jr., 'Martial Sons: Tennessee Enthusiasm for the War of 1812," *Tennessee Historical Quarterly* no. 20 (March, 1961), pp. 20-37.
34. Samuel Cole Williams, *Beginnings of West Tennessee, In the Land of the Chickasaws, 1541-1814* (Johnson City: Watauga, 1930), p. 81.
35. Elizabeth H. Peeler, *Tennessee Historical Quarterly*, pp. 317-318.
36. Ibid.
37. Marquis James, *Andrew Jackson–The Border Captain* (New York, 1933), p. 152.
38. W. A. Walker, p. 36.
39. Ibid., p. 33.
40. Peeler, Thesis, p. 70.
41. Lacy, pp. 129-131.
42. Peeler, *Tennessee Historical Quarterly*, pp. 320-323.
43. Folmsbee, Corlew, and Mitchell, p. 138.
44. Ibid., p. 138.
45. Clement Eaton, *A History of the Old South* (New York, 1975), p. 152.
46. Arrell Morgan Gibson, *The West in the Life of the Nation* (Lexington, Massachusetts, 1976), p. 129.
47. Phelan, p. 250.
48. Peeler, Thesis, p. 71.
49. G. R. McGee, *History of Tennessee from 1663-1914* (New York, 1889), p. 129.
50. Ibid., p. 122.
51. Peeler, *Tennessee Historical Quarterly*, p. 327.
52. Dobson, pp. xiv-xvii.
53. Walker, p. 49.
54. Dobson, pp. xiv-xvii.
55. Walker, p. 50.

BIBLIOGRAPHY

Books

Abernethy, Thomas Perkins. *From Frontier to Plantation in Tennessee.* University of Alabama Press, 1955.

Blount, Willie. *A Catechetical Exposition of Construction of State of Tennessee: Intended Principally for Use of Schools.* Knoxville: George Roulstone, 1803.

Davidson, Donald. *The Tennessee: The Old River Frontier to Secession.* Vol. 1. New York: Rinehart & Co., Inc., 1946.

Dobson, John, ed. *Tennessee Beginnings.* Spartanburg, South Carolina: reprint, 1974.

Dykeman, Wilma. *Tennessee–A Bicentennial History.* American Association for State and Local History, Nashville: W. W. Norton and Company, New York, 1975.

Eaton, Clement. *A History of the Old South.* New York: Macmillan, 1975.

Folmsbee, Stanley J.; Robert E. Corlew; and Enoch L. Mitchell. *Tennessee: A Short History.* Knoxville: University of Tennessee Press, 1969.

Gerson, Noel B. *Franklin: America's "Lost State."* New York: Crowell-Collier Press, 1968.

Gibson, Arrell Morgan. *The West in the Life of the Nation.* Lexington, Mass.: D. C. Heath and Co., 1976.

Goodspeed Publishing Company. *A History of Tennessee From the Earliest Times to the Present.* Nashville, 1889.

James, Marquis. *Andrew Jackson–The Border Captain.* New York: Literary Guild, 1933.

Johnson, Allen, ed. *Dictionary of American Biographies,* Vol. 2. New York, 1929.

Lacy, Eric Russell, ed. *Antebellum Tennessee: A Documentary History.* Berkeley, California: McCutchan Publishing Corporation, 1969.

McGee, G. R. *History of Tennessee From 1663-1914.* New York: American Book Company, 1899.

Masterson, William Henry. *William Blount.* Baton Rouge, Louisiana: State University Press, 1954.

Phelan, James. *History of Tennessee.* Boston: Houghton, Miflin, and Company, 1888.

Putnam, A. W. *History of Middle Tennessee or Life and Times of General James Robertson.* University of Tennessee Press, 1971.

Ramsey, James G. M. *Annals of Tennessee to the End of the 18th Century.* First American Frontier Series, 1853: reprint edition. New York: Arno Press, 1971.

Smith, Sam B. *Tennessee History, A Bibliography.* Knoxville: University of Tennessee Press, 1974.

Walker, Nancy Wooten. *Out of a Clear Blue Sky.* Cleveland, Tennessee, 1971.

Williams, Samuel Cole. *Beginnings of West Tennessee, in the Land of the Chickasaws, 1541-1814.* Johnson City: Watauga, 1930.

Wright, Marcus J. *Life and Services of William Blount.* Washington, D.C.: E. J. Gray, 1884.

ARTICLES

Peeler, Elizabeth H., "Policies of Willie Blount as Governor of Tennessee," *Tennessee Historical Quarterly* no. 1, 1942.

Walker, W. A., Jr. "Martial Sons: Tennessee Enthusiasm for the War of 1812." *Tennessee Historical Quarterly* no. 20. March, 1961.

UNPUBLISHED WORKS

Peeler, Elizabeth H. "The Policies of Willie Blount as Governor of Tennessee, 1809-1815." Thesis: Vanderbilt, 1936.

Portrait of Joseph McMinn, painted in Philadelphia by Rembrandt Peale. *Photograph by George W. Hornal, courtesy Tennessee Department of Transportation.*

5

JOSEPH McMINN
Governor of Tennessee,
1815-1821

by Nancy Boswell Kincaid

"Wonderful to tell, I was elected in twenty-six days . . . without having the wish or expectation of being elected." These words were spoken by Joseph McMinn, who at the age of 57 became Tennessee's fourth governor. His reference was to the fact that 26 days after receiving a letter from friends asking him to put forth his name for the governorship, he was elected.[1] Although these remarks might seem to indicate that the new governor was an inexperienced dark horse, he was no stranger to the state's political scene. He had, in fact, been significantly involved in the shaping of Tennessee's early history.

Joseph McMinn, in his own handwriting, gave the date of his birth as June 27, 1758. In a family Bible, he listed his birthplace as near Westchester, Pennsylvania. He was the son of Robert and Sarah McMinn and the fifth child in a family of ten. He had a Quaker background and received a "sound education."[2] In 1785, Joseph married Hannah Cooper, daughter of James and Rosannah Cooper. A little more than a year later, Jane, the couple's only child, was born.[3] The McMinn family moved to Hawkins County, Tennessee, in 1787, following Joseph's brother who had already settled there. After purchasing a small farm, Joseph and Hannah, like many pioneer husbands and wives, worked together in the fields.[4]

In a meeting at which the boundaries of Hawkins County were fixed, Territorial Governor William Blount commissioned McMinn a lieutenant of the Hawkins County militia on November 30, 1790. A year later, in 1791, he was promoted to captain. In the succeeding years, he became, in order, second major of the militia, justice of the peace (1792), and first major (1793). *The Blount Journal* also recorded his appointment as a representative from Hawkins County to the Territorial Assembly in 1794.[5] *The Commission Book of Governor John Sevier* continues Joseph McMinn's record of military and public service under the first state governor. Page 22 of this historic book lists McMinn's appointment as justice of the peace on May 6, 1796. Later that year, his name was listed with a commission as first major of the Hawkins County Militia.[6] McMinn represented his county at Tennessee's first Constitutional Convention when it assembled in Knoxville in 1796. It was his motion that secured the addition of a Bill of Rights to the new Constitution.[7] William Blount, who presided at the convention, entrusted the new Constitution to McMinn to be delivered to Secretary of State Timothy Pickering in Philadelphia.[8]

McMinn did not spend his time at Philadelphia in idleness. While there, he had his portrait painted by Rembrandt Peale. The only clear image of the governor, the portrait was acquired by the Tennessee Historical Society in 1945. As an observer, Joseph McMinn noted the opposition facing Tennessee's admission. The Federalists feared that the new state's electoral vote would be cast for Thomas Jefferson. After considerable delay, Tennessee was admitted to the union on June 1, 1796.[9]

McMinn also served in the first eight general assemblies of the new state, serving three times as the Speaker of the Senate. His common sense and loyalty to the state won him this post. His rulings while Speaker were noted for their fairness and respect for the rights of minorities. It was through this office that Joseph McMinn made friends from all parts of the state, friendships that would later help him win the office of governor. The period of McMinn's military and legislative service continued through the administrations of Territorial Governor William Blount and the first three governors of the state—John Sevier, Archibald Roane, and Willie Blount.[10]

Although McMinn was doing well in public life, his personal life was not as happy. His wife Hannah died February 27, 1811, at the age of 49. A year later, McMinn married again. His new bride was Rebecca Kincade, the daughter of David and Mary Kincade and a native of Hawkins County. Rebecca was 18 at the time of her marriage, but her youth did not protect her from an outbreak of influenza which, after only three years of marriage, claimed her life. Rebecca's death in 1815 was followed in just weeks by the death of Joseph's only child, Jane McMinn Cambell.[11] Perhaps the bereaved planter's only solace was Hetty McMinn, his niece, who had been adopted into his family and who, McMinn said, was treated in all respects as one of its members.[12]

Until 1815 the gubernatorial contests of Tennessee had not, with the exception of the Sevier-Roane race, drawn much attention, but the contest in 1815 followed the Battle of New Orleans, which had focused national attention on Tennessee. There was much interest in the governor's chair, as evidenced by an initial field of four contestants. These aspirants were Jesse Wharton, Robert Weakley, Robert C. Foster, and Thomas Johnson—all outstanding men.[13]

Added to the race was a late entrant. Joseph McMinn's candidacy was announced only one month before the election, and no circulars or customary advertisements were made. In a personal letter to his brother-in-law, Joe Bailey, McMinn spoke of his candidacy:

> I wished to spend the balance of my days in retirement. But to my utter astonishment on the 6th of July a very lengthy address was handed me from a large and respectable class of my fellow citizens soliciting me to offer for Governor of Tennessee. Having been frequently chided for leaving my countrie's service, I thought I would give my name and did so."[14]

In the *Scrapbook of Tennessee Governors,* McMinn is described as "being the only Eastern Tennessee candidate, which counted for much in that day."[15] McMinn won the election by an overwhelming margin, as the Middle Tennessee vote was divided among the other candidates. The final tally was McMinn, 15,600; Robert Weakley, 7389; Jesse Wharton, 7662; Robert C. Foster, 4184; and Thomas Johnson, 2987.

McMinn was inaugurated September 27, 1815, with the General Assembly convening in Nashville on November 17, 1815. He was to return to the state governor's office for two additional terms. In the 1817 race he met Robert C. Foster for the second time. The returns gave McMinn the office with a vote of 28,402 to Foster's 15,460. The third race McMinn waged was in 1819. For a time it seemed that former governor Willie Blount might be his opponent; however, Blount declined to run, making Enoch Parsons of Knoxville the only opposing candidate. In this race McMinn's showing was even more impressive, with a vote of 33,524 against Parsons' 8079.[16]

In his first gubernatorial speech before a joint session of the House and Senate, McMinn called attention to some of the problems awaiting the legislature and governor. North Carolina had been challenging settlers in the French Broad area about the validity of their land claims. Because of the settlers' services to the state, McMinn felt that they deserved consideration. Another item of high priority was the extinguishment of Indian claims within the state's borders. To accomplish this goal, McMinn requested the aid of the state legislators and suggested that Congress be enlisted to act on behalf of the white citizens. The Kentucky-Tennessee border dispute was another problem that the governor outlined for the legislators. He also recommended transportation projects involving new roads and river navigation.[17]

It has been said that "the financial history of the state of Tennessee began with Governor McMinn's administration."[18] Certainly the most perplexing problem in finances was the balance, or lack thereof, between specie (gold and silver) and paper money caused by a speculative boom and financial panic following the War of 1812.[19] During the period after the war the population had increased dramatically. In 1800 the total was 105,602, but by 1820 it had almost tripled to 261,727. Tennessee was no longer merely a frontier state where a system of barter sufficed. The increasing population produced a surplus of goods and demanded a more sophisticated means of exchange.

Before Governor McMinn came to office, the Bank of the State of Tennessee was chartered in Knoxville in 1811. Its capital was fixed at $400,000 with shares selling at $50 each. The bank had begun operations when $25,000 was paid in gold and silver by bank subscribers. The state itself had bought one-tenth interest by purchasing shares. The bank's stipulation was that notes of less than five dollars could not be issued. A supposed safeguard existed in the restriction that bank debt (not including deposits) was limited to double the bank's capital. This legislation also created bank branches at Clarksville, Columbia, and Jonesboro.

Boom years were beginning as Governor McMinn took office. By 1817, cotton prices had risen to 34 cents per pound. With settlers pouring in, the demand for land drove prices up. Many who could not afford the purchase price bought with bank loans. Trade expansion followed the growing population. Borrowed capital allowed merchants to purchase additional inventories to supply the expanded market. In 1814 there had been a general suspension of specie payments across the United States. The banks of Tennessee, however, were able to avoid this measure. New banks were created in Tennessee with offices in Fayetteville and Franklin. Yielding to public pressure, the legislature permitted the state banks to issue notes as low as one dollar.

The chartering of the Second Bank of the United States in 1816 eased the banking situation elsewhere. One purpose of a strong national bank was to curb the policy of issuing money without adequate deposits. Fearing the competition and strict regulations a national bank would impose, public opinion in Tennessee favored the local institutions.[20]

Controversy flared in the legislature over state versus federal banking. Felix Grundy, the voice of the merchants, hoped to establish a branch of the United States Bank in Nashville. The president of the Knoxville State Bank, Hugh Lawson White, led the opposition. To substitute for a branch of the national bank, a group of state banks was chartered in 1817 in Gallatin, Murfreesboro, Carthage, Rogersville, Winchester, Columbia, Shelbyville, and Knoxville. Capital stock for these new banks was fixed at $400,000, with shares selling at $50 each. These eight new banks could become part of the State Bank or Nashville Bank, or they could choose to remain independent. Notes of less than one dollar were prohibited. Although the newspapers criticized the legislature for creating banks in towns removed from the centers of commercial interest, the main offices at Knoxville and Nashville were enough to keep the commercial interests placated.[21] While Governor McMinn's approach to the question of state versus federal banking was to let the legislature decide rather than make an arbitrary decision himself, he did recommend in a speech before a joint session that the state maintain a fund of $7500 for such small banks as those at Jonesboro and Franklin; if the need arose the state could help meet demands on them, he said.[22]

In 1819 the price of cotton fell drastically; land value also declined. A depression first hit New Orleans and then moved up the river. The western portion of the state, where land was suited to cotton cultivation, was the most seriously affected.[23] Banks were forced to call in loans, and they faced increased demand for redemption of bank notes for specie. The Farmers and Mechanics Bank of Nashville suspended specie payments. Citizens meeting in Nashville suggested that the other banks stop specie payments as well. The

Nashville branch of the State Bank followed the recommendation of the public on June 29th, as did the Nashville Bank. The State Bank at Knoxville, under the leadership of Hugh Lawson White, was the only bank that continued to redeem its notes for specie.[24] Efforts were made to determine the cause of the panic. The Nashville Bank charged that overwhelming debts Tennesseans had incurred to Easterners were the cause. Continued redemption of bank notes held by Easterners would mean the loss of all gold and silver from Tennessee within a period of 90 days, according to the bank's estimate. Suits were brought against debtors by creditors and merchants. Many who could not pay found their property auctioned and sold for a price less than they had paid for it.

In 1819 the legislature acted by passing an "endorsement law," which dictated that at least two years should lapse before the enactment of a judgment unless the creditor would accept the depreciated notes of the Nashville Bank or the State Bank. The law was intended to act as a reprieve for the debtors. Unfortunately, some debtors did not possess even the depreciated Tennessee or State Bank notes to hold off the creditors. Using the endorsement laws to hold off Eastern creditors, heavily indebted merchants fared better than did farmers and landowners. To deal with the dilemma, Governor McMinn called a special session of the legislature in 1820. The plan was to create a new state bank which, unlike the earlier version, would be entirely owned by the state. Loan offices were to be maintained in Nashville and Knoxville, with branches or agencies in each county. These loan offices could lend up to a maximum of $1 million at six percent interest. In addition, paper money would be backed with the proceeds from public land sales. Governor McMinn proposed a "property law" whereby creditors would be forced to accept property at a value determined not by the creditors but by an arbitration committee, thereby insuring a measure of fairness to both the debtor and creditor. In addition, he suggested that the circulation of paper money be increased and that the state issue treasury notes through a loan office.[25] McMinn's contention was that someone needed to intervene between the debtor and ruin and that this responsibility properly belonged to the state government.[26]

The legislative debate on Governor McMinn's proposals became an example of both political and sectional rivalry. East Tennesseans protested the special session itself. They questioned the origin of the petition for the special session and the signatures affixed to the petitions. The "honest, industrious, and prudent" man, they contended, needed no aid and wanted no special session. Suggestions were made that those favoring a special session had made purchases without capital and now wanted the legislature to keep the creditor from collecting his just receipts.[27] The conservative element in the controversy, including Andrew Jackson and his friend Edward Ward, believed debt relief would damage credit abroad and cause further depreciation of bank notes. Felix Grundy, a former Congressman and a criminal lawyer, became the champion for the debtors.

Although the legislature did not follow Governor McMinn's suggestion for a "property law," it did establish a new state bank in Nashville, the Bank of the State of Tennessee; there was to be a branch in Knoxville and agencies in the counties. The new bank had power to issue up to $1 million and to lend at six percent interest. The legislation specified that security for loans could be either real or personal property, but mortgages on this property could not exceed one-half of its "unencumbered" value. Bank notes would no longer be secured by gold or silver but by the proceeds from public land sales and other state revenues. The law placed a limit of $500 on personal loans and regulated the amount of loans any county agency could make. The bill further provided that the new state bank would be the depository for all state funds.

The newly proposed legislation did not win complete acceptance. Among its opponents were Andrew Jackson and Edward Ward. They stood with the supporters of the "old State Bank" who felt their financial interests would suffer under the new plan. Jackson and Ward, under criticism from the debtors, recorded their violent opposition to a new bank by lodging a formal protest in the legislature, but their efforts were in vain. The measure passed. The Nashville Bank and the "old State Bank" reacted by refusing to accept the notes issued by the new bank. Refusing to accept the notes of the bank and calling in loans, the established banks defeated the purpose of the new State Bank legislation by reducing the amount of money in circulation.[28]

The Davidson County grand jury reproved the "two private corporations, managed by a few merchants" for disregarding "the laws, the will, and the strength of the country." The banking issue continued to be an area of dispute among the political figures of the state and figured in the gubernatorial and legislative races of 1821.[29] Governor McMinn, in a final speech before the legislature on September 21, 1821, indicated that it would be prudent for that body to examine all banking institutions in order to formulate improvements.[30]

Although he has been accused of lacking foresight in the banking issue, McMinn's proposals for internal improvements for the state indicated his vision of the future needs and growth of Tennessee. County courts had borne the responsibility for constructing roads and building bridges in accordance with an act of 1804.[31] The result of designating the counties as the responsible party for roads was that overland travel was at times tedious and in the winter impossible. In a message on September 27, 1815, McMinn spoke to the state lawmakers on the importance of "opening public roads and keeping those already opened in best possible repair." Expenses to the government would be offset by a small toll which "would in a very short time remunerate the expenses. . . ."[32]

Governor McMinn recognized Tennessee's great potential in river navigation. An 1807 article in Nashville's *Impartial Review* contrasted the expense of land and water transportation. It cited the example of a merchant shipping 2000 pounds from Murfreesboro to Nashville. The 34-mile trip cost $9.50 for transportation by water—a savings of $150.50 over the charge for transportation overland.[33] In his first inaugural address, Governor McMinn cited the "country produce" of the East and the "surplus property" of the West, which could be exchanged. What stopped the exchange, according to Governor McMinn, was the obstructions in the channels which made water transportation hazardous. McMinn advocated a navigation company. If the state permitted the company to charge a toll, the cost to the state would be minimal. Unfortunately, no action was taken on the measure by the legislature at that time.[34]

Two years later, in 1817, McMinn once again pressed the issue of river navigation before the legislature. He believed that the legislature's inaction was due to its belief that only merchants would benefit. As further encouragement he pointed to the benefits the residents of West Tennessee derived from the Mississippi River. In the end, he stated that he would leave the implementation of the project, whether by toll or by some other means, to the legislature's choosing.

By means of a joint resolution, McMinn appointed a committee for river investigation. Its duty was to report on existing obstacles and the expense of their removal. Half a million dollars was to be appropriated for the project.[35] For improvements on the Tennessee River, lotteries were held and special taxes levied. A small amount of the receipts from land sales south of the French Broad River were set aside in 1817 for improvements of the Tennessee River between Knoxville and the Alabama state line.[36] In 1819 a bill was introduced appropriating $500,000 for improvements on all the rivers in the state, but the depression and a natural reluctance on the part of the legislature to appropriate funds which were not in the treasury prevented enactment of the plan.[37] Another idea credited to Governor McMinn was the construction of a canal that would unite the Holston and Tennessee rivers. Free navigation from Muscle Shoals to the mouth of the Tennessee River was another proposal that he supported. During his last year in office, 1821, he continued his appeal for improved river navigation in a report to the United States Treasury on the navigable waters in the state.[38]

But Governor McMinn's lengthy campaign to improve river transportation was defeated by the state's limited finances. Financial consideration also hampered the development of a statewide road system. The legislature's decision in 1819 to allow the roads to remain under the control and responsibility of the counties meant that the roads would remain as they were—impassable. It was not until 1831 that the first macadam road was built and the movement for a state network of roads found support.[39]

Governor McMinn was not only interested in internal improvements but humanitarian reforms as well. A speech in 1819 focused on the need for a state penitentiary. Part of the text reads:

> I think it is my duty to bring the subject before you, and with earnest hope, that in your wisdom, and in your love, for the principles and practice of humanity and justice, you will lend your aid in commencing a work which will do lasting honor to its founders.[40]

An examination of the penalties for certain crimes reveals why reform was desperately needed. Punishment was not commensurate with the crime. For example, both murder and horse stealing convictions brought death by hanging. No discrimination was made between the first offender and the habitual criminal. Lesser offenses were punishable by whippings, brandings, and the pillory. For "willful perjury" the offender had his ears nailed to the pillory, and then, after his public display, the ears were severed from the head.[41] An example of the barbarity in punishments was the case of a Negro man named Moses. Charged with murder, he was sentenced to be hanged; after the subject's death, the sentence decreed that his head was to be severed and attached to a pole for public viewing. According to the directions of the court, the sheriff of Montgomery County displayed the severed head on a pole where it remained until only the skull was left.[42]

The idea behind severe punishments was to deter crimes, but, because of the barbarity of the sentences, the actual effect was that jurors were hesitant to find defendants guilty. Governor McMinn addressed this problem when he spoke in 1819 of the likelihood that few of the prisoners on trial would be convicted even if they had committed a serious crime. His pleas for reform were joined by the editorial voices of the *Tennessee Advertiser* and the Nashville *Whig*. Governor McMinn was able to use the sentiment for reform in an 1819 meeting of the legislature at Murfreesboro. For the proposed penitentiary, he suggested a loan from the state, the use of prison labor to enlarge the facilities when necessary, and the hiring-out of prisoners to create a future source of income.[43]

The legislature met in 1819 to consider not only penal reform but the construction of a state prison facility as well. The measure under the consideration of the House of Representatives would retain the death penalty for first degree murder and provide for a prison facility where prisoners would be segregated according to age, sex, and crime. The House passed the bill with only one dissenting vote. But in the Senate sectional differences surfaced, causing the defeat of the proposed prison. East and Middle Tennessee Senators differed over the site of the prison, each group determined that the prison would be constructed in its district. Since the two groups refused to compromise, the measure was tabled and a state prison act was not approved until 1825.[44]

Of no less interest to Governor McMinn was the education of the state's youth. He foresaw "advantages incalculable" arising from the education of the citizens of the state. Tennessee's problems in providing educational opportunities were related to the sale of public lands. The Compact of 1806, formulated by Congress to settle land disputes between the states of North Carolina and Tennessee, reserved 640 acres in each township for supporting public schools. In addition, the compact stated that one of the two tracts of land of 100,000 acres each in the Cherokee reservation would be used to support one college in East and one in Middle Tennessee and that the other tract was to support an academy in each county of the state.

Subsequent acts of the state legislature chartered academies in each of the 27 counties of the state. A curriculum of English grammer, philosophy, mathematics, Latin, astronomy, and logic illustrates the classical education these schools attempted to provide. Although the academies received state funds from land sales, they were essentially private schools for a limited number of white males only, and interest in them was not widespread. In some cases, as many as 25 years lapsed between the chartering of the academy and its actual establishment. Some never materialized. Because most of the desirable landholdings had already been taken, the revenue from sales was much less than had been anticipated. Some "squatters" refused to pay anything for the land, and the state was reluctant to force these voters to pay.[45]

The beginnings of a common school movement in Tennessee are found in a bill "to provide for the education of the orphans of those persons who died in the service of their country" during the War of 1812. The phrase "poor orphans who have no property to support or educate them" was designed to discourage individuals from taking advantage of the bill; however, the act was a step forward in that it was the first instance in Tennessee of a proposal for schooling based on state funds—on taxes rather than land sales.[46]

In 1817, when the legislature approached the problem of school revenues derived from land sales, it shifted the task to Governor McMinn. The legislature requested that the governor provide them with the acreage surveyed and reserved for schools. In a detailed report, Governor McMinn stated that 93,000 acres had been set aside for colleges and another 93,000 had been set aside for academies. In 1819, when the topic of schools arose again, the legislature's question concerned the number of sections of 640 acres that had been set aside in the different counties. Governor McMinn's reply was that he could neither locate nor provide a source for the answer. His feeling toward the school issue was made clear in a speech in 1821:

> We all know two hundred thousand acres of land south of French Broad and Holston, at the price of one dollar per acre, was appropriated to the establishment and support of Colleges and Academies; but in what manner collections on the sale of these land have been made, and to what amount; how much of the land has been granted; how much of the principal or interest has been voluntarily or otherwise paid; or how much still remains due or to become due, is scarcely known to any individual within the state. . . .[47]

Although Governor McMinn called for an investigation, he found no response on the part of the legislature.

In spite of the impractical system of funding, progress in education was made during his administration. During his second term, the trustees of Nashville Female Academy were named. Scholarship was also encouraged by the incorporation of a library in Knoxville and the founding of the Tennessee Antiquarian Society, the forerunner of the Tennessee Historical Society.[48] Among the many academies founded during this period, one bore the Governor's name—McMinn Academy, located near Rogersville. Years later, he remembered the school with a bequest in his will.[49]

In addition to dealing with the problems of education, Governor McMinn sought to solve the long-standing boundary dispute between Kentucky and Tennessee. He corresponded with the governor of Kentucky and kept the legislature advised of the negotiations. In 1818 the region of disputed territory was opened to settlement, and confusion arose as to whether these settlers lived in Tennessee or Kentucky. McMinn proposed a compromise based on the retention of the previously surveyed Walker's Line.[50] Although details of the settlement, including a survey conducted by representatives of both Tennessee and Kentucky, were not worked out until years later, it was his proposal that provided the basis for settling the dispute.

Although he was concerned with finances, education, internal improvements, and boundaries, the treaty providing for removal of the Cherokee was considered the greatest accomplishment of his administration. Concerning his efforts, the governor commented: "No portion of time is spent without affording the pleasing reflection of believing that the best interests of my Beloved Country is to be promoted when I shall be mouldering in the dust. . . ."[51] At the beginning of his gubernatorial administration in 1815, Governor

McMinn asserted that the "extinguishment of Indian claim to land lying within the limits of this state has always been a very desirable object."[52]

Land-hungry Tennesseans had found their ambitions checked by the Indian territories and the North Carolina land grants. When North Carolina ceded the Tennessee territory to the United States, it reserved its grants to Revolutionary War soldiers. North Carolina's right to reserve these Tennessee grants was upheld in 1806 when the federal government worked out a compromise; moreover, North Carolina also had reserved three sections of Tennessee land for the Cherokees, including the district south of the French Broad and Holston rivers, the Hiwassee District (between the Hiwassee and Little Tennessee rivers), and the Ococee District (between the Hiwassee and Tennessee rivers). Because the right of the North Carolina grants had been upheld, the only hope for Tennessee settlers to seize more land was to induce the Indians to move.[53] In fact, before Governor McMinn came to office, Indian Agent Return J. Meigs had been successful in securing some Indian land in exchange for payments.[54]

Following his announced intention of securing Indian removal, Governor McMinn in December of 1815 enlisted John Williams and G. W. Campbell to negotiate a treaty with the Cherokees. Negotiations were terminated when the Cherokee chief contended that he could not release lands he did not own.[55] With the aid of the president of the United States, negotiations were resumed, but in a period lasting more than two weeks nothing was accomplished. The reluctance of the Indians did not dim McMinn's determination to acquire land "which served them for no other object . . . than hunting ground."[56]

On July 14, 1816, in a letter to John Williams, McMinn informed him that Return J. Meigs had notified him that negotiations were about to resume and that there was a possibility of a new treaty:

> Object of the treaty is to obtain from the Cherokee nation a cession of the land north of the Tennessee River, which I deem of vital importance to the State of Tennessee, and, having commissioned you to negotiate with the Cherokee Chief last winter at Washington City, I deem unnecessary to invest you with additional authority, and will therefore take the liberty of asking you to attend in character of Commissioner on behalf of the state of Tennessee. For myself, I will attend in person.[57]

In correspondence dated August 30, 1816, Governor McMinn appointed a man whose firmness he greatly admired as commissioner to negotiate with the Cherokees—Andrew Jackson. Jackson accepted the task and received instructions from Governor McMinn to offer $20,000 for their "entire claim" north of the Tennessee River, $5,000 as "equivalent" for improvements on the land, and $5,000 to be distributed among the members of the nation.[58]

Governor McMinn, David Meriwether, and Andrew Jackson concluded the Cherokee Treaty on July 18, 1817. Under the treaty, signed by a few Cherokees, they ceded to Tennessee the rich Sequatchie Valley land in exchange for unknown territory in Arkansas. Each Indian migrating across the river was to be issued a rifle with ammunition, a blanket, and a brass kettle or beaver trap. Each head of a family group was entitled to 640 acres in the new area. A census was to be taken of those who emigrated to insure that they would receive their share of the money to be paid to the tribe.[59]

Few of the Cherokees were willing to accept the treaty as valid; certainly few of them wished to be deprived of their ancestral lands. And, because they had traditionally been given the status of a separate nation by the government of the United States, they appealed directly to President James Monroe for protection against the terms of the treaty. McMinn appealed to the Secretary of War, John C. Calhoun, arguing the necessity to Tennessee whites of the treaty and promising that the Indians would be treated justly. The Indians' Washington delegation was disappointed when President Monroe refused them aid, answering only that he wished to be a friend to both parties of the controversy. The Cherokees were thus abandoned to the mercies of those who coveted their land.[60]

The governor appeared before the legislature to report on the progress of the Cherokee affair. To the House and Senate he said, "We are now prepared to put into practice the theory of that illustrious statesman, Mr. Jefferson, by whom the principal of exchanging land was first suggested. . . ."[61] In order to facilitate matters, the governor suggested that the legislature appoint someone to oversee the collection and delivery of articles that had been promised to the migrating Indians. The legislature making no move to comply, Governor McMinn assumed the duty himself. With the idea of either forming a new treaty or enforcing the existing one, he left for the Cherokee Agency on December 10, 1817. On his arrival, he announced that books would be opened to record the names of those who wished to migrate to the land in Arkansas.[62] His interest in removing the Indians was so strong that he remained at the agency to supervise arrangements personally.[63]

At the Cherokee Agency some 3500 Indians were removed under Governor McMinn's auspices. However, most Cherokees refused to leave, even though an offer of $200,000 was made to secure their agreement. These Cherokees took their grievances to Washington where they were defeated by Secretary of War Calhoun's demand for additional Cherokee cessions as compensation for the remaining Indians who also would need new homes in the West. The resulting Calhoun Treaty of 1819 ended Cherokee claims to an area including the Jackson-McMinn Treaty line and a tract north of the Little Tennessee River. This action left the Cherokees in Tennessee with only the Hiwassee District, which they retained until 1835.

While the Cherokee negotiations were continuing, McMinn was simultaneously bargaining with the Chickasaws, the tribe that owned the land between the Tennessee and Mississippi rivers. In a tribal council meeting Governor McMinn advised the Chickasaws that he could no longer prevent "encroachments by whites" on their lands.[64] General Andrew Jackson and Governor Isaac Shelby of Kentucky, acting United States Commissioners, formulated the treaty that would secure Chickasaw claims to what is now known as West Tennessee on October 19, 1818.[65] In exchange for the Chickasaw lands, the United States was to make annual payments of $20,000 for a period of 15 years. In addition, two debts incurred by the Chickasaws to Captain John Gordon and Captain David Smith in the amounts of $1115 and $2000, respectively, were to be settled. Certain individual members of the tribe were to receive $4264. These last payments apparently were bribes needed to secure signatures for the treaty. All payments to the Chickasaws now were to be made in cash rather than trade goods. Only a small area of about four square miles was reserved by the tribe because the area supposedly contained salt deposits. Three small tracts also were allowed to remain in the hands of tribal owners, provided that these individuals accepted the laws of the United States.[66]

McMinn's letters from the Cherokee Agency, where he personally oversaw the enrolling of migrating Indians, reflect the concern he had that the government keep the promises it had made to the

Indians. In one of these letters he wrote, "I have at this time a large number here who look up entirely to me, for everything they require, and I feel it so much my duty, and the interest of all parties concerned, that they should leave here with their wants well supplied, and their affections well secured to the Government. . . ."[67]

In 1819, McMinn gave his assessment of his actions regarding the Chickasaw and Cherokee cession:

> In a long life of labor and active employment, more than thirty years of which have been devoted to the faithful service of my country, I have never been engaged in any other public duty from which I had reason to expect so much substantial good and lasting advantage to my fellow-citizens; and that it will prove the most useful part of my public life. . . ."[68]

The governor had indeed worked long hours on the scene at the agency and had displayed great persistence in encouraging the federal government and the state legislature to take the land from the Indians.

With the acquisition of the Chickasaw territory, the boundary of the state changed. Formerly the Tennessee River marked the western boundary of the state, but with the "Chickasaw Purchase," or the "Western Purchase" as the area was often called, the Mississippi River became the new western boundary of the state. The area included roughly about 10,000 square miles, almost one-fourth of the land area of the state. The two rivers, the Tennessee and the Mississippi, afforded the new area with great opportunities for the development of trade.[69]

Because the Chickasaws had only used the territory for hunting grounds, the area was sparsely populated. Enthusiastic newspaper accounts stirred the interest of Middle and East Tennesseans, North Carolinians, and others. The Nashville *Clarion* compared the soil to the best in Alabama, while the Raleigh *Register* encouraged readers to reap the "rich rewards."[70] Descriptions and appeals like these brought settlers both from within and from outside the state.[71]

In an attempt to provide local governments for the new territory, the legislature began to create new counties in the area. In 1817 and 1819 the legislature created the counties of Marion, Monroe, and one which bore the governor's name (McMinn) from the Cherokee lands.[72] Starting in the eastern portion of the Chickasaw Purchase, the legislature created the county of Hardin which at the time reached from the eastern boundary to the Mississippi River. Later it was subdivided into the counties of McNairy, Hardeman, Fayette, and Shelby. As the number of settlers increased, new counties were added, including Henry, Carroll, Madison, Henderson, Haywood, Dyer, Gibson, Weakley, Obion, and Tipton.[73]

While he was in office Governor McMinn married Nancy Glasgow Williams. Governor McMinn was 58 and his bride was 46; like the governor, she had lost a previous spouse. Mrs. Williams' son was Colonel Willoughby Williams, a sheriff of Davidson County and a friend of Andrew Jackson. The governor's marriage was not as successful as his negotiations with the Cherokees and Chickasaws.[74] His duties as negotiator kept him away from home frequently, and Mrs. McMinn spent considerable time away from home visiting her relatives. Each one blamed the other for the marriage's failure. In the governor's petition of divorce to the legislature of October 16, 1821, he cited his wife's absence of eight months and her announced intention of remaining away. In response, Mrs. McMinn had her attorney present a defense of her faithfulness and of the governor's shortcomings. Each party had support among the legislative members. Despite the controversy it caused, the divorce petition was labeled "reasonable" and the request granted. In a letter to a friend, the Governor reported, "I had on former occasion advised you of my marriage to a third wife, and now I have the painful task of stating to you that we are separated, by her resolving to remain in Nashville with her relations, instead of coming to this place; upon which, I returned every article of property which came into my hands by this marriage, and gave her $2000 out of my estate."[75] Nancy McMinn continued to reside in Nashville until her death in 1857.

Having served the constitutional limit of three terms, Governor McMinn retired from office. He purchased a farm near Calhoun, Tennessee, where he cultivated about 100 acres with the help of 20 slaves. In conjunction with the farm he operated a tavern and a grocery. In 1823 Lucian Minor, a traveler from Virginia, recorded his impressions of the former Governor in the *Atlantic Monthly,* describing him as "bustling about the tavern, at once landlord, bar-keeper, and head-waiter, administering entertainment to guests of every degree."[76]

After retirement, Governor McMinn joined the Presbyterian

Church. His religious convictions seem to have been deeply held, as evidenced by his frequent references to divine guidance and providence in his messages and speeches. He held family prayers before the assembled members of the household each night. On one of these routine occasions, while the Governor was down on his knees in prayer, his supplications were interrupted by the loud snores of a young servant. McMinn paused, turned to a person nearby, and said, "Wake that damn nigger up." Resuming his posture, the governor continued to the end of his prayer.[77]

Even after retirement, McMinn was still involved in Indian affairs. Appointed in 1823 as the Cherokee agent, he continued in this position until his death at the Cherokee Agency headquarters on October 27, 1824. Seated at his desk, he was said to have fallen back in his chair, stricken with "dropsy of the heart." Joseph McMinn was buried close to the agency in a cemetery overlooking the banks of the Hiwassee River.[78]

The three decades of Joseph McMinn's public service were eventful ones. It was to his credit that he promoted education, penal reform, and internal improvements. But in his own estimation, his greatest achievements lay in the realm of Indian affairs. It should be noted, however, that the Indians may not have agreed with this view. He must have been a capable mediator, as indicated by his serving as Speaker of the Senate, struggling with the Kentucky-Tennessee border dispute, and acting as agent in the Cherokee and Chickasaw negotiations. John Allison, in his *Notable Men of Tennessee,* stated, "His administration was noted for its uprightness and for certain measures in the interests of the masses of the people."[79] In describing Governor McMinn's contributions, the historian Dr. J. G. M. Ramsey referred to him as "a man remarkable for the best of all endowments, great and good common sense. . . ."[80]

Governor McMinn's administration spanned a period of transition in Tennessee. During the period from 1815 to 1821, the land area of the state was increased by one-fourth. This new land made possible the formation of several new counties. Tennessee took on the shape it has today with the three grand divisions of the state— East, Middle, and West Tennessee. McMinn's efforts with the Chickasaws made possible the founding of the great metropolitan city of Memphis in 1819. The governor initiated several social and internal improvements which succeeding governors saw fit to continue. Although two historical markers point out the governor's home, New Market, and the place of his early settlement in Hawkins County, the two most obvious memorials are the county which bears his name and the town of McMinnville.[81] During a period of service spanning 30 years, the tabulation of votes in each of his campaigns showed his overwhelming popularity with the people.

NOTES

1. Edwin M. Murphey, Jr., "Joseph McMinn," *Tennessee Historical Magazine* (October, 1930), 1:6.
2. Ibid., p. 3.
3. Lucy Womack Bates, *Roster of Soldiers and Patriots of the American Revolution Buried in Tennessee*, State Regents Bicentennial Project (NSDAR: 1974), p. 278; Zella Armstrong, *Some Heroes of the Revolution*, (Chattanooga: Lookout Publishing Co.), 4.
4. Murphey, p. 4.
5. Tennessee, *The Blount Journal*, pp. 37, 52, 64, 67, 84, 92.
6. Tennessee, *The Commission Book of Governor John Sevier*, (Nashville: Benson Printing Company, 1957), pp. 22-23.
7. J.G.M. Ramsey, *The Annals of Tennessee* (Kingsport: Kingsport Press, 1967), p. 652.
8. William E. Beard, "Joseph McMinn," *Tennessee Historical Quarterly*, no. 4 (1945), 158.
9. Cynthia McCarlie Sloan, "Governor Joseph McMinn," (Thesis, George Peabody College, 1938), p. 2.
10. Beard, p. 154.
11. Ibid., p. 158.
12. Jeanette Tillotson Acklen, ed., *Bible Records, Tombstones, Inscriptions* (Baltimore: Genealogical Publishing Co., 1967), p. 145.
13. John Trotwood Moore and Austin P. Foster, *Tennessee the Volunteer State* (Nashville: S. J. Clarke Publishing Co., 1923), 1:368.
14. Murphey, p. 6.
15. *Scrapbook of the Governors of Tennessee*, p. 137, quoted in Cynthia McCarlie Sloan, "Governor Joseph McMinn."
16. Phillip M. Hamer, ed., *Tennessee—A History*, (New York: The American Historical Society, 1933), 1:229.
17. Robert H. White, *Messages of the Governors of Tennessee* (Nashville: Tennessee Historical Commission, 1952), 1:447.
18. Will T. Hale, *A History of Tennessee and Tennesseans* (New York: Lewis Publishing Co.) 2:267.
19. Stanley J. Folmsbee, Robert E. Corlew, and Enoch L. Mitchell, *Tennessee: A Short History*, (Knoxville: The University of Tennessee Press, 1969), p. 140.
20. Hamer, p. 230.
21. Folmsbee, Corlew, and Mitchell, p. 141.
22. White, p. 484.
23. Thomas Perkins Abernethy, *From Frontier to Plantation in Tennessee* (University of Alabama Press: 1967), p. 225.
24. Hamer, p. 231.
25. Ibid., p. 233.
26. Ibid.
27. Joseph H. Parks, "Felix Grundy and the Depression of 1819 in Tennessee," *East Tennessee Historical Society Publications* no. 2, (1938), p. 27.
28. Hamer, p. 234.
29. Ibid., p. 235.

30. White, p. 450.
31. Federal Writers Project, *Tennessee* (New York: Hastings House: 1949), p. 92.
32. White, p. 450.
33. Federal Writers Project, p. 93.
34. White, p. 451.
35. Ibid., p. 483.
36. Beard, p. 10.
37. Abernethy, p. 243.
38. Beard, p. 11.
39. Abernethy, p. 244.
40. White, p. 531.
41. E. Bruce Thompson, "Reforms in the Penal System of Tennessee, 1830-1850," *Tennessee Historical Quarterly*, no. 1 (1942), p. 292.
42. Ibid., p. 293.
43. White, p. 531.
44. Thompson, p. 296.
45. Folmsbee, Corlew, and Mitchell, p. 274.
46. Robert H. White, *Development of the Tennessee State Educational Organization 1796-1929* (Kingsport: Southern Publishing Co., Inc., 1929), p. 25.
47. Ibid., p. 23.
48. Beard, p. 161.
49. Federal Writers Project, p. 311.
50. W. R. Garrett, "Northern Boundary of Tennessee," *Tennessee Old and New* (Kingsport: Kingsport Press, Inc.), p. 417.
51. "Correspondence of Governor Joseph McMinn," *The American Historical Magazine*, no. 4, (1899), p. 330.
52. Folmsbee, Corlew, and Mitchell, p. 148.
53. Slone, p. 13.
54. Folmsbee, Corlew, and Mitchell, p. 148.
55. Murphey, p. 6.
56. White, *Message of the Governors of Tennessee*, p. 481.
57. "McMinn's Correspondence on the Subject of Indian Treaties," *The American Historical Magazine*, no. 8, p. 377.
58. Ibid., p. 384.
59. Murphey, p. 7.
60. Slone, p. 21.
61. White, *Messages of the Governors of Tennessee*, p. 527.
62. Ibid.
63. Ibid., p. 6.
64. Murphey, p. 7.
65. James D. Porter, "The Chickasaw Treaty of 1818," *The American Historical Magazine*, no. 9 (1904), p. 252.
66. Murphey, p. 7.
67. "Correspondence of Governor Joseph McMinn," *The American Historical Magazine*, p. 330.
68. Robert H. White, *Messages of the Governors of Tennessee*, p. 527.
69. Samuel Cole Williams, *Beginnings of West Tennessee* (Johnson City: The Watauga Press, 1930), p. 94.
70. Ibid., p. 98.
71 Moore and Foster, p. 375.
72. *General History of Tennessee* (Nashville: Goodspeed Publishing Co., 1887), p. 361.
73. Ibid., p. 362.
74. Nancy Wooten Walker, *Out of a Clear Blue Sky* (Cleveland, Tenn.: By the Author, 1974), p. 57.
75. Murphey, p. 12.
76. Ibid.

77. Ibid.
78. Beard, p. 166.
79. Judge John Allison, ed., *Notable Men of Tennessee* (Atlanta: Southern Historical Association, 1905), 1:64.
80. Beard, p. 166.
81. Tennessee Historical Commission, *Tennessee Historical Markers,* 6th ed., (1972), p. 19.

BIBLIOGRAPHY

BOOKS
Abernethy, Thomas Perkins. *From Frontier to Plantation in Tennessee.* University of Alabama Press, 1967.
Acklen, Jeanette Tillotson, ed. *Bible Records, Tombstones, Inscriptions.* Baltimore: Genealogical Publishing Co., 1967.
Alderson, William T. and Robert H. White. *A Guide to Study and Reading of Tennessee History.* Nashville: Tennessee Historical Commission, 1959.
Allison, Judge John, ed. *Notable Men of Tennessee,* Vol. 1. Atlanta: Southern Historical Association, 1905.
Armstrong, Zella. *Some Heroes of the Revolution,* Vol. 4. Chattanooga: Lookout Publishing Co., n. d.
Bates, Lucy Womack. *Roster of Soldiers and Patriots of the American Revolution Buried in Tennessee.* State Regents Bicentennial Project, NSDAR, 1974.
The Blount Journal. State of Tennessee.
The Commission Book of Governor John Sevier. Nashville: Benson Printing Company, 1957.
Dictionary of American Biography, Vol. 12. New York: Charles Scribners Sons, 1933.
Folmsbee, Stanley J.; Corlew, Robert E.; and Mitchell, Enoch L. *Tennessee, A Short History.* Knoxville: University of Tennessee Press, 1969.
Hale, Will T. *A History of Tennessee and Tennesseans,* Vol. 2. New York: Lewis Publishing Company, n. d.
Hamer, Phillip M. *Tennessee, A History,* Vol. 1. New York: The American Historical Society, 1933.
Harlan, A. H. *Genealogy of the Harlan Family.* Baltimore: Lord Baltimore Press, 1914.
McBride, Robert Martin. *Tennessee County Data for Historical and Genealogical Research.* Nashville: State Library and Archives, 1966.
Moore, John Trotwood and Austin P. Foster. *Tennessee, the Volunteer State,* Vol. 1. Nashville: S. J. Clarke Publishing Co., 1923.
Ramsey, J. G. M. *Annals of Tennessee.* Knoxville: East Tennessee Historical Society, 1967.
Scrap Book of Governors of Tennessee. State of Tennessee.
Smith, Sam B. *Tennessee History, a Bibliography.* Knoxville: University of Tennessee Press, 1974.
Tennessee. Federal Writers Project. New York: Hastings House, 1949.
Tennessee Historical Markers. Tennessee Historical Commission, 1972.
Walker, Nancy Wooten. *Out of a Clear Blue Sky.* Cleveland, Tenn.: By the Author, 1974.
White, Robert H. *Development of the Tennessee State Educational Organization, 1796-1929.* Kingsport: Southern Publishing Co., Inc., 1929.
————. *Messages of the Governors of Tennessee,* Vol. 1. Nashville: Tennessee Historical Commission, 1952.
Williams, Samuel Cole. *The Beginnings of West Tennessee.* Johnson City, Tenn.: Watauga Press, 1930.

ARTICLES
Beard, William E. "Joseph McMinn." *Tennessee Historical Quarterly,* no. 4, 1945.
"Correspondence of Governor Joseph McMinn," *The American Historical Magazine,* Vol. 4, 1899.

Garrett, W. R. "Northern Boundary of Tennessee." *Tennessee Old and New.* Kingsport: Kingsport Press, n. d.

"McMinn's Correspondence on the Subject of Indian Treaties." *The American Historical Magazine,* Vol. 1. October, 1930.

Murphey, Edwin M. "Joseph McMinn." *Tennessee Historical Magazine,* Vol. 1. October, 1930.

Parks, Joseph H. "Felix Grundy and the Depression of 1819 in Tennessee." *East Tennessee Historical Society Publications* no. 2, 1938.

Porter, James D. "The Chickasaw Treaty of 1818." *The American Historical Magazine,* Vol. 9, 1904.

Thompson, Bruce E. "Reforms in the Penal System of Tennessee, 1820-1850." *Tennessee Historical Quarterly,* Vol. 1, 1942.

NEWSPAPERS
Nashville *Whig.* Nashville: September 25, 1819.

UNPUBLISHED WORKS
Slone, Cynthia McCarlie. "Governor Joseph McMinn." Thesis, George Peabody College, 1938.

6

WILLIAM CARROLL
Governor of Tennessee, 1821-1827 and 1829-1835

by Harriet W. Stern

On the Fourth of July in 1829, a large crowd gathered at the First Presbyterian Church of Nashville for special festivities honoring one of Tennessee's most popular heroes of the War of 1812. The honoree, Major General William Carroll, became the recipient on this patriotic occasion of a ceremonial gold sword—a rare presentation in the state's history. His sword, handsomely designed, was sheathed in a scabbard adorned with medallions of gold. A golden eagle head formed the handle of the sharp, steel blade. On one side of the blade was inscribed the dedication "Presented by the State of Tennessee to Major General William Carroll as a testimonial of high respect for his public services" and, on the other, the battles in which Carroll had earned this gratitude were listed: New Orleans, Talladega, Emuckfau, Enotochopco, Tohopeka.

William Carroll had distinguished himself in three of the six terms he was to serve as governor. This was the Jacksonian Era—a time of rapid growth and change in the state. Carroll proved to be a stabilizing but progressive helmsman as the state grew from a frontier region to the fifth most populous state, from an agricultural area to one also having business and commercial interests, and from a single- to a two-party state. He exerted his influence for judicial, educational, and humanitarian reform. During his time in office the state Constitution underwent a major revision, bringing a broadening of democracy. Carroll has been referred to as "Tennessee's Reform Governor" and "Tennessee's Business Governor," but, in the minds of the people he served, he seems always to have been their military hero and their general in peace—a Washingtonian figure in Tennessee.

The first half of the 19th century was a time of national prominence for a number of Tennesseans, among them Andrew Jackson
and James Polk, Felix Grundy and John Bell, Sam Houston and
Hugh Lawson White. Carroll moved in the political arena with these
men, working diligently for the Democratic party and serving as its
champion in Tennessee. Although Carroll never attained national
office and was never offered an appointed position of prominence,
his power was secure in the state for many years. While Jackson ran
the nation, Carroll ran Tennessee.

William Carroll was born in 1788 near Pittsburgh, Pennsylvania,
to Thomas and Mary Montgomery Carroll; he was the eldest of that
union which was to produce seven surviving children. The Constitution of the United States was then a year short of passage. The vast
wilderness north of the Ohio River and east of the Mississippi had
just been opened for settlement the previous year by the passage of
the Northwest Ordinance. What was to be in eight years the state of
Tennessee then was a barely explored frontier country of isolated
settlements. The population was something less than the 35,691
enumerated in the 1790 census.

Accounts differ as to the origin of Thomas Carroll, William's
father. According to one account, the elder Carroll emigrated to the
colonies from Ireland shortly before the Revolution. It was said that
he had been a British soldier but had joined the Colonial Army and
fought first at Bunker Hill, then with the Delaware brigades through
the rest of the war. When advised to change his name by friends who
feared the consequences if Carroll was captured by the British, he
reportedly declared, "No, I'll keep me own name. They'll be welcome to hang what's left of me when they get me."[1]

A genealogical history prepared for the family differs from this
account, tracing further and more illustriously back to a Daniel
Carroll, father of Thomas and a member of the outstandingly patriotic Carroll family of Maryland. Daniel Carroll was a member of
the Continental Congress, signer of the Articles of Confederation,
and one of the two Catholic signers of the Constitution. He was a
cousin of John Carroll, who led in the establishment of the Catholic
Church in the States, and Charles Carroll "of Carrollton," signer of
the Declaration of Independence. According to family memoirs,
Governor William Carroll in 1832 took his 11-year-old son Charles
to visit his namesake, the famous Charles Carroll of Carrollton, only

Portrait of William Carroll. *Photograph by George W. Hornal, courtesy Tennessee Department of Transportation.*

to arrive two weeks after the elderly patriot had died.

Whether or not William Carroll was himself a second or a third generation patriot, it is generally agreed that his father, Thomas, of Irish descent and revolutionary devotion, moved with his wife, Mary, the daughter of his captain, from Maryland to a settlement near Pittsburgh around 1783 or 1784. On the banks of the Monongahela, he set up a nail foundry. Soon he entered the employment of another hardy immigrant, Albert Gallatin, and later became his partner in a hardware business. It may have been a tribute to Gallatin that Thomas Carroll named his first son William for William Tell, the hero of Gallatin's native Switzerland.[2] Gallatin soon literally left Thomas Carroll to mind the store when he entered his long career of public service to the new nation. In 1810 Gallatin was Madison's Secretary of the Treasury. He proposed using the Treasury surplus for a broad program of improved transportation, including the rivers of the frontier. This plan would surely have added to the commercial prospects of Nashville, where the Pittsburgh to Nashville river trade was already valuable as one of the main outlets between East and West—a fact which perhaps influenced Thomas Carroll's eldest son's decision to move South.

William Carroll, then 22, emigrated to Nashville in 1810 to start his own business after five years of mercantile employment in Pennsylvania. He began his life in Tennessee with a keg of nails and a letter of introduction to Andrew Jackson from Gallatin. His education was, according to most sources, meager. It probably consisted of bookkeeping, surveying, math, and apparently a background in language and grammar which made his "clarity and vigor of thought and expression" possible.[3] His education also included some instruction in military tactics[4] and, one assumes, the usual farming skills of the time. The Nashville *Whig* at the time of his death stated

> His native sense and perseverence overcame all the difficulties of a defective education in early life, so that the style and language of his public documents, as well as his private correspondence, so far from denoting the want of scholarship, reflect the highest credit upon his literary taste.[5]

"An interesting man with steel blue eyes, and a fastidiously dressed figure,"[6] Carroll became "one of the best-dressed sparks in Nashville."[7] He was noted for his tall, athletic figure, refined face, and graceful bearing.[8]

The move downriver from Pittsburgh brought Carroll into Middle Tennessee, an area which was moving into prominence as the most thriving commercial and manufacturing area of the new state. Settlement and trade were expanding. In Nashville, the center of the Cumberland area, a hardware business for the sale of such things as pots and kettles, hatchets and nails, spikes and hammers could thrive. William Carroll soon became established. His "nail factory," the first among Nashville's 1100 people, was tremendously successful. Zadok Cramer of the *Pittsburgh Navigator and Almanac* of 1814 cited the store as one of the main businesses: "William Carroll & Co. in connection with Mr. Cowan of Pittsburgh, have a nail manufactory and an extensive ironmongery store."[9]

By 1816 William Carroll was a highly regarded businessman. When Nashville citizens decided to investigate the development of steamboat trade, he was one of a committee of five chosen to explore the feasibility of the project. As a result, he himself invested in the first steamboat to arrive at the Nashville landing. This boat, the *Andrew Jackson,* was named for the dominant political figure in the state, Carroll's future patron. Although the steamboat reached the mouth of the Cumberland in 1818, low water over the Harpeth Shoals prevented passage to Nashville until March 11, 1819. Carroll had helped promote a new and successful means of transportation in the area. Although the *Andrew Jackson* made a number of runs to New Orleans in good time, it was another two years before a second trip could be made up the entire stretch to Nashville. Carroll's role was played early, for in 1821, when his business was bankrupt, he sold the boat. This may have been a fortunate necessity, for the *Andrew Jackson* sank in an accident shortly thereafter.

Another early venture of Carroll's was more personal. In September of 1813, he married Cecelia Bradford in a ceremony performed by her father, a civil official. Of Cecelia herself almost nothing is recorded in the histories of either her husband's career or his family. It is known, however, that she was born in 1787 on her father's farm near what is now Hendersonville, Tennessee. Her mother's family were Scottish immigrants to Virginia, and Cecelia is said to have been a devout Presbyterian. Her maternal grandfather, Josias Payne, had once served in the Virginia House of Burgesses before moving to Tennessee to take possession of a land grant after the Revolution. Her mother, Elizabeth Chichester Payne, was a widow with a small daughter when she married Cecelia's father in 1785 and settled with him on the farm in Sumner County. From this union Cecelia had five brothers and sisters.

Cecelia's father, Henry Bradford, was of Virginia background. As a boy of 12 he had apprenticed himself to a tailor, later leaving his indenture in his teens to fight in the Revolution. Wounded and discharged, he received a land grant for military service. In the fall of 1784 he migrated along the Cumberland Gap Trail, where his party was attacked by Indians. Young Bradford was seized in his own tent but managed to break away and escape on horseback. By morning he had arrived safely in the camp of other migrant settlers, bearing with him a bleeding comrade he had rescued on the way. When the journey ended in Middle Tennessee, Bradford and his neighbors immediately fortified their new settlement with a stockade.

Like her husband, Cecelia came from sturdy, ambitious, and patriotic stock. Henry Bradford was capable and industrious. He served the federal government as Internal Revenue Officer for the Mero District and the state as a major in the militia. His farm prospered in maize and cotton, and at his death in 1815 he was able to leave an estate of land, slaves, and personal property to each of the five children who survived him. This inheritance must have been an asset to Cecelia and William Carroll, particularly during the depression of 1819.

William and Cecelia Carroll had three sons. The youngest son, Charles, lived most of his life in Memphis, where he served in the militia and held the rank of colonel during the Civil War. Thomas, the middle son, was mayor of Memphis from July of 1856 until he died in office in April of 1857. The oldest son, William Henry, also moved to Memphis, went into the real estate business, and served as postmaster. He rose to the rank of brigadier general in the Civil War, but the severity of his command ruined him. While at Knoxville, he executed several citizens who, as Union sympathizers, had burned railroad bridges. As the victorious Union forces advanced to the South, he was declared an outlaw and fled to Canada, where he died in 1866.

William Carroll was not only successful in business, river transportation, and marriage, but in the military as well. Soon after his arrival in Nashville, he, who was "much given to military affairs,"[10] helped to organize the local militia and was elected a captain. In 1811 he and two other militia leaders requested Jackson's aid in procuring arms for drill and training. Jackson obliged, declaring that the three officers were "gentlemen of Property and standing in society."[11] Carroll's concern for a well-organized and well-trained militia continued through all his years as governor.

In 1812 Carroll accompanied other Tennessee troops under Jackson to Natchez in readiness for possible maneuvers by the British near Mobile.[12] The troops traveled by river for a month to reach Natchez, where they camped for a long, cold winter. In February they learned that the British threat in the South had failed to materialize and they were to disperse without firing a shot. Jackson refused to discharge his troops, and returned them in military order to Tennessee. Carroll, like the others, saw no active service on this expedition.

When he arrived home, however, there was action of another sort. Carroll was challenged to a duel by Lyttleton Johnson, a fellow officer. The basis for this challenge seems difficult to determine. Carroll is said to have told Jackson that certain people wanted to drive him out of town. There may have been some jealousy among the ranks because of Jackson's favoritism in appointing Carroll brigade inspector, a position which the future president had held before Natchez. Buell rumored that a woman might have been involved. Parton thought that Carroll aroused dislike for other reasons:

> With all his powerful frame and superior stature, there was an expression of delicacy in his smooth, fair countenance that found small favor in the eyes of the rougher pioneers. . . . Perhaps, too, in those days there was a touch of dandyism in his attire.[13]

As it developed, however, the dispute turned into a political quarrel revolving around Jackson—which it probably had been from the start.

At first Carroll refused the challenge as not coming from a gentleman. Finally, Jesse Benton, a friend of the challenger, accepted. Carroll could not deny Benton's stature as a gentleman. He asked Jackson to act as his second, but Jackson instead made efforts to settle the affair peacefully. His overtures were rejected when Benton allowed friends to persuade him to fight—friends who were probably Jackson's enemies by virtue of his duel, which had been fatal to John Dickinson in 1806.

The duel took place, and it was a farce. Benton fired the first shot, injuring the ball of Carroll's left thumb. Carroll then fired at Benton who, having turned and crouched, suffered a painful and embarrassing injury in the rear portion of his anatomy. With no serious injury beyond Benton's humiliation, the parties retired from the field. The situation, however, was further inflamed by Jackson's enemies who alerted Jesse's brother, Thomas Hart Benton, to what was happening. A former companion-in-arms and close friend of Jackson's, Thomas was at this time in Washington on a mission partly intended to aid Jackson in recovering personal funds he had spent on the Natchez expedition. He was led to anger. Bitter letters were exchanged until Jackson lost his temper and threatened to horsewhip Thomas Benton. The opposing parties met in the square of downtown Nashville, Jackson with his horsewhip and all with pistols and knives. In the mélee which followed in the City Hotel, Jackson received a near-fatal bullet wound. The incident was always an embarrassment to Jackson. Jesse Benton became his permanent enemy. Thomas Benton broke with Jackson, moved to Missouri to better his prospects at a distance from Jackson, and remained estranged from his former friend for ten years until, while both serving in Congress, they became reconciled—a reconciliation for which Jackson later gave Carroll credit.

Carroll, meanwhile, had removed himself from the quarrel. He had called upon Jackson and informed him "that an affair of a most delicate and tender nature compelled him to leave Nashville at break of day."[14] Jackson reportedly dismissed him, saying he had no need of others to fight his battles; but hard feeling between the two persisted for a time. The two men were brought together again by Carroll's effective service under Jackson's command, which began two months after the Jackson-Benton affair with a call to arms for the Creek campaign of the War of 1812. William Carroll left his brother Nathaniel in charge of the hardware business and departed in 1813 for his first active military duty.

The first engagement occurred at Talladega, where one of Cecelia's brothers died by the tomahawk. Here Carroll was placed in charge of a group of about 30 infantry scouts. Under fierce attack, they held firm in the line, then went in vigorous pursuit of the enemy. In the ensuing battle of Emuckfau, Carroll's men again distinguished themselves by aggressiveness and bravery. Carroll himself continued to display outstanding courage and a superior command of his men at the next engagement at Enotochopco and finally at the battle of Tohopeka, or Horseshoe Bend. He was slightly wounded in this decisive battle which crushed the power of the Creek Indians. To have been with Jackson at Horseshoe Bend was almost the equal of having been with him at New Orleans.

Carroll's ability to inspire his men was shown after the battles as well, for, when a large portion of the army disputed the lengths of their terms of service and went home before the end of the Creek campaign, Carroll's detachment remained active. After this large-scale "mutiny," as Jackson termed it, Jackson praised Carroll for his difficult mission of effectively raising a body of new recruits.[15] Jackson's view of Carroll's service was unequivocal:

> Too much praise cannot be bestowed upon the advance led by Colonel Carroll, for the spirited manner in which they commenced and sustained the attack. . . . I should be doing injustice to my staff, composed of Colonel Carroll (and others) not to say that they were everywhere in the midst of danger circulating my orders. They deserve and receive my thanks.[16]

When Jackson was promoted to major general in the regular army, Carroll was elected major general in command of the Tennessee militia. Yet his greatest military fame, like Jackson's, still awaited him at the Battle of New Orleans. Carroll was charged with command of 5000 troops, 2500 under his personal supervision. Volunteers were summoned to Nashville for the departure to New Orleans. Appreciating the need for speed, Carroll rapidly proceeded to take advantage of high water by building flatboats to transport the troops by river.[17] He also recognized the need for preparedness. Encountering shipment of rifles destined for the troops, but traveling slowly along the river, he had the presence of mind to request permission to requisition the guns immediately. By this foresight he arrived sufficiently armed; the remainder of the shipment reached New Orleans after the battle. Carroll also trained and drilled his men on the decks of the flatboats. Armed and ready to fight, they arrived in only 17 days to relieve a beleaguered Jackson. As battle lines formed, Carroll and his men were placed in a location which was to bear the brunt of the battle. Carroll ordered his riflemen to hold fire until the enemy advanced to within 200 yards. At this close range, the Tennessee brigades devastated the enemy.

Buell, who likes a good story even of uncertain origin, narrates an anecdote about Carroll. It seems that a grizzled old sergeant at the Battle of New Orleans observed Andrew Jackson standing on the fortifications and began to sing an old gospel song, "Deah Gaberil stannin' by de gate . . ." Carroll supposedly chided, "Shut up, Sam! If the redcoats ever once hear you trying to sing they'll run—run like hell! And we want 'em to come on."[18]

Throughout his military service Carroll had demonstrated initiative, leadership, and courage. He emerged a hero. Writing to Colonel A. F. Hayne, Inspector General of the Southern District of the US Army, regarding promotions after the Battle of New Orleans, Jackson declared, "The government and the world are sensible of the high opinion I entertain of General Carroll."[19] When news of the triumph at New Orleans reached Nashville, candles were lighted in the windows, and a long horn was sounded in the main square. Carroll returned to repair his business fortunes, which flourished until the depression of 1819.

The War of 1812 brought considerable prosperity to Tennessee and the western territory. Increased amounts of specie flowed into the state for the purchase of war provisions and began replacing barter as the chief means of exchange. With the opening of foreign trade, cotton prices rose to an unprecedented 34 cents a pound. The glorious and dangerous boom lasted until 1819 when the price of cotton fell and, throughout most of the country, currency contracted and banks called in their loans. Payment in specie was suspended, and a severe depression resulted. The state was confronted with large numbers of debtors in distress. In Davidson County alone, more than 500 suits for debts were filed. William Carroll was forced into bankruptcy, not on his own account, but as a result of having signed notes for friends. Although he could not have realized it at the time, this personal misfortune was a stroke of good luck. His status as a "poor man" would prove to be a political asset, second only to his military fame, when he chose to run for governor two years later.

Carroll had been much involved in the banking and financial issues which became focal points of the gubernatorial contest in 1821. In 1817 Carroll and Felix Grundy had led an effort to establish a branch of the US Bank in Nashville in order to obtain commercial credit on a sound basis. At that time the Overton-Blount faction of the Democratic party dominated the existing banks of Nashville and

Knoxville. They made loans to their friends and supporters. This faction succeeded in electing Hugh L. White to the state legislature, where he led the passage of a tax bill which, through an exorbitant tax, prohibited the establishment of the competing US Bank in the state. Thus Grundy and Carroll's efforts for the national bank were defeated. They and others did, however, establish a Farmers' and Mechanics' Bank in Nashville with Carroll as a director.

When the depression hit, farmers, small landowners, and businessmen were hard pressed by the calling in of credit and the cessation of specie payments. Deeply in debt, they demanded relief and blamed the banks, the speculators and the policies of special favor. They focused their anger on the clique of wealthy men of the Blount-Overton faction. By 1820, a year before the gubernatorial election, a popular outcry arose and a division into opposing groups took place. At that time Felix Grundy emerged as the champion of relief legislation for the debtor class. He led efforts to create a state "loan office" and, this failing, a state bank, which was the same thing by another name. The bank was to provide credit to debtors so that they might meet their obligations. It was based on capital from the state. Its directors were elected by the legislature, and its funds were apportioned to the counties. As a companion measure, Grundy and his followers enacted a "stay law," which provided that a creditor must allow two years' delay in debt payment or accept the depreciated notes of the state bank.

One of those allied with Grundy was Andrew Erwin, a leading anti-Jackson man. The Erwin-Grundy faction chose Carroll to represent them as candidate for governor in 1821. Grundy had been judged somewhat erratic, but Carroll was more reliable and equally popular. Against the background of financial distress and upheaval, William Carroll declared his candidacy for governor in a circular in the Nashville *Clarion,* on July 3, 1821:

> I have been your fellow citizen almost twelve years; a portion of that time many Tennesseans from almost every part of the state had the opportunity of inspecting my conduct personally under circumstances that are well calculated to exhibit a man's character in its real colors—to them I must refer those of you who are not acquainted with me. If I am your choice, fellow citizens, with the permission of providence I will serve you to the best of my abilities, in peace and in war. If you should not elect me, I will

submit with cheerfulness to the will of a majority determined still to lose no opportunity as a private citizen in an inferior status of contributing my mite toward the promotion of our happiness, and maintenance of our rights and the preservation of our liberties.[20]

Carroll did not favor the relief legislation of Grundy. Although he was the "people's candidate," he did not believe in issuing cheap paper money as did later populists. And, while he might have preferred to close all branches of the State Bank immediately, he judged this too severe. He stood for careful supervision of the banks and a return to specie payment. Careful economy on the personal level and sound money practices on the state level were his curatives. In addition, he spoke for judicial reform, educational improvement, establishment of a penitentiary, and internal improvements. With a characteristically sanguine spirit, he spoke of the good land and the habits of good hard work which would help to restore general well-being: "Some of us were born poor, and have acquired an independence; and we can maintain it if we have it, or, if we have lost it, we can acquire it again . . . with manly firmness . . . (though) assailed by the sneer of malevolence . . . ."[21] The personal references are clear.

Carroll's opponent was Edward Ward, Speaker of the State Senate from 1815 to 1819. He was a well-educated, wealthy man—a near neighbor and a good friend of Jackson's. He too opposed relief legislation, the loan bank, proliferation of paper money, and the expansion of credit. He too called for careful economy, hard work, and an end to unnecessary purchases. Like Carroll, he addressed himself to the needs in education, penal reform, and internal improvements. He identified himself as an agriculturalist who believed (as did Carroll) that the "agricultural part of society can never trade with banks but to their injury and loss."[22] He did, however, favor a centralized banking system. This preference would have most likely resulted in a continued control by the Overton-Blount faction.

Although the candidates seemed to be in agreement in many ways, they differed in ones that were of crucial importance. One was the company they kept. Another was personality. A third was their relationship to the changing time in which the campaign took place.

Ward was a wealthy aristocrat with a reputation for extravagance. His manner was cold and pompous. As a further encumbrance, he suffered politically from a prejudice against his superior education. Too, he had never been to war. Above all, he represented the wealthy aristocracy of bankers and land speculators whose activities were blamed for the depression while their own fortunes remained secure. Even the support of Andrew Jackson as an ally of the Blount-Overton faction could not help him.

Carroll, on the other hand, was an ideal man of the West for his time. Physically he stood tall. His wealth, when he had it, was self-made, not inherited. His losses made him one with the dispossessed who suffered at the hands of the old order. He had proven his leadership in battle and had fought the people's foremost enemies, the British and the Indians. He was a man of humble beginnings, and his limited education could shame no one. In manner as in allegiance, he was "popular"—open, cordial, and friendly. He greeted former soldiers, especially, in a spirit of camaraderie and often by name. Not by any means a backwoodsman, he was still a man of the people—the people's man. This fact won him the election.

The final element in Carroll's success was the time in which it occurred. The election of 1821 marked a popular revolt in Tennessee. The depression of 1819 had been a turning point in which a large segment of the populace in both the state and the nation, stirred by financial disaster, had refused any longer to allow an aristocratic oligarchy to guide it. Ironically, the democratic awakening was represented in Tennessee by Carroll, with Jackson in opposition. Its leader in the nation was Jackson.

The 1821 campaign was a popular one in another sense: the candidates sought to make a wide popular appeal. The contest was carried vigorously through the press—that in itself was an innovation.[23] In the ensuing years each faction had its "party organ" of vigorous partiality, but in 1821 this partisanship was not so clear-cut. Campaign funds were spent to circulate newspapers containing letters of support for one candidate or another, usually written under fictitious names. In the newspapers were straightforward letters and humorous ones. In the month of July "A BIG FISH" released a list of reasons in the *Clarion* for not supporting Carroll, including the following: " . . . he cannot boast of a long race of rich and illustrious ancestors . . . he has never learnt and forgot Latin and Greek . . . he will heartily shake the hand of a ragged fellow soldier; thus doing away the distinctions of rank. . . . But above all I will not vote for him because he *was broke,* and because the impudent fellow *won't stay so.*"[24]

In one issue Carroll felt the necessity of printing a detailed statement of the condition of his affairs related to bankruptcy, with supporting evidence from others.

Carroll was elected by a vote of 31,290 to 7294, the largest majority of any candidate before the Civil War.[25] He won all but two counties in the state. With this mandate Carroll entered upon his first three terms of office, from 1821 to 1827. He ran unopposed for reelection in 1823 and 1825. In this period his major contribution was firm guidance in economic and monetary matters and policy, which helped restore economic stability to the state. He advocated many reforms during this time. These, however, did not come to their varying degrees of fruition until his second period of three terms of office in the years 1829 to 1835. Had he served only the first period, he would be distinguished and well remembered. Because of the achievements of the second period, he can be highly honored.

Upon taking office as governor in 1821, Carroll directed his foremost attention to the goal of economic stability. In his first message to the legislature he opposed the issuing of paper money and also the "stay law," which he believed to be unwise as well as unconstitutional. He urged that banks be watched and be required to make regular public statements of their financial status. Building on this philosophy, his chief goal was the restoration of sound currency. The legislature in 1821 responded to this with the passage of the Specie Resumption Act, which established April of 1824 as the date by which this resumption was to be accomplished. The legislature in 1823 extended the date for resumption to 1826, but by that time Carroll's goal was accomplished as a result of his policies and an upturn in prosperity.

Another twofold goal in the area of finance was Carroll's aim to close the State Bank of 1821 (Grundy's Bank) and to establish in the state a branch of the US Bank for commercial credit. Both aims were ultimately accomplished. In 1825 the legislature finally removed the prohibitive tax against a branch of the US Bank. Branches of this bank were subsequently chartered in the state. It was ten years before Carroll achieved the closing of the State Bank. The institution endured until 1832, even after disclosures in 1829 had revealed mismanagement and embezzlement. The State Bank was succeeded by a stronger institution, the Union Bank of Tennessee. Chartered under careful provisions for public accountability, this bank was designated for public deposits with profits to be consigned for school funds. Thus Carroll's administrations left finance and banking in Tennessee on a firm basis.

Throughout all his terms as governor, Carroll called for a comprehensive system of education and a statewide program of internal improvements. A lack of funds due to the land policy in the state was one of the greatest impediments to progress in both instances.

Land policy was set by the Compact of 1806 among Tennessee, the federal government, and North Carolina. The terms of this agreement required that North Carolina land claims be satisfied and that a large section of Tennessee land be set aside as a military reservation. As time went on, many North Carolina claims were settled on lands outside of the reservation as well. All in all, little and often poorer quality land remained for Tennessee to sell in order to obtain revenue for schools and internal improvements. The compact had also provided that "where existing claims permitted" there was to be a reserve of land in each township for support of public education. Irregular surveys, however, resulted in uncertainty as to what land was school land. Furthermore, no plan of guardianship was set up for the land.

Another difficulty existed until 1823. This was the hope that the federal government would sell its vacant lands and disperse money to the states. Consequently, the legislature refrained from committing funds to education while there was a possibility of federal money. After 1823 federal sale was not anticipated, and the state assumed responsibility.

A final barrier to progress in education was the concept of public schools as pauper education. For some time public funds were sought to provide schooling only for poor orphans and other unfortunates. In advance of many others of his time, Carroll wanted to provide common education for all. Carroll pressed consistently for a system of common schools for both rich and poor (of the white race). He held a Jeffersonian belief in education as the heart of equal opportunity.[26]

In his first message to the legislature Carroll urged a survey of school lands, as had Joseph McMinn before him. James K. Polk, Carroll's ally in the Tennessee legislature, reported to him that only 22,705 acres of the 450,000 anticipated in 1806 had actually been set aside as school lands. The legislature thereupon passed its first measure of significance concerning education. It created a fund for the establishment of pauper schools through the use of taxes on school lands and sales of waste lands. County courts were directed to appoint commissioners to supervise the funds and allot them for the poor. When procedures were set up, however, the land in some counties was leased or sold for the benefit of the schools while in others nothing was done. In some locales the trustees and commissioners, themselves unpaid, mismanaged or plainly misappropriated funds.[27] A second step was taken in 1827, when the common school fund was expanded. The real financial basis of the system is dated from this point; but, in spite of good intentions and the continual adding of bits and pieces of revenue to the school fund, it was in practice never sufficient for many years.

The first major education act, passed in 1829-30, represented a change of attitude under Carroll's leadership and under the educational ferment of the times that was led by such men as Horace Mann. The act of 1830 established the principle of common schools for all white children and set up an administrative structure within the counties and townships. Furthermore, $150,000 from land sales was designated for the common school fund. Thus, under Carroll's leadership a system of common schools came to be recognized as a state responsibility.

In the work of internal improvements during Carroll's administrations, one can also observe many problems and limited success. Carroll's efforts here were hampered by sectional rivalry as well as by limited funds. Geographically, the three regions of the state differed in transportation needs. The East Tennessee region sought river access to the Gulf of Mexico at Mobile by way of the rivers of northern Alabama. Its concerns were thus focused on a canal leading to Mobile from the Muscle Shoals. West Tennessee was interested in navigation of the small rivers flowing into the Mississippi. Middle Tennessee wanted improved navigation of the Cumberland and also was interested in turnpikes, but West and East Tennessee rested many hopes on future railroad transportation. Voting on these matters in the legislature was therefore often sectional and selfish.

When he took office in 1821, Carroll stressed the importance of enabling farmers to bring their produce to market. He urged a survey of rivers, at the least, and proposed using money from present or anticipated land sales for the purpose. The survey was not achieved until 1827. Through it Carroll hoped to resolve the interests of the three sections of the state into a workable plan.

No further progress was made until Carroll returned to office in 1829. In 1831 a bill passed which apportioned $150,000 from land sales to the three divisions of the state. Sad to say, even this step had disappointing results. Only East Tennessee made a general advance by using its share of the funds to improve navigation on the Tennessee River from Muscle Shoals to Knoxville. In other areas of the state, however, the funds were parcelled out to counties for internal improvements. They were dissipated in projects of minor importance or for pet projects not necessarily related to transportation.[28] That so little progress was made can only be attributed to a shortage of funds and an overabundance of sectional rivalry within the state.

Although education and internal improvements were important to William Carroll, his most passionate efforts were directed toward penal reform and the goal of a state penitentiary. He repeatedly expressed his views and his feelings to the legislature. He pleaded that the current system of punishment—including flogging, branding, and placing in stocks—produced a bad effect on both the offender and the public. The former was made vengeful and the latter callous. The penalty system was so severe that a person convicted a second time for a theft of $10 or more was sentenced to be hanged, and a man could be put to death for horse-stealing. Under these circumstances judges and juries rarely convicted anyone. Carroll urged a graduated system of punishments and the establishment of an institution of reform and rehabilitation.

Success finally crowned Carroll's long efforts. In 1829 the penal code underwent thorough revision. The death penalty was eliminated except for first degree murder. Sentences of varying severity were set for different crimes. The pillory, branding, and flogging were no longer to be used. By 1831 imprisonment for debt was abolished for women and also for men, unless debt was incurred by fraud. The new code was to go into effect when the penitentiary opened. Furthermore, a penitentiary was authorized and built quite economically. It opened its doors on January 1, 1831, to its first inmate, a tailor who had stabbed a man with his shears and assaulted him with his tailor's iron. His task on entering the prison was to make his own prison suit.

Another institution intended for humanitarian purposes was authorized in 1832. This was the first state mental hospital. It was not successful. Work proceeded so slowly that the institution was not completed until 1840 and in 1843 held only three patients after an expenditure of $56,000. Real progress did not result until 1854, following a visit from Dorothea Dix in 1847, when she criticized the legislature for the inadequacy of the institution.

Second only to penal reform, Carroll pleaded for reform in the court system. Court dockets were overcrowded, for there were few restrictions limiting matters that might be prosecuted. Members of all parties and their witnesses lost time and money waiting for a case to be heard. Then, because of overlapping jurisdiction, the same matter could be reheard in another court of original jurisdiction. Beyond this, some judges were poorly qualified. Even those who were well qualified—and especially those on the Supreme Court— were required to travel extensively and handle an unmanageable burden of cases.[29]

Judicial reform had a difficult time partly because of the conflict between the legislature and the Supreme Court. This was evidenced in the legislative refusal to void the "stay law" in 1821 and in the legislature's reenactment of the same law in 1823. In the latter year the legislature also refused to appoint anyone to a vacant position on the Supreme Court. Several years later a fierce debate ensued over the judiciary. Elements in the legislature were so frustrated in 1831 at the inability to be rid of two incompetent justices of the Supreme Court that they sought to abolish the court when impeachment failed. This served as prelude and impetus to the judicial changes made in the 1834 Constitution.

Despite Carroll's earlier efforts, significant progress began only in 1829 with a searing legislative report brought by Adam Huntsman of the judiciary committee. It declared that Tennessee's judiciary system was "the most expensive and least efficient of any in the United States." Reforms came about in the next years so that, by the end of his time in office, Carroll saw most of his desired improvements embedded in the new Constitution or enacted in separate legislation.

Carroll regarded judicial reform as a humanitarian issue. His most significant reforms were, indeed, social and humanitarian in nature. Looking over his record, one writer offers the following summation:

Many years elapsed before all these reforms were accomplished, but it is due to Carroll's liberal-minded appreciation of the necessities of the times, and his unwavering obstinacy in pressing them that they were at last achieved. All his messages from the first to the last returned repeatedly to the charge. If we divide our state history into ancient and modern periods, the credit would fall to Carroll's lot of having foreseen and ushered in the latter. He was essentially the reform governor of Tennessee.[30]

Although the new Constitution incorporated a number of Carroll's accomplishments into the basic law, he had not called for the political reforms nor the tax reform that make the 1834 document an emblem of Jacksonian democracy. Carroll actually feared the results of a Constitutional revision.[31] Despite his lack of enthusiasm, the convention produced a Constitutional revision that is one of the most significant changes of his time as governor. It codified the democratic reform movement in the state—part of an expanding popular democracy throughout Jacksonian America.

One of the most significant of the reforms was the change in taxation. According to the 1796 Constitution, all property was taxed equally by acre except for town lots, which could be taxed slightly more per acre but still equally as a group. Thus with equal acreage, a farmer of poor, swampy bottomland would pay the same taxes as a prosperous cotton planter with more fertile farmland. The law had worked as a special privilege for large landowners and speculators. It was primarily these interests that had been able to defeat repeated attempts over almost 30 years to gain the votes needed to call a Constitutional Convention. The new Constitution provided for taxation by value.

Another democratic reform in the 1834 Constitution was the provision for popular election of the leading county officials: justices of the peace, constables, sheriffs, trustees, registers, and clerks of the inferior courts. By the previous Constitution the members of the county courts had been chosen for life by the legislature, and they in turn chose the other county officials. Greater popular control was established by the accompanying new power to elect these county officials for a specific term, rather than for life as before.

A much-contested reapportionment article of the 1834 Constitution also represented a democratic adjustment. Under the 1796 document a county of small size could have the same number of representatives in the legislature as a large county. Consequently, the Eastern division of the state was over-represented in comparison with the more recently settled Middle and Western divisions, where large counties were the rule. With the changes of 1834, apportionment was to be based on the "qualified voters," not the former "taxable inhabitants." The number of representatives could increase from 40 to a potential 99, and senators from 20 to one-third the number of representatives.

Still another democratic reform was the removal of property ownership as a requirement for voting and holding office. This expansion of the electorate and potential office-holding population aplied, however, only to free white male inhabitants. The new Constitution withdrew previous rights from free "men of color." The latter were disenfranchised except for those who were then "competent witnesses in a court of justice against a white man." Further shadows of the slavery question also fell across the Constitution in the item which deprived free "men of color" of the right to bear arms.

Among the judicial reforms for more effective justice were provisions for three Supreme Court justices and a designation of three places only in which they were to meet. This court also was declared an appellate body. All of these were reforms which Carroll had eagerly sought. He had also worked for the establishment of separate chancery courts. While this last provision was not written into the Constitution, the legislature did create a number of such bodies and would continue to do so under its power to establish courts. The new Constitution further declared an official responsibility for internal improvements and education that Carroll had urged over the years. It committed the revenue that might come to the state through sale or division of public lands entirely to internal improvements and education.

Thus the new Constitution created more political equality and more equal taxation. It brought increased local control over county offices and a resultant decline in legislative power. Judicial independence was established as a principle. That the Bill of Rights stood first in this Constitution, not last as in 1796, was symbolic.

The story of William Carroll would not be complete without some picture of his political activities on his own behalf and on behalf of the Democratic party, nationally and within the state. Carroll's political career paralleled that of the powerful Jackson. Sometimes the two men worked in opposition and at other times in harmony of purpose. Carroll's political life rose and set beside Jackson's. Jackson was Carroll's patron when he first came to Tennessee, and it was he who saw to Carroll's merited advancement in the military. Their relationship came full circle when Carroll's last public act proved to be a speech in honor of Jackson.

Although he had urged Jackson to enter national politics in 1815, Carroll took an active role on his behalf only after Jackson was nominated by the Tennessee General Assembly in 1822. After the nomination, Carroll became Old Hickory's campaign treasurer,[32] despite the fact that Jackson had supported Ward in the governor's race the preceding year. At the same time, however, Carroll was secretly encouraging the efforts of Henry Clay to oppose Jackson as the Democratic candidate. Upon learning of Clay's nomination, Carroll wrote Clay that this step might encourage Clay forces in Tennessee and some adjoining states. He expressed confidence that Tennessee would go for Clay if Jackson failed. He stated that he would write friends in Harrisburg and Pittsburgh advising them of the sentiments of the Southern states. If Jackson could not obtain a second in caucus, Clay's name could be placed in nomination. Carroll's maneuvers did not escape Jackson's attention. He understood through friends in Alabama, Louisiana, Mississippi and Pennsylvania that Carroll was working for Clay. He also had wind of a letter written by Carroll to friends in the Louisiana legislature saying that Tennessee would go for Clay. Carroll later vehemently denied ever having written this letter or any others unfavorable to Jackson.

In 1823 Carroll and others urged Jackson to run against East Tennessean John Williams for the US Senate seat, a position they felt would fortify his chances of being elected to the White House. Jackson won the race and Carroll succeeded in removing Jackson as a possible gubernatorial candidate against him in that year's race, one who would have been almost impossible to defeat. Carroll ran unopposed and was powerful enough to help bring about the defeat of three of Williams' supporters in the legislature.

Following the Jackson-Williams contest, Carroll again sent private encouragement to Clay.[33] Openly Carroll supported Jackson in 1824 when John Quincy Adams won the presidency. In that year Carroll publicly defended Jackson's honor in connection with the

Carroll-Benton duel, a defense which countered Jesse Benton's vindictive writing during the campaign. Again in 1828 Carroll publicly supported Jackson amid rumors that he privately supported Clay. Jackson swept into office, winning 95 percent of the vote in Tennessee with an electoral turnout double that of 1824.

Carroll himself had been ineligible to run for governor in 1827, having won, again unopposed, a third term as governor in 1825. He had hoped to be chosen for the Senate by the legislature in 1826, but Jackson controlled the body and thwarted him in favor of John Eaton. It spite of this disappointment, Carroll joined Jackson in support of the successful candidacy of Sam Houston in 1827. Houston continued many of Carroll's policies, and Carroll expected to have the governorship returned to him in 1829. To his chagrin, Houston planned, with Jackson's support, to run for a second term.

Consequently, Carroll began to seek appointment as Minister to Mexico. In 1829 John McLemore wrote Jackson on Carroll's behalf. Jackson responded that ministerial appointments were curtailed because of finances. Some years later, when a new appointment was made, Jackson did not appoint Carroll. Jackson did offer him a chargé d'affaires post in South America in 1829, a position he refused. Carroll also refused an offer to become a brigadier general in the regular army and chose to stand for office against Houston. McLemore summed up Carroll's position at this time:

> Houston will be supported as a Jackson man. . . . Carroll's military fame is great and you know that he has a lot of personal friends formed in the army and you know he is very poor and absolutely needy of employment to support his family—the cry now is raised that if Maj. Eaton and Maj. Lewis are to get fat offers, and Gen. Jackson shall neglect Carroll . . . it will be very offensive to the people of Tennessee. This view of the matter will keep up the excitement—to assure his election. You very well remember the men in E. Tenn. who entertain deadly hostility to Gen. J. are united to Carroll and he to them. You remember that the same thing is true in relation to the General's enemies in West Tennessee.[34]

The situation unexpectedly resolved itself in favor of Carroll. Two months before his term ended, some ambiguous—and decidedly unhappy—circumstances related to his recent marriage caused Houston to leave the state. Hall, his brief successor, chose not to run, leaving the field to Carroll. With his reelection in 1829 he began his second and most productive period as governor; he had no significant opposition in 1831 or 1833. In an ironic way Jackson can be credited with the benefits he gave Tennessee through Carroll's good governorship, for he saw to it that Carroll did not satisfy hopes of being either a Senator or Minister to Mexico.

During the 1830s Jackson and Carroll came together as political allies to resist the increasing challenge of the Whig faction. The Whigs rose to power with several issues. One of them was Jackson's refusal to re-charter the US Bank. Although the Tennessee legislature of 1832 passed a resolution in favor of Jackson's policy, sentiment was divided. Other dissatisfaction centered about Jackson's belief in state rather than federal investment in internal improvements. Further discord entered the party with Jackson's tariff reduction policy and South Carolina's nullification stand against it. The wedge that broke the party apart, however, was Jackson's effort to hand-pick his 1836 successor, particularly since this would-be successor was the "Little Magician," Martin Van Buren from New York.

John Bell led the opposition in Tennessee which supported Hugh Lawson White against Van Buren. Carroll worked hard for the vastly unpopular Van Buren. Jackson forwarded material for Carroll to place in the hands of those who would use it against White in the legislature. Meanwhile Carroll was debating what to do in his own political career. He had refused a post of commissioner to the Indians in 1832 and hoped still for the Mexican appointment. His letters to Jackson during this time are particularly ingratiating. He considered running for the Senate against Bell, but ultimately decided to run again for governor in 1835. For once, Jackson supported him.

The Constitution allowed only three consecutive terms of office. Carroll and his supporters, however, maintained that, although this provision remained unchanged from the old Constitution to the new, the enactment of a new fundamental law in effect wiped the slate clean. The voters rejected this interpretation. It is generally agreed that Carroll's popularity was such that he could have withstood the effects of his support of Van Buren, but he could not defy the generally accepted Constitutional limit of three successive terms of office. The Whig group, however, felt that the vote gave endorsement to their position. In this, his final gubernatorial race, Carroll was defeated by Newton Cannon, a strong supporter of White as well as a pro-bank and anti-Jackson man. Revolt grew stronger. John Bell rallied the opposition against Jackson in a famous speech at Nashville's Vauxhall Garden in 1835. Although Van Buren won the presidential election in 1836, White won nomination in Tennessee and went on to win the Tennessee vote, including Jackson's own precinct. White's victory marked the birth of the Whig party in Tennessee and a two-party system in the state. Following his years as governor, Carroll carried on two major activities: the negotiation of the settlement of Indian land claims and continued work for the Democratic party. He also had several proposed and actual, but unsuccessful, candidacies during the nine years from the time he left office until his death.

Carroll accepted appointment as a commissioner to the Indians after his electoral loss in 1835. As such, he was one of the two officials who concluded the Treaty of Removal at New Echota with the Cherokees. By this treaty the Indians ceded all their lands east of the Mississippi for $5 million in return for land in the Indian Territory in the West. In 1838 they were forced on their "Trail of Tears" in fulfillment of this treaty which most of the Cherokee nation had repudiated. Carroll favored Indian removal, as did the general populace. The removal accomplished for the state a relinquishment of all Indian claims in the Hiwassee District and, therefore, opened for sale the remainder of Indian lands, upon which such things as school funds and internal improvements had been predicated. In this sense Carroll was continuing to further his program as governor and to serve the welfare of the whites in the state. In the light of history, he must share the shame of the government's Indian policy.

In 1838 Carroll was appointed special agent to the Creeks and directed land sales until they were suspended. From 1836 to 1838 he was located at Pontotoc to negotiate with the Chickasaws regarding land titles in the western region of Tennessee and Mississippi. During this time rumors circulated but were never proven that Carroll was taking advantage of his position to enrich himself. One correspondent, John Dew, wrote Polk in 1837 that Carroll was out of touch because he was in Mississippi making money. In 1838 a virulent correspondent, Alfred Balch, wrote Polk:

> Carroll will not do. I said this before he offered the last time. He has lost his voice and cannot stump it. He cannot plead purety now as formerly for he has made a great deal of property in the

Chickasaw country. I had no objections to his making the property but I lamented that he could touch an inch of land while acting upon the claims of the Indians.[35]

In 1839, when Carroll was reluctant to commit himself as a candidate, Jackson wrote Polk: "It may be he has been speculating in lands and is afraid of Bell exposing him."[36] Such allegations remain unverified. Standard histories make no mention of ill-gotten gains on Carroll's part. A well-informed family source also knows of no accumulation of real estate from Indian lands left to Carroll's heirs.

As the fortunes of the Democratic party in Tennessee waned, more and more hope was placed on Carroll's personal popularity. In 1837 he ran for the US Senate against Whig candidate Ephraim H. Foster and was soundly defeated. In 1839 Jackson was eager for Carroll to run again for governor, but he withdrew on the basis of health and other reasons. In the same year Polk and Jackson urged him to run against Bell for the Senate, but he again refused. Carroll's defeat in 1837 and his refusal to run again reflected the rise of the Whigs. In 1840 he served as chairman of the Democratic convention which nominated Van Buren, who was defeated by Harrison. Carroll, the loyal Democrat, saw Whig governors elected in 1841 and 1843 and a partisan warfare of such an extent that no Senators were elected by the Tennessee legislature in 1841 and 1842. Even when Polk was elected Democratic president in 1844, he did not carry Tennessee. Carroll was a fighter to the end, but the tide had turned.

His health became a problem by the early 1830s, when he began suffering from arthritis. He continued, however, to speak and campaign for the party as much as his health would permit. Andrew Johnson described him in October of 1841 as bravely defending the "Immortal Thirteen" diehard Democrats in the legislature against accusations of being tories, "tottering into the Senate chamber . . . arms that are stiff and almost useless . . . legs that are weak . . . eyes that are sunken . . . a physical wreck. . . ."[37]

William Carroll died at his home in Nashville on March 22, 1844, a week after speaking at the Jackson Jubilee in that city. In the City Cemetery, where he is buried, an imposing monument reads in tribute:

> As a gentleman, he was modest, intelligent, and courteous
> As an officer, brave and daring
> As a statesman, firm, wise, and just

> To commemorate her estimation of his character,
> the State of Tennessee has caused this monument
> to be erected.

Carroll's greatest monument, however, is the record of his accomplishments as governor in the areas of financial stability and responsible, business-like management; erection of the first penitentiary; reform of the penal code; reform of the judiciary and the court system; and advancement of education and development of internal improvements. That the democratic reforms of the 1834 Constitution were no part of his work is a striking omission in the career of one whose achievements as governor were exceptional.

Few in history share the long popularity and influence of William Carroll. A man of optimistic spirit and great vigor, he was patiently and persistently dedicated to the welfare of his state, thorough politician though he was. In his graceful valedictory to the legislature in 1835, Carroll said

> In calmly reviewing my official acts in peace and in war, during a period of almost 20 years, I can lay my hand on my heart and declare that I am unconscious of a single intentional error. That I have often erred, I cannot doubt; but my countrymen have been charitable and thrown over all my errors and shortcomings the kind mantle of forgetfulness . . . . I shall always be ready to serve my country and if necessary to pour out my blood as I have heretofore done, in support of the liberties of our *glorious Union*.[38]

William Carroll was a devoted public servant, a dedicated politician, an outstanding governor, and a fervent patriot.

NOTES

1. Augustus Buell, *History of Andrew Jackson* (New York: Charles Scribners & Sons, 1904), 1:283.
2. Ibid., p. 284.
3. Allen Johnson, ed., *Dictionary of American Biography* (New York: Charles Scribners & Sons, 1929), pp. 529-30.
4. Isabelle Green Kegley, "The Work of William Carroll as Governor of Tennessee" (Master's Thesis, Vanderbilt University, 1933), Ch. 1.
5. The Nashville *Whig* as quoted in Wallace Rolland Rogers, "A History of the Administration of William Carroll, Governor of Tennessee, 1821-1827, 1829-1836" (Master's Thesis, University of Tennessee, 1925), p. 93.
6. Nancy Wooten Walker, *Out of a Clear Blue Sky* (Cleveland, Tennessee: By the Author, 1971), p. 63.
7. Marquis James, *The Life of Andrew Jackson* (Indianapolis: Bobbs, Merrill & Co., 1938), p. 151.

8. James Phelan, *History of Tennessee* (Boston: Houghton Miflin Co., 1888), P. 254.
9. Byrd Douglas, *Steamboatin' on the Cumberland* (Nashville: Tennessee Book Co., 1961), p. 1.
10. James Parton, *Life of Andrew Jackson* (New York: Mason Brothers, 1860), p. 386.
11. James Bassett, ed., *Correspondence of Andrew Jackson* (May 10, 1811), 2.
12. S. G. Heiskell, *Andrew Jackson and Early Tennessee History* (Nashville: Ambrose Publishing Co., 1920-21), 1:330.
13. Parton, p. 386.
14. Phelan, p. 253.
15. James, p. 813.
16. Samuel Putnam Waldo, *Memoirs of Andrew Jackson, 1818,* letter to Willie Blount, as quoted in Rogers, "History of William Carroll," p. 4.
17. Bassett, *Correspondence* (October 25, 1814), 6:443.
18. Buell, p. 156.
19. Parton, pp. 275-6.
20. Nashville *Clarion,* July 3, 1821.
21. Ibid.
22. Ibid., June 13, 1821.
23. Nashville *Gazette,* July 7, 1821.
24. Nashville *Clarion,* July 4, 1821.
25. Robert H. White, *Messages of the Governors of Tennessee* (Nashville: Tennessee Historical Commission, 1952), 2:15.
26. Ibid., p. 49.
27. D. M. Doak, "The Development of Education in Tennessee," *American Historical Magazine* 8:48.
28. White, p. 421.
29. Ibid., p. 9.
30. Phelan, p. 302.
31. Heiskell, p. 318.
32. Buell, p. 186.
33. James F. Hopkins, ed., *Papers of Henry Clay* (October 1, 1823), 3:492.
34. Powell Moore, "The Political Background of the Revolt Against Jackson in Tennessee," *East Tennessee Historical Society Publications* no. 4 (January 1932), p. 49.
35. Herbert Weaver, ed., *Correspondence of James K. Polk* (Nashville: Vanderbilt University Press, 1977), 4:477; originally June 15, 1838.
36. Bassett, *Correspondence* (February 1839), 5:5.
37. Leroy P. Graf and Ralph W. Haskins, ed., *Papers of Andrew Jackson* (Knoxville: U.T. Press, 1967), 1:42; originally October 27-8, 1841.
38. White, *Messages,* 2:664-5.

BIBLIOGRAPHY

BOOKS
Abernethy, Thomas P. *From Frontier to Plantation in Tennessee.* Chapel Hill: University of North Carolina Press, 1932.
Allison, John, ed. *Notable Men of Tennessee.* Atlanta: Southern Historical Association, 1905.
Alderson, William T. and White, Robert H. *Guide to Study and Reading of Tennessee History.* Nashville: Tennessee Historical Commission, 1959.
Bassett, J. S., ed. *Correspondence of Andrew Jackson,* 6 vols. Washington: Carnegie Institute, 1926.
Bassett, J. S. *Life of Andrew Jackson.* Archon Books, 1967.
Blum, John M.; Catton, Bruce; Morgan, Edmund S.; Schlesinger, Arthur M., Jr.; Stampp, Kenneth M.; and Woodward, C. Vann. *The National Experience.* New York: Harcourt, Brace, and World, Inc., 1963, pp. 212-34.
Brinkley, Wilfred E. *American Political Parties.* New York: Alfred A. Knopf, 1951.
Buell, Augustus C. *History of Andrew Jackson,* 3 Vols. New York: Charles Scribner's Sons, 1904.

Byrd, Douglas. *Steamboatin' on the Cumberland.* Nashville: Tennessee Book Co., 1961.
Combs, W. H. and Cole, W. E. *Tennessee: A Political Study.* Knoxville: University of Tennessee Press, 1940.
Folmsbee, Stanley J. *Sectionalism and Internal Improvements in Tennessee 1796-1845.* Nashville: George Peabody Teacher's College, 1939.
Folmsbee, Stanley, J.; Corlew, Robert E.; and Mitchell, Enoch L. *Tennessee: A Short History.* Knoxville: University of Tennessee Press, 1969.
Goodspeed's General History of Tennessee. Nashville: The Goodspeed Publishing Co., 1887.
Graf, Leroy P. and Haskins, Ralph W., eds. *Papers of Andrew Johnson,* Vol. 1. Knoxville: University of Tennessee Press, 1967.
Heiskell, James G. *Andrew Jackson and Early Tennessee History.* 4. Vols. Nashville: Ambrose Printing Co., 1920-21.
Hopkins, James F., ed. *The Papers of Henry Clay,* 3 Vols. Lexington: University of Kentucky Press, 1963.
James, Marquis. *The Life of Andrew Jackson.* Indianapolis: Bobbs, Merrill Co., 1938.
Johnson, Allen, ed. *Dictionary of American Biography.* New York: Charles Scribner's Sons, 1929.
Lacy, Eric R., ed. *Antebellum Tennessee: A Documentary History.* Berkeley: McCutchan Publishing Co., 1969.
McRaven, Henry. *Nashville.* Chapel Hill: Scheer & Jervis, 1949.
Moore, John Trentwood and Foster, Austin F. *Tennessee, the Volunteer State* Vol. 1. Chicago: The S. L. Clarke Publishing Co., Inc., 1923.
Morris, Eastin. *Tennessee Gazeteer, 1834, and Matthew Rhea's Map of the State of Tennessee 1832.* Nashville: Gazeteer Press, 1971.
National Cyclopedia of American Biography Vol. 2. New York: James T. White Co., 1897.
Parton, James. *The Life of Andrew Jackson.* New York: Mason Bros., 1860.
Phelan, James. *History of Tennessee.* Boston: Houghton, Mifflin, Co., 1888.
Schlesinger, Arthur M., Jr. *The Age of Jackson.* Boston: Little, Brown, & Co., 1946.
Sellers, Charles Grier, *James K. Polk,* Princeton: Princeton University Press, 1957.
Sobel, Robert and Raimo, John. *Biographical Directory of the Governors of the U.S. 1789-1978.* Westport: Meckler Books, 1978.
Smith, Sam. *Tennessee: A Bibliography.* Knoxville: University of Tennessee Press, 1972.
Walker, Nancy Wooten. *Out of a Clear Blue Sky.* Cleveland, Tennessee: By the Author, 1971.
Weaver, Herbert, ed. *Correspondence of James K. Polk.* 4 Vols. Nashville: Vanderbilt University Press, 1977.
White, Robert H. *Messages of the Governors of Tennessee.* Vol. 2. Nashville: Tennessee Historical Commission, 1952.

MANUSCRIPTS
State of Tennessee. Archives. Letters and Papers of Governor William Carroll.

ARTICLES
Abernethy, Thomas P. "Andrew Jackson and the Rise of Southwestern Democracy," *American Historical Review,* Vol. 33, no. 1, October 1927.
Abernethy, Thomas P. "The Early Development of Commerce and Banking in Tennessee," *Mississippi Valley Historical Review,* Vol. 15, June, 1927 to March, 1928.
Abernethy, Thomas P. "The Origins of the Whig Party in Tennessee," *Mississippi Valley Historical Review,* Vol. 12, June, 1925 to March, 1926.
Golden, Gabriel Hawkins. "William Carroll and His Administration," *Tennessee Historical Magazine,* Vol. 9, no. 1, April, 1925.
Goodpasture, A. J. "Andrew Jackson, Tennessee, and the Union" *Tennessee: Old and New,* Vol. 1, 1946.
Goodpasture, A. J. "Education and the Public Lands in Tennessee," *American Historical Magazine,* Vol. 4, no. 3, July, 1899.
McClure, Wallace Mitchell. "The Development of the Tennessee Constitution," *Tennessee Historical Magazine,* Vol. 1, December, 1915.

Moore, Powell. "James K. Polk and Tennessee Politics 1839-41," *East Tennessee Historical Society Publications,* no. 9, 1937.
Moore, Powell. "The Political Background of the Revolt Against Jackson in Tennessee," *East Tennesse Historical Society Publications,* no. 4, January 1932.
Sellers, Charles Grier, Jr. "Banking and Politics in Jackson's Tennessee," *Mississippi Valley Historical Review,* Vol. 41, 1954.
Souissant, St. George L. "Some Phases of Tennessee Politics in the Jackson Period," *American Historical Review,* Vol. 14, no. 1, October, 1908.
Tucker, Emma Carroll. "Governor William Carroll," *American Historical Magazine,* Vol. 7, no. 4, October, 1902.

OFFICIAL DOCUMENTS
Public Acts of the State of Tennessee 1831 and 1832. Nashville: Allen A. Hall and F. S. Heiskell, 1831 and 1832.

NEWSPAPERS
"The Carroll Family 'Of Tennessee'," *Commercial Appeal,* 18 July 1976, sec. G, p. 7.
"Carroll Served Longest; Jones Was Youngest," *Nashville Tennessean,* 9 November, 1969, sec. B, p. 1.
The Church Today (Diocese of Alexandria-Shreveport), Vol. 9, no. 8, 26 June, 1978.
Nashville Clarion, July 3, 1821; July 13, 1821; July 4, 1821.
Nashville Gazette, July 7, 1821.
Tennessee Gazette, September 14, 1813.

INTERVIEWS
Austin, Mrs. A. L. III. 251 West Cherry Circle, Memphis, Tennessee. November 26, 1978.
Page, Carlisle. 1766 Vinton, Memphis, Tennessee. November 2, 1978.

UNPUBLISHED WORKS
Kegley, Isabelle Green. "The Work of William Carroll as Governor of Tennessee." Master's Thesis, Vanderbilt University, 1933.
Page, Carlisle S. III. "General William Henry Carroll." Senior History Class Paper, Memphis University School, May 14, 1960. Personal papers of Carlisle Page, 1766 Vinton, Memphis, Tennessee.
Rippa, Sol Alexander. "The Development of Constitutional Democracy in Tennessee 1790-1835." Master's Thesis. Vanderbilt University, 1950.
Rogers, Wallace Rolland. "A History of the Administartion of William Carroll, Governor of Tennessee 1821-1827, 1829-1836." Master's Thesis, University of Tennessee, 1925.
Vance, Mary Pillow Carroll. "Carroll Family and Ancestors." Family history secured and composed about 1931. Personal papers of Carlisle Page, 1766 Vinton, Memphis, Tennessee.

Portrait of Sam Houston. *Photograph by George W. Hornal, courtesy Tennessee Department of Transportation.*

7

SAM HOUSTON
Governor of Tennessee, 1827-1829

by James Alex Baggett

S am Houston, the seventh governor of Tennessee, was one of antebellum America's most extraordinary leaders. His colorful and controversial life spanned the years from early nationhood to the Civil War. Born during Washington's administration, he was at one time or another a citizen of five nations, a hero of two wars, and the creator and president of a southwestern republic. He served as the governor of two states and as a United States Army Officer, Congressman, and Senator.[1]

Houston's personal life, however, was often unhappy, and he found domestic tranquility only with age and a third wife. Frequently he sought contentment from the bottle, and on two occasions he turned to the Cherokee Indians for refuge, living with them for a total of six years. He married late—at age 35—and his young wife departed after fewer than three months. He left his next mate, a common-law Cherokee wife, after only three years. He changed religions on several occasions. Refused baptism by the faith of his family, he later was baptized by two other denominations. Twice, while still in office as governor, he was led by his convictions to resign: once because of marital problems and again 30 years later because he refused to take an oath to the Confederacy. One who knew him during his last decade said of the old general: "He was the product of strange environments which have disappeared in the progress of society, and for that reason we will not see his like again."[2]

Sam Houston's Scottish forefathers sojourned a time in Ireland before sailing for the New World where they joined a southwesterly migration of Scotch Irish Presbyterians. Sam's paternal great grandfather, John Houston, an immigrant of modest means from a large family, landed at Philadelphia in 1730, where they resided a few years before moving beyond the Blue Ridge Mountains to Rockbridge County, Virginia. John Houston prospered in Virginia, and the family lived there for three generations. He built a house seven miles from the county seat of Lexington, acquired large land-holdings, purchased slaves, served as local magistrate, soldiered in the militia, and led in the planning and construction of roads and the building of a community church.[3]

Before John Houston died at 65, he bequeathed his Timber Ridge plantation to his son, Robert, who improved upon it and willed it to his son, Samuel, a veteran of the Continental Army and the father of Sam Houston. After the Revolution, Captain Samuel Houston had married Elizabeth Paxton, the tall 18-year-old daughter of Squire John Paxton, one of the county's most prosperous citizens. Although the captain retained Timber Ridge, his greatest passion was not planting but soldiering. He loved the military, and, following the war, he continued in the army as an inspector of Virginia's frontier troops. Yet much of his time was spent at home. He fathered nine children: six sons and three daughters; Sam, born on March 2, 1793, was the fifth child and fifth son.[4]

The Houston household was comfortable but hardly affluent. Along with others, black and white, slave and free, Sam worked in the fields much of his youth. Beginning at age eight he attended briefly each winter a nearby school which had been built on land donated by his father. There he learned only the most rudimentary of "the three Rs," and his arithmetic, as he later admitted, he learned only "imperfectly." He also received some religious instruction as he worshiped with his family at the community church.[5]

Although Sam's father farmed and was promoted to major in 1803, he was not a financial success. The productivity of the plantation decreased steadily as the family's expenses rose. At first, Major Houston sold some of the land and a few of the slaves to meet his debt, but he finally decided that the best solution was to sell the entire plantation and to follow some of his more prosperous relatives to East Tennessee.[6] Thus in September of 1806 Samuel Houston sold Timber Ridge plantation for a thousand pounds and began negotiations for the purchase of a 419-acre tract ten miles beyond Maryville on the western slope of the Great Smoky Mountains. Being in ill health he instructed his executor to set aside most of his estate if he should die for the Tennessee tract (a portion of which would belong to each child upon maturity), with the remainder to provide for the family's immediate livelihood. Then, in 1807, while on a frontier inspection tour, Major Houston died.[7]

Widow Houston, her famous son would later say, was "not a woman to succumb to misfortune." Within weeks the Houston clan crossed the mountains and settled on the previously selected site a few miles north of the Tennessee River, a boundary which separated the whites from the Cherokees. At first, young Sam Houston helped his brother "in breaking up the virgin soil," but he disliked the "hard work" of farming. Later he briefly attended Porter Academy, and, although dissatisfied with formal learning, he acquired a love for the classics, particularly Pope's translation of Homer's *Iliad*. He also became fascinated with the ways of nearby Indian tribes.[8] Most of all, at this particular time, Sam resented what he called the "fraternal tyranny" of his brothers. During his 16th year they secured for Sam, much to his consternation, the position of clerk in a general store partially owned by the family. To their bewilderment, however, he soon disappeared to dwell with the Cherokee, a people who progressed greatly in the ways of civilization, while remaining less restricted and inhibited than whites. When his brothers went in search of Sam and questioned him about the reasons for his disappearance, he answered that "he preferred measuring deer tracks, to tape—that he liked the wild liberty of the Red men, better than the tyranny of his own brothers . . . [and that] he could, at least, read a translation from the Greek in the woods, and read it in peace."[9] Yet Houston soon came home to replace his threadbare clothing, remaining with his family for some months before being confronted once again by what the six-foot lad believed to be the overbearing ways of his brothers. He returned to the Cherokees and in a short time was adopted by Chief Oolooteka (known to the whites as John Jolly) who renamed Sam "The Raven," a bird which in Cherokee mythology is a symbol of good fortune. The Raven met others who would remain his longtime friends, including the two half-white Rogers brothers, John and James. Occasionally he visited his family to secure clothing and to purchase on credit gifts for his Indian friends.[10]

Because of concern over his growing debt (probably owed to his mother), Sam left the Cherokees at age 18 and engaged himself from May to November of 1812 as a teacher in a one-room school

near his white family's home. Although his formal education was
limited and despite the fact that Sam's tuition was higher than the
going rate, parents sent their children to him. He charged eight dollars per pupil for the term, one-third in corn, one-third in cash, and
one-third in colored cotton cloth which he used for his shirts. According to Houston, his "sense of authority over" his pupils caused
him to "experience a higher feeling of dignity and self-satisfaction
than from any other office" he was to occupy.[11]

After clearing his debt and completing his term of teaching,
young Sam felt a need to receive further education. In the fall of
1812 he returned to Porter Academy. He soon was discouraged,
however, from becoming a "scholar" because of his difficulty with
geometry.[12] Yet it was the tide of events and not his scholastic woes
that soon swept him from the ranks of the student into those of the
soldier. During the summer of 1812, the United States had declared
war upon Great Britain, and young men everywhere were urged to
join the army. Therefore, shortly after his 20th birthday on March
24, 1813, after he and a younger friend had listened to patriotic
drum and fife music and a recruiting appeal by an army sergeant,
Sam stepped forward and grasped from a drumhead a silver dollar
bounty—a token of his enlistment in the United States Army. His
brothers scorned Sam for joining the army as a common soldier
rather than as an officer like his father, but his mother gave him, in
addition to her signature of consent, a musket and a simple gold
ring. On the inside of the ring was engraved one word, *Honor*.[13]

Sam Houston, along with other local recruits, reported for training to the Seventh United States Infantry at Knoxville. In only four
weeks he was promoted to drill sergeant. Meanwhile, his neighbors
and friends had appealed to President Madison to promote him, and
when the Seventh Infantry merged into the Thirty-ninth Infantry a
few months later, he was given an army commission as ensign. Before the end of the year his rank was raised to third lieutenant. His
commanding officer, Colonel Thomas Hart Benton, later remembered that he saw in the young officer "soldierly and gentlemanly
qualities." Houston, he said, was "ready to do, or to suffer . . . to
answer the call of honor, patriotism and friendship."[14] It was not,
however, the future Missouri senator who soon would most influence Houston's life, but 46-year-old ex-Senator Andrew Jackson,
commander of the Tennessee militia. In the fall of 1813 Jackson had

taken to the field of battle against the Creek Indians because of their recent massacre of 400 whites at Fort Mims on the Alabama River; the Thirty-ninth Infantry was ordered to assist Jackson's militiamen. Thus in February of 1814 Sam Houston met Andrew Jackson, the leader whom Houston would most admire and emulate.[15]

In March General Jackson led his combined forces on a long march to the Creek encampment at Tohopeka on the Tallapoosa River. There, at the Battle of Horseshoe Bend, while leading charges against the enemy, Houston was severely wounded. First, he was hit in the thigh by a barbed arrow, which he ordered a soldier to pull from the wound. Despite Jackson's request that he retire from the fray, he returned to lead yet another charge; he was then hit by two rifle balls, one in his upper arm and one in his shoulder. Soon after the battle he underwent surgery; but because of his severe pain, the army surgeon removed only one ball from his shoulder. Lieutenant Houston's courage "secured for him the lasting regard of Gen. Jackson, whose sympathies followed him through all his fortunes."[16]

For many months after Jackson's victory at Horseshoe Bend, it appeared that Houston was far more likely to die than to live. He was placed on a litter between two horses and transported 60 miles north, where he remained briefly in a field hospital before continuing, by the same mode, a two-month journey of misery to his East Tennessee home. To make matters worse, he contracted measles while enroute. A notice that he was promoted to second lieutenant for his bravery proved little consolation to the gravely wounded Houston. Adding to his gloom was the fact that when he partially recovered and reported to Washington, D.C., to receive further treatment, he found that the British had recently burned the national capitol and that the city lay in ruins.[17] However, good news of Jackson's great victory at New Orleans and the end of the war greeted Houston when, early in 1815, he returned to active duty in Tennessee.

As had his father before him, Sam requested to remain in the military, partly because his wounds had to a degree disabled him. His meritorious service and the recommendation of two Tennessee Congressmen allowed him to continue in the greatly reduced peacetime army. In May of 1815, he was transferred to the First Infantry, stationed at New Orleans; he underwent further surgery there. Fearing the loss of the use of his right arm and shoulder, he requested the removal of the remaining rifle ball. His recuperation was slow, and in the spring of 1816 the army sent him to New York for additional treatment, after which time he was furloughed to Tennessee.[18]

On New Year's Day in 1817, Houston was transferred to the Nashville headquarters of the Southern Division of the army, which was commanded by General Jackson. There Houston served in the division's adjutant general's office and renewed his friendship with "Old Hickory." In May he was promoted to first lieutenant, and in July the successful young officer joined the Cumberland Masonic Lodge. His talents, however, were soon demanded elsewhere, and in October—because of his knowledge of the Cherokees and at the urging of General Jackson—Houston accepted a special assignment as government sub-agent to aid in facilitating a recently ratified Indian removal treaty.[19] Thus, after a five-year absence, Houston returned to the Cherokee Nation. There his duties soon demanded that he accompany a dissatisfied tribal faction to Washington, D.C., where, dressed in Cherokee clothing, he appeared with the Indians before Secretary of War John C. Calhoun who reassured the faction that they would be treated fairly. For the sub-agent, however, Calhoun had only scorn. He reprimanded Lieutenant Houston for appearing in Indian dress and accused him of abetting slave smugglers operating through Spanish Florida. Actually, Houston had been recently fighting the illicit traffic, and its promoters had spread rumors in order to punish the lieutenant. At Houston's request, Calhoun began an investigation, and Houston personally presented his case to President James Monroe. Soon he was fully exonerated, but, thoroughly disgusted and discouraged with his career, he resigned from the army before leaving Washington. After accompanying the Cherokees back to Tennessee, he also resigned as government sub-agent.[20]

Houston, now a 25-year-old indebted civilian—yet by his own account "enriched by experience and observation, and a lofty aspiration"—sold his inherited share of the family's farm to his brother James and headed for Nashville. There he immediately contacted a distant relative, Judge James Trimble, and inquired about becoming a lawyer. The judge told him it would be necessary for him to study for 18 months before he could pass the bar examination. Therefore, in June of 1818, Sam Houston began the study of

Blackstone and Coke; during his limited leisure time he became a player of bit parts in the Dramatic Club of Nashville.[21]

Much to Judge Trimble's surprise and satisfaction, Houston proved ready to take the bar examination before the end of 1818. After easily passing what he called "a searching examination," Houston purchased some law books on credit and established his practice in Lebanon, about 30 miles east of Nashville. There he was befriended by Isaac Galladay, a local merchant and the town's postmaster. Houston's winning ways and Galladay's credit and friends soon made the well-attired young lawyer a great success.[22] During the next ten years, honors and achievements came rapidly to the young bachelor. A few months after locating in Lebanon, Governor Joseph McMinn appointed Houston adjutant general of the state's militia; probably through the influence of General Jackson, in October of 1819 he was elected district attorney. His election necessitated his return to Nashville, but, after only twelve months, because the work was "unceasing" and "the fees were so inconsiderable," he resigned the position and established a private practice. Soon, in addition to his busy law practice on Nashville's Market Street, he engaged in the activities of several civic-minded groups. Among these organizations were the Antiquarian Society, the Masonic Lodge, and the Tennessee Militia, of which his fellow officers elected him major general in the fall of 1821.[23]

Houston won another election in September of 1823. With the endorsement of Andrew Jackson, and the backing of William Carroll, who was the state's new governor, General Houston became Congressman Houston. The next month the General Assembly elected his idol and former commanding general to the United States Senate. In 1822 the Tennessee Senate already had unanimously recommended General Jackson as the person "most worthy & suitable to be the next President"; Jackson's Washington Senate seat would place him in the midst of upcoming 1824 presidential politics.[24]

Congressman Houston's first-year voting record in the House of Representatives largely mirrored that of his mentor, Jackson, in the Senate. Both men also served in their respective houses on the same committee, Military Affairs. Houston's time was probably about equally divided between the affairs of government and those of politics. His first-term legislative record was largely limited to yeas and nays. He performed the usual constituency chores of satisfying demands for information and recommendations, especially for patronage. Above all, he labored for his chief's election to the presidency. To this end he joined a group of Congressmen in soliciting signatures from their colleagues for a petition opposing the caucus method of selecting presidential candidates, a nomination procedure that Jackson's followers hoped to prevent.[25] Most Congressmen simply boycotted the party caucus, which nominated William H. Crawford of Georgia, and went home to support their favorite candidates who included, in addition to Jackson, John Quincy Adams and Henry Clay. The four-candidate presidential race failed to produce a majority for any of the nominees, although Jackson, the only candidate with nationwide support, led the field. No candidate having received a majority, the final determination was left to the House of Representatives, where each state delegation had one vote. The forces of Adams and Clay combined to elect Adams president; soon thereafter, Speaker Clay became secretary of state. Jackson's followers believed they had been cheated of victory by a "corrupt bargain," and Congressman Houston called for reform in the Constitutional election procedure. The present system, he said, had "resulted in the election of a candidate who had not a majority of the votes in the Electoral College. Nor had he a majority of the members in the House of Representatives, but only a majority of the States."[26]

During 1824 and 1825 the 31-year-old Congressman apparently contemplated marriage seriously for the first time. Nearly a decade earlier he had written to a friend of his family, "I will not court any of the Dear Girles before I make a fortune and if I come to no better speed than I have done hertofore, it will be some time. . . ." In the fall of 1824 Houston considered marriage to a South Carolina lady, a Miss M_____ of Cheraw, whom he wanted to accompany him to Washington. As it turned out, however, political responsibility took preference and the wedding was postponed until March or April. Then in the spring it was time for Houston to run for reelection and the couple agreed to delay the ceremony until November. By then the inclination, for one or both, had apparently passed. There was to be no marriage. Houston wrote to a friend about a year later, "I am making myself less frequent in the Lady World than I have been. I must keep my Dignity, or rather I must attend more to politics and less to love."[27]

Soon after his defeat for the presidency, Jackson stepped down as the junior Senator from Tennessee, but the record indicates that he had enough Congressional lieutenants, such as Houston, to disrupt the Adams administration. When Houston ran for reelection in 1825, he prepared a lengthy message to his constituents emphasizing his support of interstate internal improvements, the Tariff Act of 1824, and his recent call for electoral reform, an issue which closely identified him with Jackson. He easily won reelection to his second term, during which he generally followed the Jackson faction's line. For example, he opposed the Adams-Clay Latin American policy of dispatching American delegates to the Panama Congress of South American republics, and he argued that United States diplomacy could most profitably and with less risk be negotiated with the individual nations. He also opposed the administration's domestic policy of tariff adjustment and greater federal spending. Much of his opposition to the Adams administration was purely political, but his votes for fiscal conservatism would develop into a lifelong pattern.[28]

Despite his opposition to Adams and Clay, he unsuccessfully and perhaps unwisely appealed to them on behalf of federal patronage in Tennessee. He wrote to Clay requesting that certain Tennessee newspapers be given the contracts for printing in their columns the laws of the United States, a practice which had become a means of patronizing a partisan press. Clay politely replied that the contracts had already been given. Houston also, upon instruction from Jackson, recommended to President Adams that he reconsider the appointment of John P. Erwin, editor of the federally favored *Nashville Banner and Whig,* and relative of Clay, as Nashville postmaster. Houston described the editor as a man without character and public confidence, an eavesdropper, a cheating manipulator who preyed on others, and a debtor who refused to pay his debts despite his known ability to do so.[29]

When Houston returned from Washington in August of 1826, he received a demand from Erwin for a retraction. Houston replied that in opposing Erwin's appointment as postmaster he had acted in an official Congressional capacity and that he had learned nothing since to change his views. Erwin then challenged Houston to a duel through an intermediary, noted duelist Colonel John Smith, who upon his second attempt to deliver the challenge was accompanied by General William A. White, a Nashville lawyer. Houston refused to receive Erwin's note from Smith (presumably because Smith was not a resident of Tennessee but of Missouri) and threw it down. General White then made a remark which Houston took as an insult, and in the passion of the moment he advised White that he would receive a challenge from him "with pleasure."[30]

The next few days charges and countercharges appeared in Nashville newspapers. Erwin proclaimed Houston a coward and slanderer, and Houston accused Erwin of being a thief and rogue. Meanwhile, rumors spread that Houston had "backed down" General White. White, feeling that "according to the tone of public sentiment . . . a coward cannot live except in disgrace and obscurity," sent a challenge to Houston which he unwillingly but immediately accepted.[31]

Feeling forced to fight a duel he had hoped to avoid, Houston practiced on the Hermitage grounds with a pistol for a week under the tutelage of Jackson, who advised him to steady his hand by biting on a bullet as he fired. He also wrote a letter to be published only if he was killed in the duel, which provided some insight into the whole affair. "My firm and undeviating attachment to Genl Jackson," he stated, "has caused me all the enemies I have, and I glory in the firmness of my attachment . . . . I will die proud in the assurance that I deserve, and possess his perfect confidence."[32]

In order to avoid arrest in Tennessee, where dueling was illegal, the two men agreed to meet secretly with their seconds in Kentucky on September 22nd and to fire a single shot at 15 paces. At sunrise on the appointed day, in a pasture just beyond the Tennessee line, Houston, who fired first, shot and severely wounded General White, whose recovery took months. Houston, when he was later applauded at a political rally for what others believed to be his heroic action, discouraged such accolades by stating that he thanked God that his "adversary was injured no worse." Thereafter, although he averaged receiving about a challenge a year for the next 20 years (mostly because of his bitter criticism of important political enemies), he refused to engage in dueling. His customary reply became "Tell him I won't fight him, for I never fight downhill." The reply appears to have satisfied Houston's admirers.[33]

Houston suspected that the duel with General White had been plotted by those who wanted to prevent him from achieving his next political goal, one which Jackson encouraged him to seek—the governorship of Tennessee. As early as the fall of 1825 the Nashville *Whig* had announced that Houston would seek the office of governor in 1827. William Carroll, the state's popular governor, was by law ineligible to succeed himself for a fourth consecutive term; and a Jacksonian was needed to occupy the office at least until Carroll could legally hold the position once again in two years. However, an 1817 legislative act required all state officials to take an oath swearing that they had not engaged in a duel since the law's passage. While it appears that Houston was therefore legally barred from holding the office—and was soon indicted by a Kentucky grand jury for the shooting—he was nevertheless encouraged by others to enter the race. Jackson wrote Houston in December of 1826 that judging "from the voice of the people as I passed through Tennessee your popularity is Daily increasing, but you will have to return early in the spring and pass through the state."[34]

From May to July of 1827, Houston campaigned vigorously in the gubernatorial race against former Congressman Newton Cannon, who was supported by the great majority of Jackson's enemies. It was during this campaign—his first really competitive race—that Houston demonstrated the characteristics that made him a truly great campaigner. He adopted the style of the stump speaker and dressed in flamboyant attire which sometimes included a large "black beaver hat . . . ruffled shirt, black satin vest . . . silk pants . . . [and] a huge red sash . . . ."[35]

Despite the efforts of Newton Cannon to devote the campaign to state issues—Houston ran as a friend and supporter of Andrew Jackson for the presidency and as a much-abused Congressman whom the Adams administration was seeking to destroy. Perhaps as much as anything else, however, it was Houston's heroic image, meteoric rise, and personal appearance that appealed to the masses. An eyewitness of the campaign described Houston as a "well proportioned man . . . of commanding and gallant bearing" whose "fine features were lit up by large, eagle-looking eyes," and noted that Houston possessed "a wonderful recollection for persons and names, a fine address and courtly manners, and a magnetism approaching that of Gen Jackson."[36]

Houston defeated Cannon by a margin of four to three and by more than 10,000 votes, and it appears that no attempt was offered to prevent his taking office because of the Kentucky duel. He was inaugurated on October 1, 1827, in Nashville's First Baptist Church (presumably because of its large seating capacity), and he delivered a brief unmemorable address regarding support for the United States Constitution and protection from federal encroachment.[37] Two weeks later, Governor Houston spelled out his program (largely the same as his predecessor's) in his initial message to the General Assembly. He called for internal improvements, particularly the construction of a needed canal in East Tennessee, "whereby the obstructions of the Muscle Shoals would be surmounted," for West Tennessee the improvement of natural waterways and lower prices for state-owned land to speed settlement, and the use of state income for public education.[38]

Houston proved to be a capable administrator and continued in the rather conservative fiscal policies of former Governor Carroll. Much of his time during 1828, however, was spent in defending Old Hickory and promoting him for the presidency. In January, he joined General and Mrs. Jackson and a large following in a steamboat trip to New Orleans—in what really amounted to a Jackson campaign tour—to celebrate the anniversary of Old Hickory's greatest military victory. Before the year ended with Jackson's election as president, Houston had spent much of his time operating for his Old Chief what he referred to as a "literary bureau." The governor also was instrumental in the formation of a Nashville citizens' investigative committee which published a report maintaining the premarital relationship of Andrew and Rachel Jackson (which had been recently revived as an election issue) was above reproach.[39]

Shortly before the presidential election, it appears that Jackson's enemies also sought to embarrass him by reviving the episode of his friend Houston's duel with General White. Houston and White were both Masons, and the members of the local Cumberland Lodge suspended the governor from all activities for a year because of his past unmasonic, contentious behavior. An appeal by Houston to the Grand Lodge of Tennessee was denied. Still, all of the controversy seemed worth the cost when Jackson was elected president by a substantial margin over John Quincy Adams in November. The feelings of ultimate triumph, however, were soon diminished by the death of Rachel Jackson during the Christmas season.[40]

Houston was particularly grieved that Mrs. Jackson, whom he revered, had not lived to see his marriage. Houston was married in January of 1829, to Eliza Allen of Gallatin, the 18-year-old daughter of John Allen, a wealthy planter and horseman. The Jacksons had long known the Allen family, who had been among the earliest settlers of Sumner County. Governor Houston had been introduced to the family in 1824 by fellow Tennessee Congressman Robert Allen, a younger brother of John, and had visited with the Allens on a number of occasions while passing through Gallatin. The 35-year-old bachelor governor came to adore the fair, blue-eyed, blonde girl whom he had seen develop into a young lady of charm and culture—a worthy mate for the governor of Tennessee. Unaware of her strong affections for another, the governor asked Colonel Allen for Eliza's hand in marriage, and the socially prominent Allen family appeared to approve and encourage the match.[41]

The engagement was announced in December of 1828; and on January 22nd the couple were married at the Allen plantation by the Reverend William Hume, a prominent Presbyterian minister. The Houstons honeymooned for the next few days and, on January 30th, the governor announced for reelection; ex-Governor William Carroll had already declared his candidacy two weeks previously.[42]

Soon Houston found himself confronted by two great crises, personal and political: an unhappy marriage and a major challenge to his career. Doubtless, he considered his marriage a political asset, but within three months it almost destroyed him. He felt his wife was cold to him and did not love him—that she loved another man. In early April, with his stupendous vanity wounded and while in the midst of an apparent jealous rage, the governor questioned Eliza's virginity. Unfortunately, her parents heard of the nasty quarrel. On April 9th Houston wrote Colonel Allen an explanation and apology about "the most unpleasant & unhappy circumstance." He said regarding Eliza's virginity (a rather delicate subject to discuss with in-laws) that he now "was *satisfied & believed her virtuous,* and had assured her . . . ." He said he loved Eliza and would not for millions have had the quarrel made known to her parents.[43] Despite his apology Eliza returned to her parents. Houston arrived in Gallatin a short time later, but was allowed to see Eliza only on the condition that he see her in the presence of an aunt. The aunt later recalled that the governor knelt before Eliza "and with tears streaming down his face implored forgiveness . . . and insisted . . . that she return to Nashville with him." She refused. Next he sought spiritual solace, or perhaps simply a way to win Eliza's forgiveness, by requesting that the minister who had married them, Dr. William Hume, baptize him. Although he was sorry for Houston, Hume declined. Houston then applied to Reverend Obadiah Jennings, pastor of the Nashville Presbyterian Church, who also refused. The two ministers, who were friends, perhaps doubted the governor's motive as well as his conversion.[44]

Houston was so shaken—some said so insane—because of the entire affair concerning Eliza's virginity and the probability that the quarrel was known publicly (he had been burned in effigy in Gallatin) that he yielded the governor's race to Carroll by default, and, despite the protest of close friends, resigned as governor on April 16th and secluded himself from all but a few trusted individuals such as his physician, Dr. John Shelby, and Davidson County Sheriff Willoughby Williams, a boyhood friend. On April 23rd he quietly left the state for Arkansas to live with his old friends, the Cherokees. Carroll, his former opponent, commented that "poor Houston . . . rose like a rocket and fell like a-stick." Nonetheless, political retirement was the furtherest thought from Houston's mind. During February and March he had discussed his dream of conquering Texas with Daniel S. Donelson (the older brother of Andrew J. Donelson, the president's adoped son who was then serving as his private secretary).[45]

As early as 1822, only months after the first Anglo settlers entered Texas, Houston became a shareholder in the Texas Association of Tennessee, a group seeking a Texas land grant through the Mexican government. In 1827 Houston's name, as well as Dr. John Shelby's, was still listed among the shareholders by their agent in Texas, H. H. League, then negotiating with the assistance of Stephen F. Austin. According to Donelson, William Wharton of Nashville, who had previously been in Texas, had returned to the Mexican state in March of 1829, with full authority from Houston to prepare "the minds of the leading men in that country . . . and that done, he would immediately leave the U. States in order to enter upon the duties of what he called his grand scheme . . . a successful revolution. . . ."[46]

Enroute to Arkansas by steamboat, Houston drank heavily and talked profusely of his plans to use the Cherokee to create a western empire. His traveling companion, an Irishman named H. Haralson, was secretly reporting Houston's activities to the president. Houston carried with him his well-worn copy of *The Life of Caius Marius* from which he often quoted while inebriated. Perhaps he hoped that like Marius, an exiled Roman general, he would assemble an army and make a victorious comeback. Yet when Houston reached Little Rock, he wrote to the president (who by now had heard of "poor Houston's disgrace," as well as his dream of empire building) that his marriage had left him "the most unhappy man now living," but he assured Jackson that his intention in the West was not treacherous and offered himself as a peacemaker among the Indians. Old Hickory replied to Houston that he did not believe the rumors, for only a madman would attempt such a scheme. Nonetheless, the president wrote in his daybook that he had taken the precaution of notifying "the Secretary of War to write . . . to Mr. Pope, Govr of Arkansas . . . that if such illegal project should be discovered to exist to adopt prompt measures to put it down and give the government the earliest intelligence of such illegal enterprise . . . ."[47]

From Little Rock, Houston went to Fort Smith. In late May he journeyed west to Tahlontuskee village on the Grand River, a tributary of the Arkansas, where he was reunited with his adopted father, Chief Oolooteka (John Jolly), who embraced him saying, "My son . . . eleven winters have passed since we met . . . . I heard you were a great chief among your people . . . [but] that a dark cloud had fallen on the white path you were walking, and when it fell in your way you turned your thoughts to my wigwam." The old chief, who lived like a wealthy southern planter, said that the Great Spirit had sent his son, The Raven, to counsel the tribe and to use his influence with President Jackson on their behalf.[48]

Houston soon realized that the primary problem of the Cherokees had arisen from the fact that the United States government had placed them on Arkansas lands, which were the traditional hunting grounds of the warlike Osage Indians. During the 1820s the constant hostility of the Osage, coupled with the invasion of whites, had pushed the peaceful Cherokee into what is today eastern Oklahoma. In order to control the situation, the goverment had established its westernmost outpost, Fort Gibson. Houston felt that other tribal problems had resulted largely from government policy and agents regarding trade and federal subsidies. For the next four years, whatever Houston's dreams of a future empire may have been, he did not allow them to prevent his playing the role of peacemaker and reformer on behalf of the Indians.[49] Almost immediately Houston began practicing what has been described as "international law" among the Cherokee, Osage, Creek, and Choctaw nations and in their relations with the United States government and its agents. He adopted the trappings of an Indian brave, and in October of 1829, The Raven became a Cherokee citizen (he did not renounce his American citizenship, however). From January to April of 1830 he served as an unofficial ambassador of the Cherokee Nation in Washington. During the summer of 1830, Houston wrote a series of articles for the territorial newspaper, the *Arkansas Gazette,* attacking the Indian agency system of the United States government. He condemned the theft of Indian lands and funds, goverment lies and broken promises, supply scandals, overt bribery, and the sale of whiskey to the Indians.[50]

Sometime during 1830, Houston took a common-law Indian wife, Diana Rogers Gentry, a widow in her 30s and half sister of James and John Rogers, The Raven's closest friends during his first Cherokee sojourn. Sam and Diana settled in a log house-trading post which Houston called Wigwam Neosho, three miles from Fort Gibson, near the Neosho River and directly on the Texas Road. From there Houston engaged in his varied occupations of diplomat, lawyer, merchant and speculator. Sam and Diana lived together from 1830 to 1833, and, although he traveled considerably, it appears they were both satisfied with their union. When he departed for Texas in 1833, he left her the trading post and received from her a power of attorney signed Diana *Gentry.*[51]

During the spring of 1832, when Houston was in Washington with an Indian delegation, an incident occurred which brought the former Tennessee governor once again into the national limelight. Anti-administration Congressmen were stepping up their attack on Jackson's "spoils system" during the presidential election year; among those under attack was Sam Houston, who was accused by Ohio Congressman William Stanbery of attempting in 1830 to acquire by fraudulent means a contract furnishing rations to the Indians. When Houston noticed the congressman's remarks in a Washington newspaper, he demanded an explanation of Stanbery, who refused on the grounds of Congressional immunity. Stanbery did take the precaution of arming himself with two pistols. Although he threatened revenge upon Stanbery, Houston remained unarmed except for a hickory cane, which, as an inveterate whittler, he had fashioned a few weeks before on the grounds of the Hermitage.[52]

On Friday, April 13th—apparently an unlucky day for Stanbery—Houston, while returning home from an evening party, confronted the Congressman on a city street and beat him with his hickory cane. Stanbery did draw one of his pistols and pulled the trigger, but fortunately for Houston the charge failed to explode. The next day, for the first time in the nation's history, a private citizen, Sam Houston, was ordered arrested by the House of Representatives for an attack upon one of its members as a result of words spoken before Congress.[53] Houston was brought to trial before the House of Representatives. In a proceeding which lasted for days, Francis Scott Key, author of "The Star-Spangled Banner" and Houston's attorney, defended his client on the grounds that he had attacked the Congressman for remarks appearing in the press rather than for Stanbery's speech before the House. Although most representatives remained unconvinced and Houston was convicted by a vote of 106 to 89, the sentence set by the membership was merely a reprimand of Houston by the Speaker. Houston was charged and tried in a local court, however, and fined $500—a fine which Houston did not pay and Jackson remitted in 1834. Houston later assessed the political effect of the whole affair thusly: "I was dying out . . . but they gave me a national tribunal for a theatre, and that set me up again."[54]

Throughout his legal difficulties over the Stanbery beating, which consumed months, Houston planned his first journey into Texas. He was to negotiate with the menacing nomadic Comanches in San Antonio on behalf of the Arkansas tribes and to purchase land for a New York company. In August he was granted a passport to Mexico, and from mid-August to mid-September, Houston visited Nashville where he discussed his mission with President Jackson. He returned to Wigwam Neosho in October and left for Texas in mid-November, riding south to Nacogdoches. After a few days in the East Texas town, he proceeded to San Felipe de Austin on the Brazos River, where on Christmas Eve he applied as a married man for settlers' headrights in Texas. The Raven continued his journey to San Antonio, where he parleyed with a group of Comanche chiefs who promised to meet soon with other western tribes at Fort Gibson.[55]

Returning by the same route, Houston collected his approved headrights application in San Felipe and then continued to Nacogdoches, where, according to Houston, he was "warmly solicited to establish his permanent residence, and allow his name to be used as candidate for election to a Convention which was to meet in the following April." Houston reported on his trip to President Jackson from Natchitoches, Louisiana, and advised him that he would soon be present on April 1st at a San Felipe Constitutional Convention and that he would report on the proceedings. Moreover, he clearly stated his intention of settling in Texas. It appears that by this time he and Jackson had a new understanding regarding Houston's relationship to Texas.[56]

Whatever the Houston-Jackson understanding may have been, Houston returned to Nacogdoches where he was elected a delegate to the upcoming San Felipe convention, of which his old Nashville friend William H. Wharton was elected chairman. Houston chaired the committee which framed a Constitution for the new Mexican state of Texas. The separation of Texas from Coahuila, the Mexican state of which it was a part, depended of course on approval of the central government. Stephen F. Austin was sent to Mexico City to solicit this permission. In May Houston returned briefly to Fort Gibson to make a report on his conference with the Comanche chiefs and to say goodbye to Diana. Then he proceeded to Hot Springs, where he received treatment for his old war wound which had become sore. There, in late July, he wrote his favorite cousin, John H. Houston: "You want to know 'what the Devil I am going to do in Texas'? Part, I will tell you, and the balance you may Guess at. I will practice law . . . . I have a retained fee of two thousand a year . . . . I have purchased . . . choice land . . . and several minor matters I am engaged in . . . ."[57]

By the fall of 1833 Houston was back in Nacogdoches, where in November he petitioned for a Mexican divorce from Eliza Allen Houston on grounds of their four-year separation. Among his closest friends were the Sterne and Raguet families: Adolphus Sterne, a Rhinelander Jew whom Houston had first met in Nashville, was the local *alcalde,* and Henru Raguet, a Pennsylvanian whom Houston had met on a visit to New Orleans, was a landowner and town merchant. Houston seemed particularly fond of Anna, the Raguet's teenaged daughter, but through a decade of correspondence with her in the 1830s he kept his affection on a rather chivalrous level. Eventually she married another of Houston's Nacogdoches friends, Dr. Robert Irion, and the couple had the good grace to name their first child Samuel Houston Irion. Houston boarded with the Sternes, and it was Adolphus' wife, Eva Rosine Sterne, a devoted Catholic, who became Sam's godmother when he was baptized as Samuel Pablo Houston in early 1834. It is probable, although not provable, that The Raven's conversion to Catholicism at this time was a pragmatic decision born of his desire for immediate personal and political success.[58]

Houston spent much of 1834 in the United States settling diplomatic and financial matters related to his Texas trip, but by early 1835 he was busy practicing law in Nacogdoches. Stephen F. Austin, whose mission to Mexico City had failed, returned in September after months of imprisonment and called for a general consultation "of the best, calmest, and most intelligent men . . . ." Soon thereafter, a Nacogdoches public rally endorsed Austin's consultation and elected Sam Houston as their delegate. They also selected a Committee of Vigilance and Safety, which in October appointed Houston as Commander-in-Chief of the Department of Nacogdoches, comprising the territory west of the Trinity River. General Houston immediately issued an appeal for volunteers and proclaimed that "the morning of glory is dawning upon us. The work of liberty has begun."[59]

The consultation in the fall of 1834 established a provisional state government, which claimed loyalty to the Mexican Constitution of 1824, and elected Delegate Houston of Nacogdoches as commander of all military forces. For the next few months General Houston sought to organize an army of citizens—many of whom did not readily accept his command—and to discourage an unauthorized attack upon Matamoras. Houston also sought to postpone the possibility of Indian problems by negotiating with the northeast Texas tribes.[60]

In early March he attended the Convention of 1836, which declared the independence of Texas and reconfirmed Houston's command. During the Convention he rushed to the futile defense of San Antonio, then being attacked by General Antonio Lopez de Santa Anna, President of Mexico. Enroute, however, he heard at Gonzales of the Alamo's fall and the death of the gallant men. He ordered an immediate evacuation to the Colorado River, where his small army received word of the Palm Sunday massacre at Goliad of 342 prisoners of war. He retreated to the Brazos River to await the arrival of Santa Anna's army, which he allowed to cross the river without resistance and capture and burn the provisional capitol of Harrisburg. On April 19, however, Houston believed the predestined moment for attack had arrived. He wrote: "We go to conquer. It is wisdom growing out of necessity to meet the enemy now; every consideration enforces it. No previous occasion would justify it."[61]

The next day Houston approached the advanced forces of Santa Anna's army camped on the confluence of the Buffalo Bayou and San Jacinto River, where organized retreat would be difficult. A brief, indecisive cavalry skirmish occurred; the next morning 500 Mexican reenforcements entered Santa Anna's camp. Yet Houston rallied his troops with a rousing speech and a battle cry, "Remember the Alamo!" which the men continued to repeat. In the afternoon Houston spread 900 soldiers along a 1000-yard line, with a flag in the middle and a cannon on each end; a four-piece improvised band played, "Will You Come to My Bower I Have Shaded for You?" as he led his army in an 18-minute rout of 1400 Mexican soldiers.[62]

General Houston, however, was severely wounded through the ankle; a few days later, following talks with his illustrious captive, General Santa Anna, and after sending "Laurels . . . from the battlefield of San Jacinto" to Miss Raguet, Houston was forced to leave his victorious army and seek surgery in New Orleans.[63]

Shortly after his return, the Hero of San Jacinto easily won election to the presidency of the Republic of Texas, and, to placate the opposition, he appointed the other candidates to important cabinet posts: Stephen F. Austin became secretary of state, and Henry Smith, secretary of the treasury. Then, in spite of a great outcry, he released General Santa Anna to help pacify Mexico. Also, as soon as it was practical, he furloughed all but 600 soldiers of his restless, unruly army. And for the most part, despite frontier opposition to his mild policy, he preserved peace with the Indians.[64]

Yet President Houston was disappointed most in his failure to acquire Texas annexation to the United States. His friend in the White House, Jackson, who was accused of aiding and abetting (and even planning) the Texas Revolution to extend slavery, yielded the controversial question to Congress. This body agreed only to official recognition of the newly-formed, unstable Republic, and they did that only after the 1836 elections. Still, most Texans seemed satisfied with Houston's administration (at least enough to elect him again when he became eligible three years later). The government was established; the Republic survived.[65]

From 1836 to 1861, antebellum Texas politics revolved around the Hero of San Jacinto. Of the early period one observer wrote: "We here in Texas had nothing to do with parties in the United States. We were Sam Houston or anti-Sam Houston; Eastern Texas was largely for and Western Texas against him." Mirabeau Buonaparte Lamar, former Georgia editor, Texas general, and the Republic's first vice president, was an early leader of the anti-Houston party; he was its presidential candidate in 1838. Possibly the Houston administration's greatest failure was its inability to defeat Lamar. The Hero of San Jacinto was ineligible to succeed himself, and the pro-Houston party nominated in succession three candidates; the first refused to run, the second committed suicide, and the third drowned. Lamar won almost by default.[66]

During Lamar's stormy administration (1838-1841), Houston served two terms as a Congressman from San Augustine in the Texas House of Representatives. He led his faction in opposing the capital's location at the frontier town of Austin; bitterly, but to no avail, fought Lamar's aggressive Indian policy which was aimed primarily at expelling the Cherokee; and denounced the administration's provocative and ill-fated Santa Fe expedition to conquer New Mexico.[67]

In September of 1841, Congressman Houston again was elected president by a better than two-to-one margin over Lamar-backed David Burnet. His second administration (1841-1844) reversed Lamar's expensive policies. Administrative costs plummeted because of drastic salary cuts and the dismissal of needless clerks. A friendly and less expensive Indian policy encouraged trading posts and treaties rather than shows of force, and he also pushed the United States closer to annexation through his negotiations with the British.[68] Houston's administration, however, met rebellious citizen opposition on at least two matters. His attempt to move the seat of government from Austin was thwarted by residents who hid the archives, and his effort to economize by secretly disposing of the unnecessary Texas Navy at a Galveston sale resulted only in the islanders' preventing the auction. Still, the Houston administration appeared vindicated by the election as president in 1844 of Anson Jones, a Houston party candidate, and, shortly thereafter, by the United States annexation of Texas, a decision Houston had maneuvered to effect for nearly a decade.[69]

Shortly after Houston's election to the Republic Congress, he journeyed in the spring of 1839 to Mobile, Alabama, seeking real estate investors in a proposed townsite at Sabine Pass. Among those with whom he conferred was Mrs. Nancy Lea, a shrewd businesswoman and widow of a former planter and Baptist minister. Houston soon found more to admire than Mrs. Lea's money, for accompanying the widow-investor was her tall, attractive, intelligent 20-year-old daughter, Margaret, who had three years before as a New Orleans school girl fantasied about someday meeting the famous Hero of San Jacinto. That week, in May of 1839, the bold ex-president of the Republic of Texas talked real estate with Nancy Lea and marriage to Margaret, a very religious young lady who was fascinated by the older man.[70] Nancy Lea endeavored to discourage her strong-minded daughter's affection for a man more than twice her age, but was only able to delay for a year the marriage which Margaret seemed to feel was her destiny. Houston apparently left Mobile with the good will of the mother, for Nancy Lea came to see the Texas real estate in December of 1839—much to Houston's regret, without her daughter. When Houston inquired why Margaret had not come as he had expected, Mrs. Lea responded, "General Houston, my daughter is in Alabama. She goes forth in the world to marry no man. The man who receives her hand will receive it in my home and not elsewhere." So, after a year apart and the exchange of frequent love letters, Houston went to Marion, Alabama, in May of 1840, to meet more of Margaret's relatives—an encounter he had dreaded. The family made one final, unsuccessful attempt to dissuade Margaret, and then, on May 9th, Sam and Margaret married.[71]

Few of Houston's friends and acquaintances felt optimistic about the marriage. One Texas politician wrote to Houston's physician, Ashbel Smith, that during his entire life he had "never met with an individual more totally disqualified for domestic happiness . . . ." Houston's past domestic record certainly did not forecast marital bliss, nor did the couple seem to have a great deal in common. Age was not the only disparity. For more than 20 years Houston had been a very heavy drinker and had ignored formal religion, whereas Margaret was a pious, church-going, teetotalling daughter of a Baptist minister.[72] Yet the Houston-Lea marriage more than endured. From 1843 to 1860 the Houstons had eight children, and, while the improvement of Sam's character helped fulfill Margaret's missionary zeal, her strong will and refinement answered a need in Sam's life. Early in the marriage Houston wrote relatives, "You have, I doubt not, heard that my wife controls me, and has reformed me, in many respects? This is pretty true, and I tell her, that I am willing that she should have the full benefit of my character . . . ."[73]

Margaret was a patient reformer and did not immediately transform the old general. For Margaret's sake, he imbibed intoxicants only in moderation, but, because he occasionally could not control his intake, he finally became a teetotaller. He even joined the Sons of Temperance, yet he continued to oppose temperance laws and blue law legislation. Initially, Sam attended church to please Margaret, where he often whittled to endure the sermons, but after some years he agreed to be baptized. Thereafter he remained an active communicant of the local Baptist church and a leading layman within the denomination, although he found it most difficult to stop swearing and quite impossible to forgive his enemies.[74] During 13 years of their marriage Houston served in the United States Senate to which he was elected shortly after annexation. The "trinity of his ambition," as Walter Prescott Webb phrased it, was "to be President of the United States, to be the savior of the Union, and to establish a protectorate over Mexico." Other important matters appear to have been secondary, and some, such as his frequent defense of Indian rights, were diametrically opposed to his own political self-interest.[75]

Houston strongly favored past compromises which had preserved the Union and practical approaches to abstract problems. For example, Houston and his old colonel of 1813, Thomas Hart Benton, were the only Southern Senators to vote for the organization of Oregon with an antislavery provision. Houston felt that debate over the extension of slavery into territories where it was highly unlikely to prosper was futile. He also had the somewhat dubious honor of being the only Southern Senator to vote for every provision of the Compromise of 1850. And along with John Bell of Tennessee, an old political opponent, Houston stood alone among the Southern

Senators in opposing the repeal of the Missouri Compromise by passage of the Kansas-Nebraska Act.[76]

During the Mexican War the Hero of San Jacinto strongly supported the policies of James K. Polk, an old Tennessee friend then serving in the White House. Polk offered the Texan a general's commission, which he declined. Yet Houston was disappointed with the peace treaty of Guadalupe Hidalgo which failed to protect Texas by providing for a protectorate over all of Mexico. Although his protectorate idea seemed to have won him few followers, it did distinguish him from all other potential candidates, and he continued to advocate it until the Civil War.[77]

In the mid 1850s Houston became an advocate of the American party. Unable to control the newly-organized Texas State Democratic party conventions and incapable of gaining favor with the southern-oriented National Democratic party, Houston identified with the new nationalistic movement, composed partly of Southern Whigs, which favored diverting the nation's attention away from slavery and focusing it on the immigrant threat. After his failure to gain the American party presidential nomination in 1856 and his loss in the Texas gubernatorial election in 1857, in which he had Know-Nothing backing, Houston, along with others, abandoned the American party.[78]

That the Hero of San Jacinto was not politically dead was demonstrated shortly after the expiration of his Senate term. During the Texas gubernatorial election in August of 1859 Houston's curious coalition of Union Democrats, old-line Whigs, Know-Nothings, and German Unionists triumphed over the Democratic regulars. His popularity as a heroic figure, together with the failure of the regular Democratic administration to deal with frontier defense and the activities of many secessionist-minded party regulars, led to a Houston victory. Soon his admirers began to push him for the presidency. Outside of Texas, Houston was proposed as an 1860 presidential candidate by the New York *Sun* and the New York *Express,* the *Augusta Daily Chronicle and Sentinel,* and the Little Rock *Arkansas Gazette.*[79]

Although now an independent Democrat, Houston had endeared himself to many opposition conservatives, especially Know-Nothings, by his victory over the regular Texas Democratic party. Houston had voted with the Know-Nothings in the United States Senate and had supported their candidate, Millard Fillmore, for president in 1865. His candidacy was further enhanced by his past statements that nature had already determined the boundaries of slavery and by his strong stance as governor in January of 1860 against a South Carolina-sponsored Southern conference which he regarded as a preliminary step to secession.[80]

Houston insisted (as had become his practice) that he did not wish his name submitted to a party convention and that he would only accept a call from the people. So a group of from 1500 to 2000 people met at the San Jacinto Battleground on April 21, 1860, to celebrate an important anniversary and to nominate the old general for the presidency.[81] Still, Houston delayed a decision to accept this draft from the people. A few days later, a small group of Houston's East Texas Know-Nothing friends, who were now supporting the new Constitutional Union party, assembled in the Smith County courthouse at Tyler and appointed four delegates, all of whom were close Houston associates, to the national convention at Baltimore in May. At the convention a number of pro-Houston speeches were delivered, and on the first ballot only two candidates had widespread support: Houston with 57 votes and ex-Senator John Bell of Tennessee with 68½ votes. Bell's support was geographically broader, however, and he was the second choice of most delegates. Thus, on the second ballot, he defeated Houston by a vote of 125 to 68.[82] On August 18th, Houston wrote a letter addressed "To my friends in the United States"; it began, "I withdraw my name from the list of candidates for the Presidency." In September he endorsed a Texas fusion party of Bell and Stephen A. Douglas supporters, which was easily defeated by the John C. Breckinridge ticket.[83]

Breckinridge carried only eight states of the South, and Abraham Lincoln, candidate of the antislavery Republic party, swept the North and won election to the presidency, an event which many Southerners viewed as an imminent danger to their society. But Houston remained strongly opposed to secession even after Lincoln's election, and he endeavored to keep Texas in the Union. The governor yielded to the legislature in allowing the election of a secession convention, however, and the people, in February of 1861, approved the convention's ordinance of secession. Also, Houston declined an offer of military assistance from President Lincoln; yet he refused to take a required oath of allegiance to the Confederate States of America and relinquished his office.[84]

The 68-year-old Houston and his young family returned to their farm near Huntsville in March of 1861, and, during the last two years before his death in 1863, he, on the whole, supported the Confederacy and two of his sons served in its army. As late as the early summer of 1863, however, he discussed with two close friends the possibility of evacuating Texas troops from Southern battlefields and taking the Lone Star State out of the Confederacy to recreate the Republic of Texas. Shortly after the fall of Vicksburg, which many Texans viewed as the beginning of the end for the Confederate State of Texas, Houston died of pneumonia. Margaret wrote in the family Bible: "Died on the 26th of July 1863, Genl Sam Houston, the beloved and affectionate Husband, father, devoted patriot, the fearless soldier—the meek and lowly Christian."[85]

NOTES

1. The most important biographies of Houston are Charles E. Lester, *The Life of Sam Houston: The Only Authentic Memoir of Him Ever Published* (New York: J. C. Derby, 1855); Marquis James, *The Raven: A Biography of Sam Houston* (Indianapolis: Bobbs-Merrill, 1929); Llerena Friend, *Sam Houston, the Great Designer* (Austin: University of Texas Press, 1954); Marion K. Wisehart, *Sam Houston, American Giant* (Washington: Luce, 1962); Jack Gregory and Rennard Strickland, *Sam Houston with the Cherokees, 1829-1833* (Austin: University of Texas Press, 1967); Donald Braider, *Solitary Star: A Biography of Sam Houston* (New York: G. P. Putnam's Sons, 1974); Henry Bruce, *Life of General Houston, 1793-1863* (New York: Dodd, 1891); William C. Crane, *Life and Select Literary Remains of Sam Houston of Texas* (Philadelphia: Lippincott, 1884); George Creel, *Sam Houston, Colossus in Buckskin* (New York: Cosmopolitan, 1928); and Alfred M. Williams, *Sam Houston and the War of Independence in Texas* (Boston: Houghton Mifflin Company, 1893).
2. A. W. Terrell, "Recollections of General Sam Houston," *Southwestern Historical Quarterly,* (October, 1912), 16:121.
3. James, p. 4.
4. Wisehart, pp. 6-7.
5. Lester, pp. 18-19; Oren F. Morton, *A History of Rockbridge County, Virginia* (Staunton: McClure Company, 1920), pp. 189-190; James, p. 8; Alexander Hynds, "General Sam Houston," *The Century Magazine,* (August, 1884), 28:495.
6. James, pp. 10-11; Wisehart, pp. 7-8.
7. Wisehart, pp. 7-8.
8. Lester, pp. 20-21.
9. Ibid., p. 22; Gregory and Strickland, pp. 11-21; Braider, p. 17.
10. Lester, pp. 22-23; Hynds, p. 495; James, pp. 20, 22.
11. Lester, pp. 25-26; Williams, p. 9.
12. Lester. p. 26.
13. "Letter from Col. Willoughby Williams," printed in Josephus C. Guild, *Old Times in Tennessee, with Historical, Personal, and Political Scraps and Sketches* (Nashville: Travel, Eastman, and Howell, 1878), pp. 274-275; Lester, p. 27; James. p. 29.
14. Lester, pp. 27, 303; James, p. 30; Thomas H. S. Hamersly, *Complete Regular Army Register of the United States for One Hundred Years, 1779-1879* (Washington: T. H. S. Hamersly, 1880), p. 521; "Letter from Col. Willoughby Williams," p. 275.
15. Wisehart, pp. 16-17.
16. Ibid.; Lester, pp. 34-36.

17. Lester, pp. 37-38; "Letter From Col. Willoughby Williams," p. 275.

18. Lester, pp. 38-39; James, pp. 38-39; Houston to John Rhea, March 1, 1815; Houston to Joseph Anderson, March 1, 1815; Houston to James Monroe, March 1, 1815; Houston to William H. Crawford, February 16, 1816, *The Writings of Sam Houston,* ed. by Amelia W. Williams and Eugene C. Barker (8 vols.; Austin: University of Texas Press, 1938-43), 1:1-4, 6. Hereafter cited as *Writings.*

19. Wisehart, pp. 20-21; Friend, pp. 7-8; Lester, pp. 39-40.

20. James, p. 45; Lester, p. 40.

21. Lester, p. 42-43; Wisehart, p. 25; N. M. Ludlow, *Dramatic Life As I Found It: A Record of Personal Experience, with an Account of the Rise and Progress of the Drama in the West and South* (St. Louis: G. I. Jones and Company, 1880), p. 166.

22. Lester, p. 44; James, pp. 47-48; Wisehart, p. 26.

23. James. p. 48; Lester, pp. 44-45; Friend, pp. 9-10.

24. Friend, p. 10; Crane, p. 175; Houston to Jackson, *Writings,* August 3, 1822, 1:13.

25. Crane, p. 17; *Writings,* 2:2-6; Friend, p. 10.

26. Friend, pp. 10-11; To the Freemen of the Seventh Congressional District of the State of Tennessee, *Writings,* 3:6.

27. Ernest C. Shearer, "The Mercurial Sam Houston," *East Tennessee Historical Society Publications,* (1963), 35:6; Houston to Alexander Campbell, April 25, 1815, *Writings,* 1:4-5; Houston to A. M. Hughes, January 22, 1825, *Writings,* 1:24; Houston to William J. Worth, January 24, 1826, *Writings,* 1:28; Wisehart, pp. 30-31.

28. Braider, p. 59; To the Freemen of the Ninth Congressional District of the State of Tennessee, *Writings,* 3:1-7; Friend, pp. 12-13; Speech on the Congress of Panama, February 2, 1826, *Writings,* 1:28-40; Crane, p. 181.

29. Houston to Clay, December 9, 1825, *Writings,* 4:3; Houston to Adams, March 18, 1826, *Writings,* 4:4; Wisehart, p. 31.

30. Houston to John P. Erwin, August 18, 1826, *Writings,* 4:5; To The Public, September 12, 1826, *Writings,* 1f:6-8; The Answer to a Toast at Telico, Tennessee, *Writings,* 1:113-114; "Letter From Col. Willoughly Williams," p. 277; "Letter From General William White," published in *Guild, Old Times in Tennessee,* pp. 286-287.

31. Braider, p. 61; "Letter From Col. Willoughby Williams," p. 277; "Letter From Gen. William White," p. 287.

32. James, pp. 64-66.

33. Ibid., p. 66; The Answer to a Toast at Telico, Tennessee, *Writings,* 1:113-114; Terrell, pp. 128-129.

34. The Answer to a Toast at Telico, Tennessee, *Writings,* 1:113-114; Evelyn Wiley "Sam Houston's Career in Tennessee," (Master's Thesis, Vanderbilt University, 1939), pp. 77-80; Jackson to Houston, December 15, 1826, *Correspondence of Andrew Jackson,* ed. John S. Bassett (7 vols; Washington: Carnegie Institute of Washington, 1926-35).

35. Wiley, pp. 81-83.

36. Philip M. Hamer, *Tennessee—A History, 1673-1932* (4 vols; New York: American Historical Society, 1933), 1:273; Guild, *Old Times in Tennessee,* pp. 262-263.

37. Hamer, 1:273; Friend, p. 16; Inaugural Address as Governor of Tennessee, *Writings,* 4:9.

38. To the Legislature of Tennessee, October 15, 1827, *Writings,* 1:115-121.

39. Marquis James, *Andrew Jackson: Portrait of a President* (New York: Bobbs-Merrill, 1937), pp. 160-161; Friend, p. 17-18; Braider, p. 68.

40. Braider, p. 68; Shearer, p. 19; Wisehart, p. 36.

41. Wisehart, pp. 37-39; James. p. 73.

42. Wisehart, pp. 39-40.

43. Houston to John Allen, April 9, 1829, *Writings,* 1:130; Wisehart, p. 41; John T. Moore, ed., *Tennessee, the Volunteer State* (4 vols; Chicago: S. J. Clarke Publishing Co., 1923), 1:400-401.

44. James, pp. 81-82, 139; Ernest C. Shearer, "Sam Houston and Religion," *Tennessee Historical Quarterly,* (Summer 1961), 20:40-41.

45. Wisehart, p. 50; Shearer, p. 9; Houston to William Hall, April 16, 1829, *Writings,* 1:131-132; Letter From Col. Willoughby," pp. 278-279; Hamer, 1:279; Stanley F. Horn, ed., "Hold-

ings of the Tennessee Historical Society," *Tennessee Historical Quarterly*, (December, 1944), 3:349-351.

46. Friend, p. 41; League to Austin, September 10, 1827, *The Correspondence of Stephen F. Austin, American Historical Association Annual Report, 1919*, ed. by Eugene C. Barker (2 vols; Washington: Government Printing Office, 1924); Horn, p. 350.

47. Gregory and Strickland, pp. 6-7, 143, 147-148; Wisehart, pp. 116-117; Houston to Jackson, May 11, 1829, *Writings*, 1:132-134; Jackson to Houston, June 21, 1829, Henderson Yoakum, *History of Texas, from Its First Settlements in 1685 to Its Annexation to the United States in 1846* (2 vols; New York: J. S. Redfield, 1855) 1:307; Jackson's Manuscripts, "Executive Book," Library of Congress, cited in Richard R. Stenberg, "The Texas Schemes of Jackson and Houston," *Southwestern Social Science Quarterly*, (December, 1934), 15:230.

48. Gregory and Strickland, pp. 15-21, 61-69.

49. Ibid., pp. 20-21, 68-69.

50. Ibid., pp. 21-31, 104-109; *Writings*, 1:155-185.

51. Gregory and Strickland, pp. 41-46, 134-135.

52. Roger M. Busfield, Jr., "The Hermitage Walking Stick: First Challenge to Congressional Immunity," *Tennessee Historical Quarterly*, (June, 1962), 21:122-124.

53. Ibid., pp. 122, 124-126; Paul H. Bergeron, "A Test For Jacksonians: Sam Houston On Trial," *East Tennessee Historical Society Publications*, (1965), 38:19-20.

54. Busfield, "The Hermitage Walking Stick," pp. 126-129; Bergeron, "Sam Houston on Trial," pp. 22-23, 27-29; George W. Paschal, "Last Years of Sam Houston," *Harper's New Monthly Magazine*, (April, 1866), 32:631; *Writings*, 1:199-257; *The Autobiography of Sam Houston*, ed. by Donald Day and Henry H. Ullom (Norman: University of Oklahoma Press, 1954), pp. 66-71.

55. Friend, pp. 43-56; Application for Headright in Austin's Colony, *Writings*, 1:271.

56. Lester, pp. 64-65; Houston to Jackson, February 13, 1833, *Writings*, 1:274-276.

57. Friend, pp. 57-59; Houston to John Houston, July 31, 1833, *Writings*, 5:5-6.

58. Divorce Petition, *Writings*, 1:277-279; Friend, p. 59; James, p. 199; Martha A. Turner, *Sam Houston and His Twelve Women; the Ladies Who Influenced the Life of Texas' Greatest Statesman* (Austin: Pemberton, 1966), pp. 25-45; Shearer, "Sam Houston and Religion," pp. 41-42; Shearer, "The Mercurial Sam Houston," p. 9; *Writings*, 1:400-401.

59. Friend, pp. 60-63; Lester, pp. 70, 73; Barker, pp. 480-481; Wisehart, p. 123; Nomination As Commander-In-Chief Of The Troops Of The Department Of Nacogdoches, October 6, 1835, *Writings*, 1:303; To The Troops Of The Department of Nacogdoches, October 8, 1835, Ibid., 1:304-305.

60. Friend, pp. 63-67.

61. Ibid., pp. 67-69; Houston to Henry Raguet, April 19, 1836, *Writings*, 1:413-414.

62. Rupert N. Richardson, Ernest Wallace, and Adrian N. Anderson, *Texas: the Lone Star State* (3d ed.; Princeton: Prentice-Hall, 1970), pp. 96-98; Official Report Of The Battle Of San Jacinto, April 25, 1836, *Writings*, pp. 416-420.

63. Friend, pp. 70, 72; Houston to Anna Raguet, undated note, *Writings*, 1:415.

64. Richardson, Wallace, and Anderson, pp. 106-109; Wisehart, p. 277, 281-285; Friend, p. 682.

65. Friend, pp. 118-119; Stenberg, p. 229; Seymour V. Connor, *Texas: A History* (New York: Thomas Y. Crowell, 1971). pp. 129-130.

66. Stanley Seigel, *A Political History of the Texas Republic, 1836-1845* (Austin: University of Texas Press, 1956), pp. 50, 100-102; Richardson, Wallace, and Anderson, pp. 109-110.

67. Richardson, Wallace, and Anderson, pp. 113; *Writings*, 2:354-362, 365-367, 372-373, 391-397.

68. Richardson, Wallace, and Anderson, pp 113-115; Friend, p. 134.

69. Dorman H. Winfrey, "The Texan Archive War of 1842," *Southwestern Historical Quarterly*, (October, 1960), 64:169-184; Richardson, Wallace, and Anderson, pp. 114-115.

70. William Seale, *Sam Houston's Wife: A Biography of Margaret Lea Houston* (Norman: University of Oklahoma Press, 1970), pp. 10-13.

71. Ibid., pp. 13-31; James, p. 313.

72. Friend, p. 97; Shearer, "Sam Houston and Religion," p. 43; Shearer, "The Mercurial Sam Houston," p. 15; F. N. Boney, "The Raven Tamed: An 1845 Sam Houston Letter," *Southwestern Historical Quarterly*, (July, 1964), 68:90-92.

73. Boney, p. 91.
74. Shearer, "Sam Houston and Religion," pp. 43-47; Terrell, pp. 121-122, 133; Georgia J. Burleson, *The Life and Writings of Rufus C. Burleson, D.D., Ll.D., Containing a Biography of Dr. Burleson by Harry Haynes* (privately printed, 1901), pp. 166-167, 224-226, 285-286, 289; Crane, pp. 240-245.
75. Walter P. Webb, *The Texas Rangers: A Century of Frontier Defense* (Boston: Houghton Mifflin Co., 1935), p. 197; Wisehart, p. 551.
76. Walter P. Webb and H. Bailey Carroll, *The Handbook of Texas* (2 vols.; Austin: Texas State Historical Association, 1952), 1:846-847.
77. Ibid.
78. Ralph A. Wooster, "An Analysis of the Texas Know Nothings," *Southwestern Historical Quarterly*, (January, 1967), 70:414-423.
79. James Alex Baggett, "The Constitutional Union Party in Texas," *Southwestern Historical Quarterly*, (January, 1979), 82:236-239.
80. Ibid., p. 239.
81. Ibid., pp. 239-240.
82. Ibid., pp. 240-241.
83. Ibid., pp. 242-243.
84. Friend, pp. 331-346; Terrell, pp. 134-135.
85. Terrell, pp. 122-123; Seale, p. 233.

BIBLIOGRAPHY

BOOKS

Barker, Eugene C., ed. *The Correspondence of Stephen F. Austin, American Historical Association Annual Report, 1919.* 2 vols. Washington: Government Printing Office, 1924.
———. *The Life of Stephen F. Austin, Founder of Texas, 1793-1836: A Chapter in the Westward Movement of the Anglo-American People.* Nashville: Cokesbury Press, 1926.
Bassett, John S., ed. *Correspondence of Andrew Jackson.* 7 vols. Washington: Carnegie Institute of Washington, 1926-35.
Binkley, William C. *The Texas Revolution.* Baton Rouge: Louisiana State University Press, 1952.
Braider, Donald. *Solitary Star: A Biography of Sam Houston.* New York: G. P. Putnam's Sons, 1974.
Bruce, Henry. *Life of General Houston, 1793-1863.* New York: Dodd, 1891.
Burleson, Georgia J. *The Life and Writings of Rufus C. Burleson, D.D., Ll.D., Containing a Biography of Dr. Burleson by Harry Haynes.* Privately printed, 1901.
Connor, Seymour V. *Texas: A History.* New York: Thomas Y. Crowell, 1971.
Crane, William C. *Life and Select Literary Remains of Sam Houston of Texas.* Philadelphia: Lippincott, 1884.
Creel, George. *Sam Houston, Colossus in Buckskin.* New York: Cosmopolitan, 1928.
Day, Donald, and Ullom, Henry H. *The Autobiography of Sam Houston.* Norman: University of Oklahoma Press, 1954.
Friend, Llerena. *Sam Houston, the Great Designer.* Austin: University of Texas Press, 1954.
Gregory, Jack, and Strickland, Rennard. *Sam Houston with the Cherokees, 1829-1833.* Austin: University of Texas Press, 1967.
Guild, Josephus C. *Old Times in Tennessee, with Historical, Personal, and Political Scraps and Sketches.* Nashville: Travel, Eastman, and Howell, 1878.
Hamer, Philip M. *Tennessee—A History, 1673-1932.* 4 vols. New York: American Historical Society, 1933.
Hamersly, Thomas H. S. *Complete Regular Army Register of the United States for One Hundred Years, 1779-1879.* Washington: T. H. S. Hamersly, 1880.
James, Marquis. *Andrew Jackson: Portrait of a President.* New York: Bobbs-Merrill, 1937.
———. *The Raven: A Biography of Sam Houston.* Indianapolis: Bobbs-Merrill, 1929.
Lester, Charles E. *The Life of Sam Houston: The Only Authentic Memoir of Him Ever Published.* New York: J. C. Derby, 1855.

Ludlow, N. M. *Dramatic Life As I Found It: A Record of Personal Experience, with an Account of the Rise and Progress of the Drama in the West and South.* St. Louis: G. I. Jones and Company, 1880.

Moore, John T., ed. *Tennessee, the Volunteer State.* 4 vols. Chicago: S. J. Clarke Publishing Co., 1923.

Morton, Oren F. *A History of Rockbridge County, Virginia.* Staunton: McClure Company, 1920.

Richardson, Rupert N., Wallace, Ernest, and Anderson, Adrian N. *Texas: the Lone Star State.* 3rd ed. Princeton: Prentice-Hall, 1970.

Seale, William. *Sam Houston's Wife: A Biography of Margaret Lea Houston.* Norman: University of Oklahoma Press, 1970.

Siegel, Stanley. *A Political History of the Texas Republic, 1836-1845.* Austin: University of Texas Press, 1956.

Turner, Martha A. *Sam Houston and His Twelve Women: the Ladies Who Influenced the Life of Texas' Greatest Statesman.* Austin: Pemberton, 1966.

Webb, Walter P. and Carroll, H. Bailey. *The Handbook of Texas.* 2 vols. Austin: Texas State Historical Association, 1952.

Webb, Walter P. *The Texas Rangers: A Century of Frontier Defense.* Boston: Houghton Mifflin Co., 1935.

Williams, Alfred M. *Sam Houston and the War of Independence in Texas.* Boston: Houghton Mifflin Company, 1893.

Williams, Amelia W., and Barker Eugene C., ed. *The Writings of Sam Houston.* 8 vols. Austin: University of Texas Press, 1938-43.

Wisehart, Marion K. *Sam Houston, American Giant.* Washington: Luce, 1962.

Yoakum, Henderson. *History of Texas, from Its First Settlement in 1685 to Its Annexation to the United States in 1846.* 2 vols. New York: J. S. Redfield, 1855.

ARTICLES

Baggett, James Alex. "The Constitutional Union Party in Texas." *Southwestern Historical Quarterly* no. 82, January, 1979.

Bergeron, Paul H. "A Test for Jacksonians" Sam Houston on Trial." *East Tennessee Historical Society Publications* no. 38, 1965.

Boney, F. N. "The Raven Tamed: An 1845 Sam Houston Letter." *Southwestern Historical Quarterly* no. 68, July 1964.

Busfield, Roger M., Jr. "The Hermitage Walking Stick: First Challenge to Congressional Immunity." *Tennessee Historical Quarterly* no. 21, June, 1962.

Horn Stanley F., ed. "Holdings of the Tennessee Historical Society." *Tennessee Historical Quarterly* no. 3, December, 1944.

Hynds, Alexander. "General Sam Houston." *The Century Magazine* no. 28, August, 1884.

Paschal, George W. "Last Years of Sam Houston." *Harper's New Monthly Magazine* no. 32, April, 1866.

Shearer, Ernest C. "The Mercurial Sam Houston." *East Tennessee Historical Society Publications* no. 35, 1963.

————. "Sam Houston and Religion." *Tennessee Historical Quarterly* no. 20, Summer, 1961.

Stenberg, Richard R. "The Texas Schemes of Jackson and Houston." *Southwestern Social Science Quarterly* no. 15, December, 1934.

Terrell, A. W. "Recollections of General Sam Houston." *Southwestern Social Science Quarterly* no. 15, December, 1934.

Terrell, A. W. "Recollections of General Sam Houston." *Southwestern Historical Quarterly* no. 16, October, 1912.

Winfrey, Dorman H. "The Texan Archive War of 1842." *Southwestern Historical Quarterly* no. 64, October, 1960.

Wooster, Ralph A. "An Analysis of the Texas Know Nothings," *Southwestern Historical Quarterly* no. 70, January, 1967.

UNPUBLISHED WORKS

Wiley, Evelyn. "Sam Houston's Career in Tennessee." M. A. Thesis, Vanderbilt University, 1939.

8

WILLIAM HALL
Governor of Tennessee, 1829

by Michael O. Sanders

Since his selection as Speaker of the Senate to the 18th General Assembly, William Hall's duties had been varied. Most had been ordinary, but now he was faced with a duty which no other Speaker had ever confronted in the young history of the state. He had received a letter of resignation from the governor of Tennessee, Sam Houston. By the state Constitution, William Hall, Speaker of the Senate, would now become governor of the state of Tennessee.[1]

Who was this man whom fate had selected to be Tennessee's least known governor? He has been characterized as "an Israelite in whom there was no guile"[2] and described by the man he was replacing as a "Patriot, soldier, gentleman, and an honest man."[3] He was born February 11, 1775, in Surrey County, North Carolina, the son of William and Thankful Doak Hall,[4] pioneer parents who greatly influenced the life of the future Indian fighter, general of the Tennessee militia, United States Congressman, and governor of Tennessee. Both classic examples of the frontier personalities of the time, his father and mother shared close relationships with all their five children, two of whom they would bury in the soil of Tennessee. William Hall, Sr., served in the American Revolution, attaining the rank of major, a title by which he would always be addressed in Tennessee. His marriage to Thankful Doak was indeed a wise one, for she was able to give him the moral support and his children the guidance they would need in the rugged frontier of the Cumberland Valley. She was the sister of Reverend Samuel Doak, a prominent early clergyman and educator in East Tennessee. Doak had come to Tennessee in the early 1780s and had established the first school in

the Tennessee country. Chartered as Martin Academy, it later became Washington College. While riding his circuit, he brought both
religion and education to the backwoods of Tennessee.[5] William Hall
and his brother John would continue the family interest in education
as William served as a trustee for several academies and John Hall
became the first schoolmaster in Gallatin, Tennessee.[6]

In 1779 William Hall sold his possessions in North Carolina and
started for Kentucky. Because of troubles with the British and the
ever-present Indian danger, Hall decided to stop in New River, Virginia. The halt lasted until 1785 when he sold his plantation there
and moved on to the area which would soon become Sumner
County, Tennessee.[7] He probably followed the old road which
passed Fort Blount at Gainesboro and continued on to Bledsoe's
Lick. Leaving his family at the fort there, Major Hall went a mile east
where he selected a beautiful and commanding site on Lick Creek
and during the winter erected buildings before moving his family to
the site.[8] This was the beginning of Hall's Station which stood 184
years until it was destroyed by fire during the night of April 15, 1969.
At the time of its burning it was possibly the oldest building in Middle Tennessee, and one of the oldest in the state.[9]

The Hall family had reached Bledsoe's Fort on November 20,
1785. By January 1, 1786, Hall's Station was ready for them to occupy. It appears that Hall was assisted in building the house by James
Harrison and William Gibson.[10] Typical of the log farmhouses of its
period, it had no stockading or protection against Indian attack. For
security the Halls, like others, relied on the nearest fort. Frontier
defense was often a community effort. With the threat of Indian
attack, the settlers would spread the alarm and retreat to the walls of
the stockade.[11] Two hundred yards to the northeast was a big spring
which provided water for the family.[12] In 1956 the Hall's Station
structure was examined by Nashville historian, Stanley F. Horn, and
the president of the Tennessee Historical Society, Albert Ganier.[13]
Ganier, along with other historians who examined the building over
the years, concluded that the southern end was built first and the
second story and northern end added later, perhaps within a year or
two.[14] The log structure itself measured 50 feet across the front and
at the south end was 20 feet wide. Its southern end was separated
from the northern end by a huge stone chimney. The large room
which was the south end of the lower floors showed evidence of

Portrait of William Hall. *Photograph by George W. Hornal, courtesy Tennes-see Department of Transportation.*

being built hurriedly. Its construction was unique for Middle Tennessee. With the bark still remaining on top and bottom, the logs of the house were no more than dressed trees smoothed on two sides. The method of joining the logs at the corner had consisted of trimming the trees at the ends with an ax until they had been reduced to half their original diameter. This completed, the ends were notched and joined. Originally the house was floored with split logs with the smooth side up. Later they were covered with tongue and groove boards. Neatly beaded overhead beams highlighted the interior. The north room and the second story appear to have been built by men skilled in cabin construction. As the heavy logs were completely trimmed, the bark was removed and the joints were prefitted before the walls were put up. The logs were numbered with Roman numerals that were struck with a chisel or hatchet, and the joints were made with tight notches.[15] In his later years Governor Hall lined the cabins with wooden paneling and built a roof and porch which joined the two structures. A dim photograph of this expanded structure appears in Cisco's *Historic Sumner* and Albright's *History of Middle Tennessee*.[16]

The area of Tennessee in which Major Hall chose to settle was one of beauty, of danger, and of growth. Since the expeditions of John Donelson and James Robertson had reached the French Lick in early 1780, more and more settlers had followed into the rich fertile area of the Cumberland. The coming of the white man posed a problem for the Indians. For countless years the major tribes of the area had shared Middle Tennessee as a common hunting ground. Each spring the Shawnee, Creek, and Cherokee tribes had come to the Cumberland. In the spring of 1780 the whites also were there; Donelson and Robertson had built Fort Nashborough during the previous winter. For the Indians the only logical answer to the white presence was war. The Hall family found themselves in the midst of the struggle for the land of the Cumberland. Almost 15 years were required to break the power of the Indians, and future governor William Hall would play a vital role in their defeat.

The land of the Cumberland Valley was well worth the struggle to win it from the Indians. Isaac Bledsoe, who discovered the lick where present-day Castalian Springs is located, wrote that herds of buffalo in the bottoms surrounding the sulphur springs were so numerous that he was afraid to alight from his horse lest he be trampled beneath the hoofs of the restless beasts.[17] The sulphur springs and the accompanying salt licks were especially numerous in Sumner and Davidson counties. This fact, together with the proximity of the Cumberland River, was largely responsible for selection of this area for pioneer settlement.[18]

By an act of the North Carolina legislature, the county of Sumner was established in November of 1786.[19] It was the second county to be formed in Middle Tennessee and the fifth county to be organized in the state. In April of 1787, the First Court of Pleas and Quarter Sessions of Sumner County met at the home of John Hamilton, near Station Camp Creek. The fact that Major Hall was already a respected leader of the settlement is evidenced by his being recommended by James Robertson as a magistrate for the county. The North Carolina legislature also appointed Hall, along with others, to serve as commissioners to select a site and build a courthouse, prison, and stocks.[20] According to records of the time, the first legislative body of the county was composed of men with character and ability; they were given credit for ruling both wisely and well.

Death and tragedy came to the Hall family as the Indians of the Cumberland struck out against the white encroachment into their hunting grounds. In 1769 Robert Crockett was killed by Indians on the headwaters of the Roaring River in Overton County. His was the first recorded death of a white at the hands of the Indians in Middle Tennessee.[21] In January of 1786, members of the Hall family had their first problem with Indians. During the night a band of Creeks, returning from a war in Georgia and looking for other areas to raid, stole all 12 of Major Hall's horses.[22] Fearing for the safety of his family, he moved them to the protection of Bledsoe's Fort where they remained until fall when they again returned to the homestead.[23]

Young Hall would find himself becoming a man quickly in this rugged area of danger and adventure in the summer of 1787. The area of Sumner County became a storm center of savage fury. Death came quickly to many settlers as the Indians launched an all-out attack to drive the pioneers from their land. The first incident occurred when a Mr. Price and his wife were killed at the town creek just south of Gallatin. Judge Haywood, in recording the incident, states that the Indians also "chopped the children."[24] Stories of terror were on the lips of everyone. A Mr. Radcliff from Gallatin went to volunteer his services in the defense of the people of Nashville. As he stood listening to the stories of anguish from his neighbors, "there came to him one who said that, only twelve hours after leaving his home, his own house had been broken into, and his young wife and their babies had been slaughtered, and that when the messenger left, they were still lying on the hearthstone of his dwelling, weltering in their blood."[25]

It is certain that young Hall heard many such tales of atrocities, but in June of 1787 he observed the horrors of the frontier firsthand when his brother, James, became the first white person killed in the Sumner area after the Indian wars began in Middle Tennessee. The two young boys had gone to a field near their home to retrieve some horses they had tethered there the day before. Lying in ambush along the road was a war party. Ten of the Indians were waiting beside the road while five more were hiding in a treetop. As William turned to speak to James, he spotted ten of the warriors stalking them. Feeling the situation to be hopeless, young Hall first thought of surrender. He quickly changed his mind as two of the braves jumped forward and tomahawked James, sinking their war axes into his forehead. Hall decided to make a dash for freedom. Being smaller and quicker, he felt he could lose the Indians in the cane-brake. Running wildly through the heavy brush, grapevines grabbing at him, he finally reached the safety of the house. The Indians had chased their quarry to within 100 yards of the cabin. Fortunately for the future governor of Tennessee, a group of young men and women had just arrived to visit the family. Seeing the size of the group and noticing that the men of the party were armed, the Indians turned away. A force was quickly organized to try and retrieve the body of James Hall and to pursue and punish the Indians. After a short period of time they surprised the Indians at Goose Creek near the fort. Not wanting to fight, the Indians fled leaving behind one of their horses on which was tied the bloody scalp of James Hall.[26]

Major Hall was not home when his son was killed. He was attending a peace conference with General James Robertson and Little Owl, a Cherokee chief.[27] When he returned, he quickly moved to provide security for the family. He, along with two neighbors, hired several young men to serve as scouts and guards. For two months there was no further danger. But on the morning of August 2nd the scouts advised Major Hall to move his family to the safety of the fort, for a force of 30 Indians was reported to be in the area. The family loaded sleds with their possessions and started the dangerous trek to Bledsoe's Station. On the first trip young William became alarmed when the horses began to act strangely. He was sure the animals had smelled Indians. However, his brother Richard insisted that they continue; four additional trips were made.

With five men serving as a guard they began the last and fatal trip, the moving of the members of the family. Young William was leading the horses when suddenly a dog belonging to one of the younger boys began to bark excitedly. Richard Hall started forward to investigate and was promptly shot. A group of 40 to 50 Indians was waiting in ambush. One of the guards, a Mr. Henderson, foolishly chose the open road to make his stand. He was quickly dispatched by the Indians, falling with six or seven shots through his body. Acting quickly, William took his younger brother and sister and placed them behind the other men, including Major Hall, who were fighting to hold the Indians at bay. The horse upon which Mrs. Hall was mounted bolted and carried her to the safety of the fort. Major Hall's body was pierced by 13 shots. The Indians quickly scalped him and fled as a force from the fort approached.[28] The death of Major Hall had a tremendous impact on the community. In his *History of Middle Tennessee*, James Phelan notes the death of Major Hall in a mystifying account: "The mangled and bloody bodies of these men were brought into Bledsoe's Station, and laid upon the floor in the presence of three pregnant women, whose after born children, were marked, one as if a bullet had been shot through the head, and the two others upon the backs with red streaks, as of blood streaming down from scalped heads."[29] After the death of Major Hall and two of his sons, Mrs. Hall decided to move to the safety of Greenfield Fort.[30] Amid such scenes of terror, William Hall continued on the path to manhood. In the next eight years he was to have more encounters with the Indians.

Early in the 1790s Hall was commissioned an ensign in an infantry regiment from Sumner County.[31] Before the Indian wars were over he would be promoted to major in the Sumner Light Horse.[32] In the fall and spring of 1793 when smallpox came to the settlements around Nashville, Hall decided to rest from his duties as a scout for Governor William Blount and to take advantage of the inoculations being given at Greenfield. For several months he and William Neely had spent long nights in the woods watching for signs of Indians. Their usual procedure was to leave on a Monday morning and return on a Saturday morning. George Winchester, writer of Hall's obituary for the Nashville *Christian Advocate,* vividly described Hall's experiences as a frontier scout: "Often in his later years as Governor Hall would—'shoulder his crutch and fight his battles o'er'—the writer has heard him recite the incidents of some perilous foray, or military bivouac in the mighty forest, as he tracked the cunning savage in his mission of plunder and massacre, or watched him in his night camp, as in mystic signs and unintelligible jargon he plotted the death of the paleface."[33] As he rested at the fort one evening, Hall decided to go out to the fields where the slaves were working under a Mr. Jarvis. The field was next to a canebrake about 15 feet in height. While he was speaking with Abraham, one of the slaves, a group of dogs in the field began to bark and growl. Quickly Hall ordered Jarvis to take the workers to the fort, for he was sure there were Indians lurking nearby. Early the next morning, over the protests of Mrs. Clendenning, one of the matrons of the fort, Jarvis ordered the workers back to the field. Hall was aroused from his bed by one of the neighbors who requested that he go after Jarvis. Hearing gunfire, he seized his rifle and shot-pouch and met William Wilson, another soldier who was running to the field. When they arrived at the canebrake, Hall, Wilson, and two others who had joined them saw Jarvis and the slaves being pursued by a large body of Indians. A race for the protection of a fence that separated the two groups ensued. The four soldiers reached the fence first and fired a volley at a party of onrushing Indians, forcing them to turn back up the hill. Running to another angle of the fence, they encountered a group of 25 Indians. Choosing a bold plan of action, Hall called for Wilson and the others to follow his lead and to charge straight at the warriors hoping that "disconcerted by our audacity, they might miss us." The Indians fired, the bullets whistling past the four men's ears. After delivering their fire, the Indians turned and fled.

Much-needed assistance came when William Neely and James Hays arrived to relieve the soldiers' desperate situation. Concentrating on Neely and Hays as they approached, one group of Indians failed to see Hall and his men approaching their side. One of the startled braves, when he noticed Hall, turned and fled. He had gone some ten steps when Hall fired: "I saw the bottoms of his moccasions fly up in the air as he went over on his face, shot through his body." Another group of Indians was at the same time trying to cut Jarvis and the others off before they reached the fort. Turning after them, Hall and his men were too late to save Jarvis, but a quick shot by James Hays rescued the mulatto slave, Abraham. Hall then proposed that they fire in volley on his command to drive the Indians away from the body of Jarvis. The Indians turned to fire at the whites, one shot striking a rail and sending bark flying close by William Hall's ear. As they retreated toward the fort, Hall called for the group to turn and fire one more round. As they did the Indians also fired, one ball taking a lock from Hall's hair. By this time Neely and the others were ahead and Hall quickly followed. As he crossed the creek near the fort, bullets splashed water on his legs before he reached the safety of the fort.

It was estimated that the Indian force at Greenfield was at least 260, making it one of the largest ever mustered in Middle Tennessee. Commenting on the fight years later, Hall said, "It seemed almost miraculous that we were able with such slim numbers to keep them at bay. The fort was poorly calculated to stand a regular siege and if they had any bravery equivalent to their numbers they might have taken it at the first assault." Deciding at that time not to follow the Indians, Hall and a group of others waited until evening. Tracking the war party, they found where they had lain in ambush waiting for the whites. An extended search turned up the body of the Indian that Hall had killed; it was hidden under a decaying log.[34]

Two months later Hall had another encounter with war parties roaming the area. In company with seven other members of the Light Horse at Greenfield, he was having dinner when James Steele, Steele's son, his daughter Betsey, and his brother Robert entered declaring that they were going on to Morgan's Station. They did so, despite the warnings of Hall that they should wait for an escort before they continued their journey. Hearing gunfire, Hall and his men jumped up from dinner and ran down the road to find James Steele dead and Betsey, a beautiful girl of 17, lying in the road scalped and bleeding. Taking off his hunting shirt, Hall wrapped it around her in a futile attempt to save her life.[35]

It was obvious that it would take a concentrated push to drive the Indians out of Middle Tennessee. William Hall played a vital role in this struggle; he was repeatedly engaged in warfare against the Indians from the age of 12 until he was 19. In his *Annals of Tennessee,* J. G. M. Ramsey says that the actions of Hall and the others at Greenfield were "definitely a heroic effort unparalled."[36] James Phelan, writing about the Indian wars in his *History of Middle Tennessee,* commented that "Hall having lost a father and two brothers by the savages; was ready and nerved for a desperate fight, whenever opportunity was afforded."[37] In his later years, when commenting on his frontier days, Hall said, "I am proud I have never been driven from my heritage."[38]

In late 1803 William Hall married Mary Brandon Alexander. When the ceremony took place at Locustland, the Hall plantation, Hall was 29 and Mary, or Polly as she was called, was 17. Her father, William Locke Alexander, had served in the American Revolution as a commander of the "Volunteer Spies" against the Cherokee Indians and was wounded in a battle at Seven Mile Mountain. Later commissioned a captain in Colonel Wade Hamptons' cavalry regiment, he served in several other major battles, including that of Cowpens.[39] The marriage of William and Polly produced eight children, three girls and five boys. One of them, Robert Hall, died during Hall's short term as governor. The second son, William Harrison Hall, served as a colonel in the Seminole War.[40]

A devout Methodist like her husband, Polly was also a model frontier housewife. In a marriage that lasted for more than 50 years, she supervised the household and was herself adept at such things as candlemaking, baking, and sewing the clothes.[41] According to Nancy Walker in her book on the governors' wives, *Out of a Clear Blue Sky,* Mrs. Hall's admirable traits characterized her as a "woman of virtue, forgetful of self, a dignified lady with a heart full of sympathy for her family and friends."[42]

Both Hall and Polly enjoyed horse racing. Hall would, after leaving Congress, serve as an officer in the Gallatin Jockey Club.[43] In the fall of 1804 horse racing was introduced to Gallatin. In one particular race General Jackson's prize filly, Indian Queen, was running against another popular horse, Polly Medley. The race attracted a large crowd including Hall and his petite young wife. As the horses started for the track, Mrs. Jackson reportedly said, "She is too little to run with Indian Queen." Petite Polly replied quickly, "Horses are like people, the smallest are usually the smartest." The exchange of comments did not create any problems. That night at a banquet to honor the opening of the races, General Jackson danced the first dance with Polly Hall.[44]

On the early frontier, relationships were quickly formed as men and women were caught up in the struggle to survive and in the need for companionship. A strong friendship could be a lasting thing and prove beneficial to both parties. The friendship between Hall and Andrew Jackson was just such a relationship. The campaign against the Creeks and the Battle of New Orleans would serve as the major forces in binding the two men together. Their first encounter probably occurred when both men were struggling to establish themselves. Throughout their lives each man held the other in high regard. Jackson would speak highly of Hall's conduct as an officer during the Creek War,[45] and Hall would later campaign vigorously for Jackson in his campaigns for the presidency.[46] Despite the mutual admiration, Hall did not always approve of Jackson's feuding ways. In the power struggle between John Sevier and Andrew Jackson which culminated in a duel, Hall was caught in the middle. Hall was a political follower of Sevier and felt that Jackson was in the wrong in the quarrel. In a report drawn up by Hall and four other legislators, they defended the actions of Sevier in the duel with Jackson.[47]

Years later, however, Colonel William Martin tried to get Hall to give incriminating evidence against Jackson concerning the mutiny of Tennessee volunteers in the Creek War. Hall indignantly replied that he refused to give "any statement of facts that took place fifteen years since, with a view to injure General Jackson's election to the presidency."[48] Hall and Jackson tacitly agreed to omit the Sevier quarrel from their conversations.[49]

On June 18, 1812, the United States declared war on Great Britain. For the second time in 40 years America was to engage England in conflict, this time not to win independence but to gain respect and to secure her place among other nations of the world. Numerous Tennesseans had been instrumental in persuading President Madison to support a declaration of war. Congressman John Rhea and Felix Grundy were members of the "War Hawks," a sabre-rattling group of Congressmen anxious to punish England for disrupting United States trade and impressing American sailors and to gain new lands for the growing young American nation. When the call came for volunteers, Tennessee was ready.

The state was divided into eastern and western military districts. Each had a "division" commanded by a major general. The eastern commander was William Cocke; the western, and senior, commander was Andrew Jackson. In reality the divisions were strong brigades. By 1811 each division's forces were organized into two regiments of foot riflemen, each having 900 men and a strong regiment of mounted cavalry. Commanding Jackson's infantry were William Hall and Thomas H. Benton. Jackson's old friend, John Coffee, was in charge of the mounted rifles, and Major William Carroll served as inspector general.[50] With the impending threat of British invasion in Louisiana, Secretary of War John Armstrong ordered Governor Willie Blount to dispatch 1500 men to lower Mississippi. More than 2000 answered the call.[51]

Hall had been elected "Colonel Commanding." The newly elected officer was described by Augustus Buell as a "solid citizen, an original pioneer of Tennessee. . . ."[52] His staff included nine officers.[53] They received their marching orders on January 7, 1813. Colonel Coffee was to take his cavalry regiment to Natchez via the Natchez Trace while the infantry moved down the Cumberland, floating by day and tying up at night.[54] The *Tennessee Gazette* reported that Hall's regiment arrived at Smithland, Kentucky, where the Cumberland empties into the Ohio, on January 18, 1813.[55] Early the next day Colonel Hall and Lieutenant Colonel Bradley inspected the river and found it so heavy with ice floes that further movement was delayed. On January 25th the trip continued. Four days later the forces reached the Mississippi in a snowstorm.

On January 27th Hall, along with General Jackson and Lieutenant Colonel Bradley, met to question Chaplain Lerner Blackman concerning the harshly moralizing manner in which he spoke to the critically ill. However, little came of the meeting. Blackman continued to counsel the sick and commented in a letter home that Jackson may have been a great general but that he knew very little about the need for salvation of men's souls.[56]

When the infantry reached Natchez, they found the cavalry was already there waiting. Also waiting was an order from General James Wilkinson to halt in the Natchez vicinity and to wait for further orders.[57] While in Natchez the armies received devastating news of the River Raisin defeat in the north and of the reported death of General James Winchester. Many of the volunteers wrote home telling their families that they yearned to go north and rectify the embarrassing defeat.[58] This news was followed by a war department order dismissing the Sumner County volunteers in Hall's regiment. Jackson refused to dismiss his volunteers so far from home without necessary provisions and did not start north until the materials needed were acquired. Because of hardships he shared with his men and the determination he showed on the return trip, he earned the nickname "Old Hickory."[59]

Fortunately the reports of Winchester's death proved false; instead he had been taken prisoner and held in Canada. Upon his release in April of 1814, Winchester returned to the United States to answer the charges of William Henry Harrison concerning his defeat. Winchester then returned to his mansion, Cragfont, and a series of testimonial dinners. Serving on the arrangement committee, Hall superintended a dinner for Winchester.[60]

Hall once again was called to serve in the military when on August 30, 1814, Creek Indians massacred the inhabitants of Fort Mims, Alabama. When it reached Tennessee the news brought forth a call for volunteers, and again the state responded readily. Having been promoted to brigadier general, Hall was given command of the first brigade which included two regiments, 1410 men, under the commands of Colonels Bradley and Pillow.[61] The first brigade, along with other units under Jackson's command, marched south to Alabama, where they built two forts, Fort Deposit and Fort Strother. Jackson then proceeded to track down the Creeks. On November 11th, Hall's brigade, serving as part of the volunteers, returned to Fort Strother to find the food stocks depleted. Facing the threat of starvation, many soldiers signed a petition requesting that Jackson return them to civilization. One group, under the command of Brigadier Isaac Roberts, started for home but was turned back by Jackson and another group of volunteers. After a meeting of the brigade commanders, Coffee's Brigade voted to stay, Roberts' men voted to leave in three or four days, and Hall's men voted to leave at once. In a letter to Governor Willie Blount, Jackson outlined the problem:

> General Hall's brigade then reported that after weighing maturely all the circumstances they had determined by the vow of every officer in the Brigade with the exception of General Hall himself to march back to meet the provisions at the same time

> recommending to me to permit the men to go to their homes . . .
> I did think they would have followed me through every danger
> and hardship without a murmur. They are the first to desert me.
> But the conduct of General Hall is as usual, firm and humane,
> he says he will stay and die in the camp before he will move the
> wounded or destroy the baggage or sully the glory they have
> already acquired.[62]

When supplies did not arrive, the army headed home. Fortunately
they met a beef supply train near Fort Strother. Jackson, with the
assistance of Coffee's cavalry, still found it necessary to threaten one
company that was determined to continue the trek home. Suspect-
ing that Hall's brigade was ready to desert, Jackson utilized threats of
death for desertion.[63]

The real issue was not food but the soldiers' interpretation of
their enlistment time. The brigade wanted to count the time spent at
home after the Natchez expedition toward their enlistment because
they had not been discharged after that campaign. Jackson did not
agree. In his opinion they still had longer to serve. Despite Jackson's
pleas that they stay, the troops were determined to go home. They
felt that they had a legal right to leave when their terms expired, and
they intended to exercise that right. As the day approached for the
terms to expire, Jackson became more determined to hold the volunteers with him. He wrote to General Coffee: "What may be attempted tomorrow I cannot tell, but should they attempt to march
off in mass, I shall do my duty, should the mutineers be too strong,
and you should meet any officers or men, returning without my written authority, you will arrest and bring them back in strings, and if
they attempt to disobey your order you will immediately fire on them
and continue the fire until they are subdued, you are to compel
them to return."

On December 9th General Hall informed Jackson that his
brigade planned to slip away during the night. Acting quickly,
Jackson ordered the volunteers' brigade into a formation facing the
fort's two brass cannon. Moving up and down the line Jackson at
first spoke pleadingly to the troops. Reminding the brigade of their
honor, he warned them to think of the disgrace that would fall on
each man who left. But they would never leave, he said in a matter-
of-fact tone, except over his dead body. Raising his voice he told the
brigade that he "was done with entreaty, it has been used long

enough, I will attempt it no more." Demanding an answer from them, Jackson ordered the artillerists to light their matches. Knowing full well that Jackson meant what he said, the officers met and assured him that their men would stay until reinforcements arrived. Despite this promise, the conduct of the brigade had a tremendous effect upon Jackson. In a letter to Rachel he sadly informed her that "My volunteers had sunk from the highest elevation of patriots to mere, whining, complaining, Sedioners and mutineers—to keep whom from open acts of mutiny I have been compelled to point my cannon against. This was a grating moment of my life. I felt the pangs of an effectionate parent, compelled from duty to chastise his child . . even when he knew death might ensue."[64] True to their word the brigade waited for reinforcements. They would not get away without additional insults from Jackson as "he addressed the volunteers in a manner calculated to insult and wound their feelings."[65] Marquis James, in his biography of Jackson, states that Hall's brigade was "read from camp." When reinforcements arrived, the brigade was issued two days' rations and started home to Tennessee under the command of Hall.[66]

The hard feelings of Jackson toward the brigade continued past the battlefields of Alabama. He and his close friends sought to discredit the conduct of Hall's men and publicly referred to the men as mutineers and deserters. Upon their return home, Hall and other officers of the brigade answered Jackson's charges on March 19, 1814, with a "statement of facts" in the Carthage *Gazette*. Siding with Hall's brigade, the editor of the *Gazette* took the position that the Tennessee volunteers were honorable and responsible men whose military service was not to be dealt with in a capricious or trifling manner by General Jackson or anyone else.[67] The argument was still continuing when Jackson was campaigning for president a decade later. Not all the wounds made by Jackson's charges had healed in Sumner County. In an effort to clear up the problem and to gain support for Jackson, his followers held a meeting in Gallatin to adopt resolutions in support of the candidate. William Hall opened the meeting with a strong statement on behalf of Jackson.[68]

With the signing of the Treaty of Ghent, war ended for Hall and his brigade. The general returned to his plantation but was not long out of the public eye. At a meeting in 1819 of delegates representing the militia companies of Sumner County, he was selected by a vote of

25-1 to serve on a committee campaigning against the Constitutional Convention at the next election.[69] He was also elected to the Tennessee House of Representatives where he served four terms before being elected in 1821 to the State Senate. He served consecutively in the 14th, 15th, 16th and 17th General Assemblies.[70] When the 17th General Assembly began, Hall was urged by several to try and gain the position of Speaker of the Senate. William Carroll wrote to him, "I have no hesitancy in saying you ought to be Speaker of the Senate. If you give authority to mention your name, I feel confident that there will be no opposition to produce that to which my best efforts shall be directed." Robert C. Foster also urged him to be a candidate. Others turned to Hall because of his close relationship with Jackson.[71] Ultimately Hall's decision to become a candidate was far more momentous than he could have imagined.

In 1827 Sam Houston was elected governor to succeed William Carroll who had served the allowed three consecutive terms. Carroll wanted to find someone who would carry on his programs, and Houston was a natural selection. Between visits with the Cherokees, Houston had served the state admirably. He had suffered a serious wound fighting the Creeks at Horseshoe Bend. While he conducted himself well in the state's political circles, few events of great magnitude occurred during his term. His downfall as governor came in 1829 when, for personal reasons, he resigned from office. Shortly after marrying Eliza Allen of Gallatin he had sent her home to her father after a serious quarrel. Despondent and suffering from the criticism of friends, Houston relinquished the governorship and returned to live with the Cherokees.

Houston's letter of resignation, delivered to Speaker of the Senate Hall, contained high praise for the Speaker who, as a result of Houston's decision to leave, ascended to the governorship.[72] William Hall was the first person from Sumner County to serve as Tennessee's chief executive. When, on April 16, 1829, he was sworn in as governor of the state,[73] the people of the county were indeed proud. On July 4, 1829, toasts were offered, one of them stating, "William Hall acting governor of Tennessee—In the field dispassionate and brave; in the state legislature his arrangements have been zealous and patriotic. May the people of Tennessee reward him according to his merits."[74]

The legislature had already ended its session when Hall became governor. A survey of his term reveals that his major duty was dealing with a large number of requests for pardons and sentence reductions. Nine pardon requests or sentence reductions were found recorded in Hall's gubernatorial papers. Of the nine requests, Hall acted on seven; he granted a full pardon in four of the cases and remitted sentences in the other three. Several of the cases merit comment: One request was for the pardon of a forger, Joseph Phillipson. The petition for his release was signed by several prominent Tennesseans, including Felix Grundy, Ephraim H. Foster, and George Washington Campbell. The penalty for forgery was harsh—30 lashes on the bare back, confinement for six months, the humiliation of enduring two hours of public display in the pillory each day for three consecutive days, and branding of the left thumb with a "T." Also a John Tompkins was convicted of fast dealing in a card game called faro but aroused so much public sympathy that Governor Hall remitted his prison term although he did have to pay court costs and a $50 fine. Another case involved a George Taylor who was convicted of manslaughter, his second such offense. Hall's judgment in this case was affected by a petition signed by one of the jurors who had found Taylor guilty.[75]

When on Monday, September 21, 1829, the 18th General Assembly met in Nashville, the leading officials of the state were William Hall, Governor; Daniel Graham, Secretary of State; Joel Walker, Speaker of the Senate; and Ephraim Foster, Speaker of the House.[76] Because Hall's full term lasted only five months and five days, few critical developments marked his short period of service. However, the General Assembly of 1829 was a progressive body and before it adjourned had passed several pieces of liberal legislation.[77] Hall's message to the assembly mentioned several key issues on which action should be taken, issues that were an extension of William Carroll's interrupted program.[78] A topical index of his speech reveals his concerns for banking, education, God, the resignation of Houston, the judiciary, loan sharks, and the state boundary dispute between Tennessee and Kentucky.[79]

Governor Hall's term lasted but ten days after he delivered his message to the legislature. With all of his legislative experience he was aware that his greatest contribution to the state would be the promotion of Carroll's program.[80] In fact, the assembly later did pass many acts that dealt with issues covered in Hall's speech, including an act providing for the building of a state penitentiary, an act to reform and amend the penal laws of the state, and one to establish a system of common schools and the appropriation of school funds. Acts were also passed to amend the Charter of the Bank of the State of Tennessee and to appropriate $150,000 for the improvement of navigation on state rivers.[81]

Throughout his life William Hall had an interest in education. His schooling was the typical country instruction of the period, but his penmanship was reported to be the best in the community.[82] His efforts to improve education in the state may have resulted from the success of his brother John who became the first teacher in Gallatin. No doubt his Uncle Samuel Doak also influenced his interest in education.[83] William Hall's participation in education came primarily through his role as a trustee for various academies. During his life he served as a trustee for Transmontania Academy, Rural Academy, and Bledsoe Female Academy. Hall was listed as one of the signers of a lottery to finance a Lancasterian School House in Cairo in 1819, but there is no indication that the school was built, the economic recession of 1819 probably ending the project.[84] He became involved in Bledsoe Female Academy, even going so far as to persuade a new principal to come to the academy from Nashville and drawing up a circular describing the school. When the school was incorporated in 1850, Hall was named as a trustee.[85] In his legislative message to the General Assembly, Hall informed the body that everyone had a duty to support education: " . . . the permanent good which necessarily results from a general diffusion of knowledge . . . makes it our duty to cherish with parental care, such resources as may be in our purpose for the encouragement of schools, colleges, and academies."[86]

After turning over the reins of government to William Carroll, Hall went home to Locustland. However, he soon returned to public service. The resignation of Sam Houston had caused considerable turmoil in Sumner County. Houston's young bride, Eliza, had been a resident of Gallatin, and many of the citizens of the community felt that Houston had besmirched her reputation. In 1830, a group assembled at the Gallatin Court House to determine whether or not Mrs. Houston's "amiable character has received an injury among those acquainted with her . . . ." A committee with William Hall as chairman was appointed to investigate.[87] When Houston received reports of the committee meeting he responded with an angry letter. At first he attacked Hall, expressing dismay at seeing his successor's name at the top of the committee's list. However, he quickly expressed his continued high estimation of Hall's character: "But upon a moment's reflection, I tended to regard it in a light, by no means prejudicial to myself, or unkind of you. And permit me to assure you sir, that no circumstance, within the scope, of remote probablity, can ever eliminate the high respect, which I have ever cherished for you, as a Patriot, a soldier, a Gentleman, and an honest man . . . ."[88]

Hall, still interested in public life after this somewhat dubious post, decided to run for Congress in 1831. He campaigned against Colonel Robert Burton, an eloquent and popular orator. Hall was not an exceptional speaker but presented his arguments in a logical manner and with such honesty and candor that the people in the district responded by electing him.[89] Although the contest was close in the district, with Hall receiving 4192 votes and Burton 3928, Hall carried Sumner County by a large margin, 1552 votes to 855.[90]

In this heated campaign, the Peggy Eaton affair was one of the issues. Mrs. Eaton, the widow of a Washington tavernkeeper, had married one of Jackson's cabinet officers and good friends, John Eaton. Her past was a much discussed item among the gossipers of the capital and became a key issue when the wives of Jackson's cabinet members refused to accept her into their social circle.[91] The blue-blooded residents of Gallatin and northeast Nashville resented the Eaton affair. One of Hall's supporters was Robert Desha, a former Congressman from the district who placed his full support behind Hall, even going on the stumping tour for him. In several speeches Desha denounced the secretary's lady as an "abandoned" woman. A Burton supporter differed with Desha and challenged him to a fight. Desha won the fight and Hall the election.[92]

When Hall reached Washington to become a member of the 22nd Congress, he was among a select group. Senators for the state were Felix Grundy and Hugh Lawson White; notable members of the House from Tennessee were John Bell, Cave Johnson, and James K. Polk.[93] Hall served only one term and no records can be found of his participation in any debates or of any laws he proposed.[94] He did, however, support a pension bill for fighters of the Tennessee Indian Wars of 1787-1795.[95]

After his term ended in Congress, Hall did not run for political office again. He returned to his plantation to farm but remained active politically and served the people of Tennessee on several occasions. During the presidential election of 1848, Hall was chosen by his fellow Democrats of Sumner County to head the party. His reputation as a Democrat was such that his fellow party members in the county felt he could swing the vote for the Democratic candidate, Lewis Cass. Cass was opposed by the Whig candidate, Zachary Taylor, a Mexican war hero. Taylor carried the national election but failed to carry Sumner County; Cass received 1994 votes to Taylor's 992.[96] In 1849 the people of the county again turned to Hall. When plans were made to charter a part of the railroad from Nashville to Louisville, Hall was selected as a delegate to attend meetings of the state legislature to campaign for the charter.[97]

The census records of 1850 show that Hall was a prosperous citizen of the county and the fifth wealthiest man in the Third Congressional District.[98] Locustland had grown from the original house and tract of 1785 to an estate covering 700 acres and valued at $17,500.[99] Hall grew tobacco and probably the other standard cash crops of Middle Tennessee.[100] He ran the estate without the aid of a professional manager, although he must have had some help; the census records for 1850 show that two of his sons, Richard and William, were also living on the farm with their families. Together they watched over the work of 49 slaves.[101]

Continued antagonisms were plaguing the country. The slavery issue had grown, and, with the acquisition of the Mexican Cession, the debate began to rage out of control. Southerners spoke in earnest of secession. In 1849 prospective secessionists held a meeting in Jackson, Mississippi, drew up resolutions concerning the land acquired from the war, and called for a second such meeting.[102] On June 9, 1845, Hall, a slaveholder, expressed his feelings toward the North and the growing rift between the North and South in a letter to Colonel William Martin. Colonel Martin had requested Hall's opinion about the pension bill for those men who had engaged in the Indian wars from 1787-1795. Hall stated that the bill had failed because of the attitude of the Congressmen from the North and East. He informed Martin that "I thought then and still think that the members in Congress from the North, never will agree that we the people of the South and West should ever enjoy equitable rights and privileges as them in anything whatever, if they can prevent it . . . ."[103]

The second meeting was held to discuss secession. Plans were made for delegates from the southern slaveholding states to meet in Nashville in June of 1850. The chief purpose of the meeting was conceded to be the presentation of a united protest from the South against the attempt to exclude slavery from the newly acquired territories, an exclusion called for by the Wilmot Proviso.[104] When the convention met for its first session on June 5, 1850, at McKendree Methodist Church in Nashville, not all Southerners were in support.[105] Sam Houston, the man Hall had succeeded, addressed a crowd in Knoxville stating in no uncertain terms how he felt about the convention. He asserted that a dissolution of the union was contemplated by those who originated the convention and that "every damned rascal who attends it, or advocates it ought to be hung with a damned rough halter."[106]

Despite Houston's attitude, Hall chose to attend. Delegates for Tennessee were chosen by the voters, and the people of Sumner County turned once again to William Hall. Hall at 75 was the oldest delegate at the convention. The typical delegate was a Democrat, 45, a Southerner by birth, well-educated, most often a lawyer or farmer, and generally a slave owner, although many of the Tennessee delegates did not own slaves. No record can be found of any part Hall played in the meeting; he apparently did not serve on any committees or propose any resolutions. The first session adopted a series of moderate resolutions and an "Address to the People" of the southern states which was more radical in tone. With the passage of the Compromise of 1850, which temporarily eased the tension in September, a November session was a dying gesture which Governor Hall did not attend.[107]

Hall went home to live out his last few years. There he recorded his early experiences on the Tennessee frontier for publication in the *Southwestern Monthly*. Many historians later used Hall's work as a major reference source. Historians such as John Carr (*Early Times in Middle Tennessee*), J. G. M. Ramsey (*Annals of Tennessee*), and Edward Albright (*Early History of Middle Tennessee*) found the work to be invaluable and a highly accurate source.[108] During his last years Hall corresponded with numerous people who requested information about the early history of the state. In one letter he noted that he would try to have a picture made but that he had lost the sight of his left eye and seldom went far from home.[109]

The comradeship of the pioneers was still strong in 1851. During that year Hall held a reunion of the "old pioneers" at his estate, establishing a custom that continued for several years.[110] As late as 1856, the year of Hall's death, the reunions were still being held and the pioneers were still in contact. John Carr, in his *Early Times in Middle Tennessee*, noted that he, James McCann, James Cartwright, Joseph and John Brown, and William Hall were the last living settlers who had come to the area in the period 1790-1795.[111]

On October 7, 1856, William Hall, accidental governor of Tennessee, died after a painful illness of twelve months.[112] Throughout his life Hall proved to be a conscientious public servant who was always ready to do his duty. Most of the people who came in contact with him found his honesty to be refreshing. His frontier upbringing greatly affected his life and taught him the value of sincerity and directness. His powers of endurance, tenacity of purpose, and high daring helped to signal him out as a scout.[113] According to George Winchester, everyone who came into contact with Hall found him ". . . simple, plain, and unostentatious in his manners; generous, confiding, and tolerant in his disposition . . . . In his private business concerns, he was rigourously just, punctual in his engagements and as sensitive of his honor, as a man of the world, as a woman of her virtue: 'his word was his bond.' " When elected to office he was "ever the incorruptible patriot and the inflexible man of honor."[114] A fellow legislator told Winchester a few days after Hall's death that the late governor was one of the few men he had ever known in public life who when he became aware that he was wrong would publicly set himself right. William Hall, eighth governor of Tennessee, was, in the words of John Trotwood Moore, "one of the purest men to ever hold the exalted position of governor of Tennessee."[115]

NOTES

1. Eric Lacy, ed., *Antebellum Tennessee* (Berkeley: McCutchan Publishing Company, 1969), p. 79.

2. Robert White, *Messages of the Governors* (Nashville: Tennessee Historical Commission, 1952), pp. 252-256.

3. Walter Durham, *Old Sumner: A History of Sumner County, Tennessee* (Gallatin: Sumner County Public Library, 1972) p. 201.

4. John Raimo and Robert Sobol, eds., *Biographical Directory of the U. S. Governors* (West Port, Connecticut: Meckler, 1978), p. 118.

5. Stanley J. Folmsbee, Robert E. Corlew, and Enoch L. Mitchell, *Tennessee: A Short History* (Knoxville: The University of Tennessee Press, 1969), p. 172.

6. Robert McBride and Don Robinson, *Biographical Directory of the Tennessee General Assembly* (Nashville, 1970), pp. 321-322.

7. "Summer Ambuscade," *Nashville Tennessean Magazine,* May 20, 1956.

8. Ibid.

9. *Nashville Tennessean,* April 17, 1969.

10. Walter Durham, *Great Leap Westward: A History of Sumner County, Tennessee from its Beginnings to 1805* (Gallatin: Sumner County Public Library, 1972), pp. 136-137.

11. Ibid.

12. "Summer Ambuscade," *Nashville Tennessean Magazine.*

13. *Nashville Tennessean,* April 17, 1969.

14. "Summer Ambuscade," *Nashville Tennessean Magazine.*

15. Ibid.

16. *Nashville Tennessean,* April 17, 1969.

17. Edward Albright, *Early History of Middle Tennessee* (Nashville: Brandon, 1909), pp. 29-30.

18. Ibid., p. 17.

19. Ibid., pp. 29-30.

20. Durham, Great Leap Westward, pp. 57-58.

21. Albright, p. 124.

22. Ibid., p. 126.

23. Ibid., p. 119.

24. Ibid., p. 126.

25. Durham, *Great Leap Westward,* p. 189.

26. Joy Cisco, *Historic Sumner County,* Tennessee (Nashville, 1909), pp. 255-258.

27. Albright, p. 128.

28. Ibid., pp. 127-130.

29. A. W. Putnam, *History of Middle Tennessee or Life and Times of General James Robertson* (Nashville: Putnam, 1859), p. 256.

30. William Hall, *Early History of the Southwest,* ed. Robert Horsley (Nashville: Parthenon Press, 1968), p. 42.

31. Durham, *Great Leap Westward,* p. 72.

32. Ibid., p. 76.

33. Hall, p. 42.

34. Ibid., pp. 21-26.

35. Ibid., pp. 26-27.

36. J. G. M. Ramsey, The Annals of Tennessee (Kingsport: Kingsport Press, 1926), pp. 601-602.

37. Putnam, pp. 416-417.

38. *Nashville Tennessean,* April 17, 1969.

39. Letter of Peytonia Barry to S. M. Young, in the William Hall Papers, Tennessee State Library and Archives, Nashville.

40. Nancy Walker, *Out of a Clear Blue Sky* (Cleveland: Nancy Walker, 1971), p. 86.

41. Ibid.

42. Ibid., p. 87.

43. Durham, *Old Sumner,* p. 307.

44. Durham, *Great Leap Westward,* pp. 178-179.

45. John Bassett, *Correspondence of Andrew Jackson* (Washington, D. C.: Carnegie Institute, 1926-1935), p. 346.

46. Durham, *Old Sumner,* p. 127.

47. William Hall Papers, TSLA.

48. Letter of William Hall to William Martin, in the William Hall Papers, TSLA.

49. Augustus Buell, *History of Andrew Jackson* (New York: Charles Scribner and Sons, 1909), p. 262.

50. Ibid., p. 231.

51. Ibid., pp. 258-259.

52. Ibid., p. 262.

53. Durham, *Old Sumner,* pp. 50-51.

54. Ibid., pp. 51-52.
55. *Democratic Clarion,* March 3, 1813; *Tennessee Gazette,* March 3, 1813.
56. Durham, *Old Sumner,* pp. 53-54.
57. Ibid., p. 55.
58. John Coffee Papers, Tennessee State Library and Archives.
59. Durham, *Old Sumner,* p. 59.
60. Ibid., p. 260.
61. Buell, p. 261.
62. Durham, *Old Sumner,* pp. 64-65.
63. Marquis James, *Andrew Jackson, Border Captain* (New York: Grossett and Dunlap, 1937), p. 172.
64. Robert Remini, *Andrew Jackson and the Course of the American Empire* (New York: Harper and Row, 1977), pp. 200-201.
65. Durham, *Old Sumner,* p. 68.
66. James, *Andrew Jackson, Border Captain,* p. 175.
67. Will Hale, Tennessee and Tennesseans (Chicago and New York: Lewis Publishing Company, 1913), p. 248.
68. Durham, *Old Sumner,* p. 127.
69. Nashville *Whig,* May 22, 1819.
70. McBride and Robinson, p. 322.
71. James Phelan, *History of Tennessee* (Boston and New York: Houghton, Miflin and Company, 1888), p. 299.
72. Ibid.
73. *National Banner,* April 17, 1829; Nashville *Whig,* April 17, 1829.
74. Durham, *Old Sumner,* pp. 210-211.
75. William Hall Papers, TSLA.
76. Tennessee, *Public and Private Acts of Tennessee, 1829-1830,* (Memphis: Memphis Public Library).
77. White, p. 255.
78. Ibid., p. 260.
79. Ibid.
80. Ibid.
81. *Public and Private Acts of Tennessee.*
82. Walker, p. 82.
83. Durham, *Great Leap Westward,* p. 136.
84. McBride and Robinson, p. 322.
85. Durham, *Old Sumner,* p. 312.
86. Ibid., pp. 322-325.
87. White, pp. 255-256.
88. Durham, *Old Sumner,* p. 201.
89. Hall, p. 44.
90. Durham, *Old Sumner,* p. 211.
91. Richard C. Wade, Howard B. Wilder, and Louise C. Wade, *The History of the United States* (Boston: Houghton, Miflin and Company, 1972), p. 244.
92. Marquis James, *Portrait of a President* (New York: Grossett and Dunlap, 1937), p. 248.
93. *Biographical Director of the U. S. Congress, 1774-1971* (Washington, D.C.: U. S. Government Printing Office, 1971), p. 118.
94. Ibid.
95. Hall, p. 242.
96. Durham, *Old Sumner,* p. 395.
97. Ibid., p. 231.
98. *United States Census Records* (Sumner County, Tennessee, 1850).
99. Thelma Jennings, "A Reappraisal of the Nashville Convention of 1850" (Dissertation: University of Tennessee, December 1968), Appendix C.
100. Durham, *Old Sumner,* p. 107.
101. *United States Census Records.*

102. Jennings, "Reappraisal of Nashville Convention."
103. Hall, Letter of William Martin.
104. Dallas Herndon, *Nashville Convention of 1850* (Reprinted from Alabama Historical Society, 1904).
105. Nashville *Union,* June 5, 1850.
106. Jennings, pp. 136-137.
107. Ibid., p. 517.
108. Hall, p. 41.
109. Ibid., p. 39.
110. Ibid., p. 41.
111. John Carr, *Early Times in Middle Tennessee* (Nashville: Parthenon Press, 1857), p. 101.
112. Ibid., p. 41.
113. Ibid., p. 42
114. Hall, p. 43.
115. John T. Moore *Tennessee, the Volunteer State* (Chicago: S. P. Clarke and Co., 1923), 2:139.

BIBLIOGRAPHY

BOOKS
Albright, Edward. *Early History of Middle Tennessee.* Nashville: Brandon, 1909.
Bassett, John. *Correspondence of Andrew Jackson.* Washington, D. C.: Carnegie Institute, 1926-1935.
_____ *Life of Andrew Jackson.* New York, 1911.
Biographical Directory of U. S. Congress, 1774-1971. Washington, D.C.: U. S. Goverment Printing Office, 1971.
Buell, Augustus, *History of Andrew Jackson.* New York: Charles Scribner and Sons, 1909.
Carr, John. *Early Times in Middle Tennessee.* Nashville: Parthenon Press, 1857.
Cisco, Joy. *Historic Sumner County, Tennessee,* Nashville, 1909.
Durham, Walter, *Great Leap Westward: A History of Sumner County, Tennessee from its Beginnings to 1805.* Gallatin: Sumner County Public Library, 1969.
_____ *Old Sumner: A History of Sumner County, Tennessee.* Gallatin: Sumner County Public Library, 1972.
Folmsbee, Stanley J.; Corlew, Robert E.; and Mitchell, Enoch L. *Tennessee: A Short History.* Knoxville: The University of Tennessee Press, 1969.
Hale, Will. *Tennessee and Tennesseans.* Chicago and New York: Lewis Publishing Company, 1913.
Hall, William. *Old Sumner: Early History of the Southwest,* 1852; reprint ed. by Robert Horsely. Nashville: Parthenon Press, 1968.
Herndon, Dallas. *Nashville Convention of 1850.* Reprint from Alabama Historical Society, 1904.
James, Marquis. *Portrait of a President.* New York: Grossett and Dumlap, 1937.
_____ *Andrew Jackson, Border Captain.* New York: Grossett and Dunlap, 1933.
Lacy, Eric. *Antebellum Tennessee, A Documentary History.* Berkeley: McCutchan Publishing Co., 1969.
McBride, Robert and Robinson, Dan. *Biographical Directory of the Tennessee General Assembly.* Nashville, 1970.
Moore, John T. *Tennessee, the Volunteer State.* Chicago: S. P. Clarke and Company, 1923.
Phelan, James, *History of Tennessee.* Boston and New York: Houghton, Miflin and Company, 1888.
Putnam, A. W. *History of Middle Tennessee or Life and Times of General James Robertson.* Nashville: Putnam, 1859.
Raimo, John and Sobol, Robert. ed. *Biographical Directory of U. S. Governors.* West Port, Connecticut: Meckler, 1978.
Ramsey, J. G. M. *The Annals of Tennessee.* Kingsport: Kingsport Press, 1926.

Remini, Robert, *Andrew Jackson and the Course of the American Empire*. New York: Harper and Row, 1977.
United States Census Records, 1850.
Wade, Richard C.; Wilder, Howard B.; and Wade, Louise C. *The History of the United States*. Boston: Houghton, Miflin and Company, 1972.
Walker, Nancy. *Out of a Clear Blue Sky*. Cleveland: Nancy Walker, 1971.
White, Robert, *Messages of the Governors of Tennessee, 1796-1921*. Nashville: Tennessee Historical Commission, 1952.

NEWSPAPERS
Democratic Clarion, March 3, 1813.
Nashville Tennessean, April 17, 1969.
Nashville Union, June 5, 1850.
Nashville *Whig,* May 22, 1819 and April 17, 1829.
National Banner, April 17, 1829.
"Sumner Ambuscade," *Nashville Tennessean Magazine,* May 20, 1956.
Tennessee Gazette, March 3, 1813.

MANUSCRIPTS
John Coffee Papers. Tennessee State Library and Archives, Nashville.
William Hall Papers, Tennessee State Library and Archives, Nashville.

PUBLISHED OFFICIAL DOCUMENTS
Tennessee. *Public and Private Acts of Tennessee, 1829-1830*. Memphis Public Library, Memphis, Tennessee.

UNPUBLISHED WORKS
Jennings, Thelma. "A Reappraisal of the Nashville Convention of 1850." Dissertation: University of Tennessee. December, 1968.

INDEX

Abingdon, Va., 64
Academies (chartered in Tn.), 107
Adams, John, 21, 24, 48, 49, 63
Adams, John Quincy, 139, 156-157, 160
Alabama, 55, 134, 139, 153, 170
Alabama River, Al., 153
Alamo, Tx., 167
Albright, Edward, 199
Alexander, Mary B., 188-189
Alexander, William, L., 188
Allen, Eliza, 194, 196
Allen, John, 161
Allen, Robert, 161
Allison, David, 23, 83
Allison, John, 113
American Party, 172
American Revolution, 64, 120, 124, 150, 179, 188
Anderson County, Tn., 66-67
Anderson, Joseph, 11, 66
Andrew Jackson (steamboat), 123
Appalachian Mountains, 1
Arkansas, 110-111, 162-163
Arkansas Gazette, 164, 172
Armstrong, James, 13
Armstrong, John, 190
Armstrong, Martin, 51
Articles of Confederation, 4, 120
Ashe, John, 10
Atkinson, Matthew, 66
Atkinson, William, 66
Austin, Stephen F., 162, 166, 167-168
Austin, Tx., 169

Bailey, Joe, 99
Baker, Ann, 83
Baker, Hannah, 80
Baker, John, 83
Baker, Lucinda, 83
Baker, William, 80
Balch, Alfred, 142
Baltimore, Md., 173
Bank of the State of Tennessee, 100, 103, 196
Bank of the United States, 128-129, 132, 141
Baptist Church, 171
Battle of New Orleans, 92
Beard, John, 18, 197
Bell, John, 120, 141-143, 171, 173
Benton, Jesse, 125-126, 140
Benton, Thomas Hart, 126, 152, 171, 190
Bertie County, N.C., 2

Big Pigeon River, N.C., 37
Blackman, Lerner, 190
Blackstone (law reference), 155
Bledsoe Female Academy, 196
Bledsoe, Isaac, 182
Bledsoe's Fort, 180, 183-184
Bledsoe's Lick, 180
Blount, Barbara Gray, 2
Blount College, 19, 76, 84
Blount, Eliza Ann, 83
Blount Hall. See Craven County, N.C.
Blount, Hannah, 80
Blount, Jacob, 2, 80, 89
Blount, John Gray, 2, 16
Blount Journal, 97
Blount, Lucinda, 83
Blount Mansion, picture of, 17; noted, 82
Blount, Reading, 9
Blount, William, picture of, 3; noted, 37-38, 44-47, 49-51, 57, 79, 82, 97-98, 185; life of, 1-27
Blount, Willie, picture of, 81; noted, 11, 25, 49-50, 98-99, 190-191; life of, 79-93
Blue Ridge Mountains, 150
Bonaparte, Napoleon, 70-71
Boone, Daniel, 2
Bradford, Cecelia, 123
Bradford, Henry, 124
Brazos River, Tx., 165, 168
Breckinridge, John C., 173
Brown, John, 200
Brown, Joseph, 200
Buchanan's Station, Tn., 18
Buell, Augustus, 125-127, 190
Buffalo Bayou, Tx., 168
Bunker Hill, battle of, 120
Burnet, David, 169
Burr, Aaron, 22
Burton, Robert, 197
Byers, James, 24

Calhoun, John C., 110, 154
Calhoun, Tn., 113
Calhoun Treaty of 1819, 111
Cambell, Jane McMinn, 98
Campbell, Ann, 64
Campbell, Arthur, 40
Campbell, David, 11, 26, 42, 64, 71-72
Campbell, George W., 90, 109, 195
Campbell, Mary Hamilton, 64
Campbell's Station, 76
Canada, 124

Cannon, Newton, 141, 159
Carey, James, 24
Carlisle, Pa., 63-64
Carondelet, Baron Hector, 15
Carr, John, 199-200
Carroll, Charles (of Carrollton), 120
Carroll, Charles (son of William), 120, 124
Carroll County, Tn., 113
Carroll, Daniel, 120
Carroll, John, 120
Carroll, Mary Montgomery, 120
Carroll, Nathaniel, 126
Carroll, Thomas (father of William), 120
Carroll, Thomas, (son of William), 124
Carrollton, Md., 120
Carroll, William Henry (son of William), 124
Carroll, William, picture of, 121; noted, 155, 159-162, 190, 194-196; life of, 119-144
Carthage, Tn., 101
Cartwright, James, 200
Cass, Lewis, 198
Castalian Springs, 182
Caswell, Richard, 38, 44
Catholic Church, 120, 167
Cavet's Station, Tn., 45
Census, of 1790, 120; of 1701, 1; of 1795, 20
Charleston, S.C., 36
Cheraw, S.C., 156
Cherokee Agency, 110-111, 114
Cherokee Indians, 13, 32-35, 41-42, 45, 54, 69, 107-112, 114, 142, 149, 151, 154, 162, 164, 169, 182
Cherokee Treaty of 1817, 110-111
Chickamauga Indians, 13-14, 17, 19, 41
Chickasaw Indians, 14, 17, 20, 67, 111-112, 114, 142
Chickasaw Purchase, 112-113
Chisholm, John, 23-24
Choctaw Indians, 15, 17, 20, 67, 164
City Cemetery (in Nashville), 143
City Hotel (in Nashville), 126
Civil War, 124, 149
Claiborne County, Tn., 66
Claiborne, William C. C., 66
Clarksville, Tn., 21, 92, 100
Clay, Henry, 139-140, 156-157
Clinch River, Tn., 13, 47-48
Coahuila, 166
Cobb, William, noted, 11, 16; home of, see Rocky Mount.
Cocke, William, 21-22, 40, 46, 84, 90, 190
Coffee, John, 190, 194
Coke (law reference), 155
College of New Jersey, 80

Colorado River, Tx., 168
Columbia, Tn., 100-101
Comanche Indians, 165-166
Commission Book of Governor John Sevier, 98
Compact of 1806, 106, 133
Compromise of 1850, 171, 199
Confederate States of America, 173-174
Constitutional Convention, of 1796, 21, 46, 64, 98; of 1824, 194
Constitutional Union Party, 173
Constitution of Tennessee, 21, 136-138, 141, 144
Continental Congress, 120
Conway, Major General George, 50-51, 72-73
Cooper, Hannah, 97
Cooper, James, 97
Cooper, Rosannah, 97
Cowpens, battle of, 188
Coyatee, 16
Cragfont, 191
Cramer, Zadoc, 123
Craven County, N.C., 2, 80
Crawford, William H., 156
Creek Indians, 7, 13-15, 17, 20, 35, 42, 45, 55, 67, 126-127, 142, 153, 164, 182-183, 191
Creek War, 189, 191-192
Crockett, Davy, 2
Crockett, Robert, 183
Cumberland College, 84
Cumberland Gap, 124
Cumberland Masonic Lodge, 154-155, 160
Cumberland River, Tn., 1, 123, 134, 183
Cumberland Turnpike, 69
Cumberland Valley, 34, 37, 41, 83, 179, 182

Dauphin County, Pa., 63
Davidson County, Tn., 7, 46, 72, 103, 113, 128, 162, 183
Dearborn, Secretary of War Henry, 52, 68
Declaration of Independence, 120
de Gardoqui, Don Diego, 43
Delaware River, N.J., 64
Democratic Party, Erwin-Grundy faction of, 129; Overton-Blount faction of, 128-131
Department of Nacogdoches, 167
Depression of 1819, 129, 131
Desha, Robert, 197
Dew, John, 142
Dickinson College, Pa., 63
Dickinson, John, 125
Dix, Dorothea, 136

Doak, Samuel, 82, 179, 196
Donelson, Andrew J., 162
Donelson, Daniel S., 162
Donelson, John, 26, 182
Donelson, Stockley, 51, 73
Douglas, Stephen A., 173
Dragging Canoe (Cherokee Chief), 35
Dramatic Club of Nashville, 155
Draper, Dr. Lyman, 57
Driver, Carl S., 52, 75
Duck River Ridge, Tn., 68
Duck River, Tn., 54, 69
Dumplin Creek, treaty of, 41
Dyer County, Tn., 113

Eaton, John, 140, 197
Eaton, Peggy, 197
Emuckfau, battle of, 119, 126
Endorsement Law, 102
Enotochopco, battle of, 119, 127
Episcopal Church, 76
Erwin, Andrew, 129
Erwin, John P., 157-158
Etowah, battle of, 45, 57
Eustis, William, 85-86, 89-90

Farmers and Mechanics Bank of Nashville, 101
Farmers' and Merchants' Bank (of Nashville), 129
Fayette County, Tn., 113
Fayetteville, Tn., 101
Federalists, 9, 21-23, 46, 98
Ferguson, Major Patrick, 36
Fillmore, Millard, 172
First Baptist Church (of Nashville), 159-160
First Court of Pleas and Quarter Sessions of Sumner County, 183, 191-194, 196-199
First United States Infantry, 153
Fisk, Moses, 69
Ford, Colonel, 50
Fort Blount, 180
Fort Deposit, 191
Fort Gibson, Ok., 163-166
Fort Mims, Al., 90, 153, 191
Fort Nashborough, Tn., 182
Fort Smith, Ark., 163
Fort Stanwix, treaty of, 32
Fort Strother, Al., 90, 191, 194
Foster, Ephraim H., 143, 195
Foster, Robert C., 99, 194
France, 11, 23, 32, 70-71
Franklin, state of, 5-7, 32, 39-42
Franklin, Tn., 67-68, 101
French Broad River, Tn., 37, 39, 45, 100, 105, 108-109

French Lick, Tn., 182
French Revolution, 71

Gainesboro, Tn., 180
Gallady, Isaac, 155
Gallatin, Albert, 122
Gallatin Jockey Club, 188
Gallatin, Tn., 101, 161-162, 180, 183, 194, 196
Galveston, Tx., 169
Ganier, Albert, 180
Garrard, James, 70
General Assembly of 1829, 195
Gentry, Dianna Rogers, 164, 166
Georgia, 6, 38, 42, 156
Ghent, treaty of, 193
Gibson County, Tn., 113
Gibson, William, 180
Glasgow, James, 51, 74
Goliad, Tx., 168
Gonzales, Tx., 167
Goose Creek, Tn., 184
Gordon, John, 111
Graham, Daniel, 195
Grand River, Ok., 163
Great Britain, 2, 11, 15, 23, 32, 34
Great Smoky Mountains, 150
Greene County, state of Franklin, 6, 42; Southwest Territory, 19; N.C., 39, 44; Tn., 55, 72; Va., 64
Greeneville (capital of Franklin), 41
Greeneville College, 19, 76
Greenfield, battle of, 186-188
Greenfield Fort, 185
Green River, Ky., 70
Grundy, Felix, 101, 103, 120, 128-130, 189, 195, 197
Guadalupe Hidalgo, treaty of, 172
Gulf of Mexico, 134

Halifax, N.C., 35
Hall, James, 184
Hall, John, 180, 196
Hall, Richard, 185, 198
Hall, Robert, 188
Hall, Thankful Doak, 179, 185
Halls Station, Tn., 180-182
Hall, William Harrison (son of William), 188, 198
Hall, William, picture of, 181; noted, 82, 140; life of, 179-200
Hall, William, Sr. (father of William), 179-185
Hamilton, David, 64
Hamilton District, Tn., 49, 64, 66
Hamilton, John, 183
Hampton, Wade, 188
Hanging Maw (Cherokee Chief), 18

Haralson, H., 162
Hardeman County, Tn., 113
Hardin County, Tn., 113
Hard Labor, treaty of, 32
Harpeth Shoals, Tn., 123
Harrisburg, Pa., 139
Harrisburg, Tx., 168
Harrison, James, 180
Harrison, William Henry, 143, 191
Hawkins, Benjamin, 10, 89
Hawkins County, Tn., 16, 97-98, 115
Hawkins, Sarah, 32, 56
Hayne, A. F, 128
Hays, James, 186-187
Haywood County, Tn., 113
Henderson County, Tn., 113
Henderson, Judge Richard, 34
Hendersonville, Tn., 123
Henley, David, 24
Henry County, Tn., 113
Henry, Patrick, 10
Hillsboro, N.C., 37
Hiwassee District, 109, 111, 142
Hiwassee River, Tn., 109, 114
Holston River, 13, 16, 32, 37-38, 58, 105, 108-109
Holston, treaty of the, 13, 24
Holston Valley, 32, 41
Hopewell, S.C., 41
Hopewell, treaty of, 7-8, 12, 41, 45, 47
Horn, Stanley F., 180
Horseshoe Bend, 91, 194; battle of, 119, 126-127, 153
Hot Springs, Ark., 166
Houston County, Ga., 38
Houston, Eliza Allen, 160-162, 166
Houston, Elizabeth Paxton, 150-152
Houston, James, 21, 154
Houston, John (great grandfather of Sam) 149-150
Houston, John H., (cousin of Sam), 166
Houston, Robert, 150
Houston, Sam, picture of, 148; noted, 21, 93, 120, 140, 179, 194, 196-197, 199; life of, 149-174
Houston, Samuel (father of Sam), 150-151
Hume, Reverend William, 161-162
Huntsman, Adam, 136
Huntsville, Tx., 174

Illiad (Pope's translation), 151
"Immortal Thirteen," 143
Indian Queen (horse), 188
Indian Territory, 142
Ireland, 63, 120, 149
Irion, Dr. Robert, 167
Irion, Samuel Houston, 167

Iroquois Indians, 32

Jackson, Andrew, 5, 16, 21, 23, 25, 27, 49-52, 55-56, 58, 64, 66, 72-75, 79, 82-83, 89-92, 103, 110-111, 113, 120, 122, 125-128, 130-131, 139-143, 152-160, 162-163, 165-166, 168, 188, 189-193, 197
Jackson County, Tn., 66-67
Jackson Jubilee, 143
Jackson, Ms., 198
Jackson, Rachel, 160, 188-189, 193
James, Marquis, 74-75, 193
Jackson-McMinn Treaty, See Cherokee Treaty of 1817.
Jay, John, 8-9
Jefferson, Thomas, 46, 63, 67, 71, 98, 110
Jennings, Reverend Obadiah, 162
Johnson, Andrew, 143
Johnson, Cave, 197
Johnson, Lyttleton, 125
Johnson, Thomas, 99
Johnston, Samuel (governor of North Carolina), 44
Jones, Anson, 170
Jonesborough, (Jonesboro), Tn., 6, 39, 64, 100-101

Kansas-Nebraska Act, 172
Kentucky, 34, 158-159
Kentucky-Tennessee Boundary, 70, 100, 108, 114
Key, Francis Scott, 165
Kincade, David, 98
Kincade, Mary, 98
Kincade, Rebecca, 98
King's College, 80
King's Mountain, battle of, 36, 57
Kirk, John, 43-44
Knox County, Tn., 16
Knox, Henry, 17, 20
Knoxville Gazette, founding of, 16; noted, 52, 74
Knoxville, Tn., 16, 19, 21, 45, 55, 57, 66, 69, 74, 98-103, 124, 135, 152

Lamar, Mirabeau Buonaparte, 169
Lancasterian School House, 196
Lea, Margaret, 170-171, 173-174
Lea, Nancy, 170
League, H. H., 162
Lebanon, Tn., 155
Lewis, Joel, 50
Lewis, William B., 140
Lexington, Va., 150
Liberty Hall Academy, Va., 64
Lick Creek, p., 180

The Life of Caius Marius, 163
Lincoln, Abraham, 173
Liston, Robert, 24
"Little Magician." See Martin Van Buren.
Little Owl (Cherokee Chief), 184
Little River, 13
Little Rock, Ark., 163
Little Tennessee River, Tn., 1, 13, 48, 109, 111
Long Island, treaty of, 35
Louisiana, 70-72, 139
Lucustland (Hall plantation), 188, 196, 198

Macadam roads, 105
Madison County, Tn., 113
Madison, James, 22, 55, 122, 152, 189
Malcom, Samuel B., 24
Mann, Horace, 134
Marble Springs, picture of, 58; noted, 57
Marion, Al., 170
Marion County, Tn., 112
Marion, General Francis, 36
Market Street (in Nashville), 155
Martin Academy, 180
Martin, Alexander (governor of North Carolina), 7
Martin, William, 189, 198
Maryland, 120, 122
Maryville, Tn., 21, 150
Masonic Grand Lodge of Tennessee, 160
Matamoras, 167
McCann, James, 200
McGillivray, Alexander, 7
McHenry, Secretary of War, 47
McKendree Methodist Church, 199
McLemore, John, 140
McMinn Academy, 108
McMinn County, Tn., 112
McMinn, Hannah, 97-98
McMinn, Hetty, 99
McMinn, Jane, 97
McMinn, Joseph, picture of, 96; noted, 21, 82, 133, 155; life of, 97-115
McMinn, Robert, 97
McMinn, Sarah, 97
McMinnville, Tn., 115
McNairy County, Tn., 113
Meigs, Return J., 67, 109
Memphis, Tn., 114, 124
Meriwether, David, 110
Mero District, 1, 11, 13, 44, 46, 49-50, 52, 66, 124
Mexico, 140-141, 165-168, 172, 198
Military Affairs Committee (Congress), 155
Minor, Lucian, 113

Mississippi River, 1, 9, 15, 23, 104, 111-112, 134
Mississippi, territory of, 67; state of, 139, 142
Missouri, 126, 152, 158
Missouri Compromise, 172
Mobile, Al., 125, 134, 170
Monongahela River, 122
Monroe County, Tn., 112
Monroe, James, 110, 154
Montgomery County, Tn., 106
Moore, John Trotwood, 200
Morgan's Station, Tn., 187
Murfreesboro, Tn., 101, 104, 106
Muscle Shoals, state of Franklin, 6; Al., 24, 38, 42, 134-135, 160

Nacogdoches, Tx., 165-167
Nashville Bank, 84
Nashville Female Academy, 108
Nashville, Tn., 1, 11, 14, 18, 21, 37, 67-69, 99, 101-104, 108, 112-113, 122-123, 127-128, 143, 154-155, 157, 160-161, 165, 184-185
Natchez, expedition of, 192
Natchez, Ms., 67, 69, 74, 125-126
Natchez Road, (later Natchez Trace), 67-69, 190
Natchez, Tn., 24, 52-53
Natchez Trace. See Natchez Road.
Natchitoches, La., 166
Neely, William, 186-187
Neosho River, Ok., 164
New Bern, N.C., 80
New Echota, treaty of, 142
New Market, Tn., 115
New Market, Va., 32
New Mexico, 169
New Orleans, La., 15, 71, 101, 123, 127, 153, 168, 170, 189; battle of, 99, 119, 127-128, 153
New River, Va., 180
New York, treaty of, 13; state of, 141, 154, 165
Nickajack, Chickamauga town of, 19-20, 45-46
Nolichucky Jack. See John Sevier.
Nolichucky River, Tn., 34-35, 38
North Carolina, 2, 10, 13, 35, 38-39, 80, 133
North Carolina-Tennessee Boundary, 70
Northwest Ordinance, 1, 120

Obed River, 52
Obion County, Tn., 113
Ococee District, 109
Ohio River, 11

"Old State Bank," 103
Oolooteka (John Jolly), 151, 163
Ore, Colonel James, 47
Oregon, 171
Osage Indians, 163-164
Overton County, 183
Overton, John, 49, 54, 70
Overton, Thomas, 49

Panama Congress, 157
Parsons, Enoch, 99
Parton, James, 125
Paxton, Elizabeth, 150
Paxton, John, 150
Payne, Elizabeth Chichester, 123
Payne, Josias, 123
Peale, Rembrandt, 96, 98
Pennsylvania, 120, 122, 139
Phelan, James, 185, 188
Philadelphia, Pa., 98, 150
Phillipson, Joseph, 195
Pickering, Timothy, 20, 24, 98
Pinckney's Treaty, 46
Pittsburgh, Pa., 120, 122-123, 139
Pleasant Forest Cemetery, 76
Polk, James, 120, 133, 143, 197
Pontotoc, Ms., 142
Porter Academy, Tn., 151-152
Postal Service, 68
Presbyterian Church, 63, 113-114, 119, 149, 161
Proclamation of 1763, 32, 34
Putnam, A. W., 57

Raguet, Anna, 166-168
Raguet, Henru, 166
Ramsey, J. G. M., 57, 114, 188, 199
"The Raven." See Sam Houston.
Revolutionary War, 4-5, 36-37
Rhea, John, 189
River Raisin, Mi., 190
Roane, Andrew, 63
Roane, Archibald, picture of, 65; noted, 21, 49, 51-52, 82-83, 98; life of, 63-76
Roane County, Tn., 66
Roane, John, 63
Roane, Margaret, 63
Roaring River, Tn., 183
Roberts, Isaac, 191
Robertson, James, 10-11, 16-17, 19, 32-34, 43, 45, 50, 85, 182-184
Rockbridge County, Va., 64, 150
Rocky Mount, picture of, 12; noted, 16, 80
Rocky Point, picture of, 80
Rogers, James, 151, 164
Rogers, John, 151, 164
Rogersville, Tn., 16, 101, 108

Romayne, Nicholas, 18, 24
Rome, Georgia. See Battle of Etowah.
Roulstone, George, 16, 93
Running Water, Chickamauga town of, 19
Rural Academy, 196
Rutledge, George, 69-71

Sabine Pass, Tx., 170
San Antonio, Tx., 165, 167
San Augustine, Tx., 169
San Felipe Constitutional Convention, 166
San Felipe de Austin, Tx., 165-166
San Ildefonso, treaty of, 70
San Jacinto, battle of, 168
San Jacinto River, Tx., 168
Santa Anna, Antonio Lopez de, 167-168
Santa Fe, expedition of, 169
Second Bank of the United States, 101
Seminole War, 188
Sequatchie Valley, 110
Seven Mile Mountain, battle of, 188
Seventh United States Infantry, 152
Sevier, George Washington, 56-57
Sevier, John, picture of, 33; noted, 2, 5-6, 10-11, 20-21, 27, 63, 69, 72-75, 82-84, 86, 88, 189; life of, 31-59
Sevier, Valentine (father of John), 32
Sevierville, Tn., 21
Shawnee Indians, 182
Shelby County, Tn., 113
Shelby, Evan, 35, 42
Shelby, Isaac, 36, 111
Shelby, Dr. John, 162
Shelbyville, Tn., 101
Shenandoah Valley, Va., 32
Sherrill, Catherine, 36, 56
Sitgraves, John, 80
Sitgraves, Samuel, 25
Slatter, Edward, 80
Slavery, recognized in territory, 11
Smith, Dr. Ashbel, 170
Smith County, Tx., 173
Smith, Daniel, 49
Smith, David, 111
Smith, Henry, 168
Smith, John, 157
Smithland, Ky., 190
Sons of Temperance, 171
South Carolina, 141, 156
Southwest Point, Tn., 52, 69
Southwest Territory. See Territory South of the River Ohio.
Spain, 1, 7-9, 11, 15, 17, 23, 42, 46, 70-71
Spanish Conspiracy, 42-43
Specie Resumption Act, 132
Stanbery, William, 164-165

State Bank of 1821 (Grundy's Bank), 132
State Bank of Tennessee, 87
State Seal of Tennessee, 66
Station Camp Creek, Tn., 183
stations, definition of, 2
Steele, James, 187
Steele, John, 10
Sterne, Adolphus, 166
Sterne, Eva Rosine, 167
Sullivan County, state of Franklin, 6; Tn., 35-36, 39
Sumner County, in Mero District, 11; Tn., 124, 161, 180, 183, 185; N.C., 179
Sumner Light Horse, 185, 187
Superior Court of Laws and Equity, 82, 87
Supreme Court of Errors and Appeals, 64, 87
Supreme Court of Tennessee, 76, 136, 138
Surrey County, N.C., 179
Switzerland, 122
Sycamore Shoals, Tn., 34

Tahlontuskee Village, Ok., 163
Tallapoosa River, Al., 55, 153
Talladega, battle of, 119, 126
Tariff of 1824, 157
Taylor, George, 195
Taylor, Zachary, 198
Tellico, treaties of, 48, 54
Tell, William, 122
Tennessee Antiquarian Society, 108, 155
Tennessee, becomes 16th state, 46; east, 53, 64, 99, 102, 114, 134-135, 138, 140, 160; middle, 99, 114, 123-124, 134; west, 104, 111, 114, 134, 138, 140, 160
Tennessee County, 10, 11, 15, 46
Tennessee Historical Society, 98, 108, 180
Tennessee Indian Wars, 178-195, 197, 198
Tennessee River, 6, 13, 38, 69, 105, 109-112, 135, 151
Territorial Assembly, 19-21, 98
Territory South of the River Ohio, 1-2, 11, 19, 23
Texas, 162, 165-174
Texas Association of Tennessee, 162
Texas Navy, 169
Thirty-ninth United States Infantry, 152-153
Thomas, Abishai, describes Knoxville, 16
Thompson, Isabel, 27
Timber Ridge Plantation, 150
Tipton County, Tn., 113
Tipton, John, 18, 41, 43-44, 56

Tohopeka, battle of. See Battle of Horseshoe Bend.
Tompkins, John, 195
"Trail of Tears," 142
Transmontania Academy, 196
Trenton, N.J., 64
Trimble, James, 154-155
Trinity River, Tx., 167
Tyler, Tx., 173
Tyrell, William, 51
Tyron, William, 79

Union Bank of Tennessee, 132
US Constitution, 1

Van Buren, Martin, 141-143
Vauxhall Garden (in Nashville), 142
Vicksburg, Ms., 174
Virginia, 1, 32, 35, 63-64, 113, 123-124, 150
Virginia House of Burgesses, 123
Virginia-Tennessee Boundary, 69
Volunteer Spies, 188
Volunteer State. See Tennessee.

Walker, Joel, 195
Walker, Nancy, 188
Walker's Line, 108
Walton Road, 69
Ward, Edward, 103, 130, 139
War Hawks, 189
War of 1812, 87-92, 100, 126-128, 152-153
Washington College, Tn., 76, 180
Washington County, state of Franklin, 6, 41, 43; N.C., 35-37, 39, 64; Tn., 76
Washington D. C., 126, 153-154, 157, 164
Washington District, Southwest Territory, 1, 13, 45; N.C., 34-35, 44; Tn., 49, 66
Washington, George, 1, 10, 11, 13-14, 21, 23-24, 45, 64, 80
Watauga Association, 32-35, 58
Watauga River, Tn., 11, 34, 38, 80
Watts, John (Chickamauga Chief), 16-17
Wayne, Mad Anthony, 46
Weakley County, Tn., 113
Weakley, Robert, 99
Webb, Walter Prescott, 171
Westchester, Pa., 97
Wharton, Jesse, 99
Wharton, William, 162, 166
Whig Party, 141, 143
White, Hugh Lawson, 11, 76, 101-102, 129, 141, 197
White, James, 16, 71, 82
White, William A., 157-158, 160

Wigwam Neosho, 164-165
Wilkinson, James, 43, 67, 90, 190
William Carroll and Company, 123
Williams, John, 109, 139
Williams, Nancy Glasgow, 113
Williamson County, Tn., 67-68
Williamson, Hugh, 10
Williams, Willoughby, 113, 162
William the Conqueror, 80
Wilmot Proviso, 199
Wilson, William, 186
Winchester, General James, 47, 49-50, 71, 90
Winchester, George, 186, 200
Winchester, James, 190-191
Winchester, Tn., 101
Wright, Marcus, 27

Xavier (grandfather of John Sevier), 32

Yorktown, battle of, 36
Yorktown, Va., 64

THE EDITOR

Charles W. Crawford, Ph.D., is Director of the Oral History Research Office and Associate Professor of History at Memphis State University. During the more than a decade that he has served as the university's Tennessee historian, he has taught several thousand students their state's history, received the distinguished teaching award, and authored three books and numerous articles on Tennessee.

Crawford is the President of the West Tennessee Historical Society and has served as a national officer or committee member of several professional organizations, including Omicron Delta Kappa, national leadership society; Phi Alpha Theta, international history honor society; the Oral History Association; the Organization of American Historians; and the Southern Historical Association. In his state, he has served as a member of the Tennessee Historical Commission, the Tennessee American Revolution Bicentennial Commission, and the Board of Trust of the Association for the Preservation of Tennessee Antiquities. As a friend and advisor to several Tennessee governors, he is familiar with the problems of gubernatorial leadership. Crawford also has served as Chairman of the Memphis Landmarks Commission and the Shelby County Historical Commission.